HEAR ALL THE BELLS

Christina Wulf

GHOST TREE PRESS

Bridgewater, Virginia

Hear All The Bells/ Christina Wulf —1st ed.
ISBN-13: 978-0692748190
ISBN-10: 0692748199

To My Family

Bipolar disorder, also known as manic-depressive illness, is a brain disorder that causes unusual shifts in mood, energy, activity levels, and the ability to carry out day-to-day tasks.

There are four basic types of bipolar disorder; all of them involve clear changes in mood, energy, and activity levels. These moods range from periods of extremely "up," elated, and energized behavior (known as manic episodes) to very sad, "down," or hopeless periods (known as depressive episodes). Less severe manic periods are known as hypomanic episodes.

Sometimes, a person with severe episodes of mania or depression also has psychotic symptoms, such as hallucinations or delusions.

-   NATIONAL INSTITUTE OF MENTAL HEALTH

CONTENTS

Hear All The Bells

PREFACE

Hear *All The Bells* is a memoir, a personal story of my diagnosis and life with manic depression. It is not written to represent the experiences of others with mental illnesses, and, beyond a basic level, I do not delve into the societal problems surrounding mental illness. The societal problems, however, are vast, close to home, and must not be ignored. For example, a recent news article reported that in my home state of Virginia, people with mental illnesses have made up almost 40% of fatal police shootings since 2010. Nationwide, the number is estimated to be at least 25%.[1]

Another example: in 2012, prisons and jails in the U.S. held approximately 356,268 inmates with severe mental illness. In comparison, state psychiatric hospitals housed only about 35,000 patients nationwide.[2] It is almost a cli-

---

[1] Gary Harki, "Virginia is Outpacing the Nation in Police Shootings of the Mentally Ill," *Virginian-Pilot* (June 4, 2016).

[2] Treatment Advocacy Center and National Sheriffs' Association, *Treatment of Persons with Mental Illness in Prisons and Jails* (Arlington, VA: Treatment Advocacy Center, 2014), 6.

ché now to say that prisons have become America's new asylums.

The first time I addressed a public audience about my experience with manic depression, I spoke to a university Justice Studies class. I explained that my story would probably be radically different if I did not occupy my particular demographic position.

I am white and cisgender female. I've had access to health insurance all my life. My family has the ability to come to my aid financially, medically, and legally should the need arise. These factors hugely boosted my chances of good treatment and recovery.

A psychiatric nurse mentioned to me once that I was lucky to have been taken to the hospital during an intense manic episode. People in extreme states of mind are regularly taken to jail. The nurse said that men and people of color are much more likely to be arrested than admitted to the hospital.

I told the Justice Studies class the story of Jamycheal Mitchell, a young man whose story haunts me because, although our diagnoses are similar, his experience is 180 degrees opposite of mine. Jamycheal, a 24-year-old, African American man from Hampton Roads, Virginia, was arrested for stealing $5 worth of snacks from a 7-Eleven. He was taken to jail. The judge ordered a psychological evaluation, which found that Mitchell was manic and psychotic. The report stated that his thought processes were "so confused that only snippets of his sentences could be understood."[3] The psychologist recommended that Mitchell be committed to a state hospital to restore him to competency before standing trial (for a $5 theft).

The state mental health and criminal justice systems went on to fail Jamycheal in almost every way. He was asked to make major decisions about his treatment while in a severely-altered mental state. Mitchell was then warehoused in jail for two and a half months, waiting for a bed to open at the nearby state hospital, while his health and mental state deteriorated. Allegedly, the jail ignored his health problems and distraught phone calls from his family members. Jamycheal stopped eating, became emaciated, and died in jail from causes probably related to heart arrhythmia and physical wasting.

It is hard to fathom allowing someone to fall between the cracks in such a drastic way. What I can imagine, all too clearly, is how the stress of incarceration could amplify symptoms and lead to rapid deterioration.

The justice issues surrounding mental illness connect up with the deep challenges we face in this country of discrimination and abuse related to race, class, ethnicity, gender identity, sexual orientation, and so on. They connect up with misunderstandings and lack of training about mental illness within the criminal justice system.

---

[3] Justin Jouvenal, "Man accused of stealing $5 in snacks died in jail as he waited for space at mental hospital," *Washington Post* (Sept 29, 2015).

Questions of safety, agency, and confidentiality of patients with mental illness also go deep. How do we balance respect for individual rights with the reality that patients in extreme mental states may not know what their best interests are? The questions are hard and painful. I have no solutions to offer beyond the need for us as individuals and a society to turn our attention and care to this problem. People with active mental illness are among the most vulnerable in our society. We can begin coming to their aid by not turning away.

As you read *Hear All The Bells*, I hope you will keep in mind Jamycheal Mitchell and the hundreds of thousands of other human beings who are incarcerated with severe mental illness. My struggles pale in comparison, yet I hope this story can still offer useful insight. Even with my many advantages, manic depression was extraordinarily traumatic, as *Hear All The Bells* illustrates.

As you read, imagine my story taking place without good medical care. Or in the context of economic hardship. Or where I am arrested and sent to jail or prison instead of being taken to the hospital or the doctor. Imagine how rapidly a deeply traumatic experience, when added to these other situations, could ruin a life, not just emotionally and spiritually, but in all ways. Imagine how incredibly difficult, if not impossible, recovery could be.

This happens. This happens all the time.

PRELUDE

At a party in December of 2012, as I wrote my way through an early draft of this book, I met a woman whose father had been a psychiatrist at Western State Hospital in the town where I live. The historic buildings and grounds of old Western State, a facility for the mentally ill, still stand just outside downtown Staunton. After the hospital moved into new space in the 1970s, the buildings housed a jail and, more recently, condos.

When it opened in 1828, the hospital was called Western State Lunatic Asylum. It was a "resort-style" asylum in the early years with beautiful architecture, graceful gardens, and weeping willows throughout the grounds. Medical theories of the time held that the restful surroundings would soothe mentally-unstable patients. But treatment models shifted over the years, moving the facility eventually toward overcrowded, prison-like conditions. For almost four decades, from 1905-1943, a famous eugenicist named Joseph DeJarnette ran Western State and carried out thousands of forced sterilizations, lobotomies, and other invasive, sometimes deadly, experiments on his patients.

My new friend described going with her father on rounds in the 1960s. It was a frightening experience for a child, she said. "There were no treatments then, only sedation," so the patients shuffled around, aimless and blank-faced, in large rooms that smelled like urine. She looked helpless and sad, staring back a few decades into the past. At that point in the conversation, I found an excuse to step away, slip out of the party, and be alone for a few moments in the chilly night. Her story hit too close to home.

A few days later, on a snowy morning, I took a detour on my way to work. As I crested a hill, I could see the grounds of old Western State spread out before me. I had known about the old cemetery behind the hospital and had even seen a picture. Blank posts—no names, no dates—marked the final resting place of those who had died inside Western State. Usually the cemetery was difficult to see, the brown posts masked beneath the trees. But against the new snow, the markers were starkly visible, and from the hilltop, I could see the whole of it. I pulled over to the side of the road, astonished—the cemetery was huge, a broad, straight-lined grid of graves.

That night, I lay in bed, staring into the dark at images of lost, lonely people, their minds bent, shuffling in the shadows and dying into nameless graves, rejected and forgotten. In that mid-space between sleep and waking, I trembled in panic, thought of lobotomies and ice picks and pressed my hands against my eyes, curled into a fetal position—the terror of literally losing one's mind at the hands of a doctor. Experimentation and sterilization, electro-shock and forced sedation, tied down, invaded in violence, no longer human.

How close I had come to the possibility of that fate—a brief span of decades, such a short time. John Cade discovered lithium's ability to stabilize manic depressives in 1948, a date so relatively recent that it made my head spin. My parents were kids in 1948. The treatment for their daughter emerged within their lifetimes. In the U.S., the Food and Drug Administration did not approve lithium for use in treating manic depression until 1970. Only in 1974, the year I was born, did the FDA approve lithium as a long-term, on-going preventative—the way I take it now. And laws surrounding the rights of mentally-ill patients were mostly passed during my lifetime. They continue to challenge and be challenged as we haggle with the rough balance between protecting safety and preventing abuse of people in extreme mental states.

I waded through an interior abyss that December night, watching my life as it might have been. During my stays in the psychiatric wards of different hospitals, I had been mostly well-treated, but echoes of psychiatry's dark history remained. On different occasions, medical professionals and legal authorities had forced me into restraints, medicated me against my will, and committed me to a psychiatric ward involuntarily. These were deeply traumatic experiences for me—despite my manic states, I remembered them clearly—and part of a terrible dilemma for my family and friends.

My parents describe these events as some of the worst experiences of their lives. What could they do? On the one hand, I was beyond control, in a confused, reckless, delusional state. Although I certainly needed some kind of help, my manic mind did not see it that way. I emphatically did not want anything to do with doctors or hospitals. On the other hand, the medical response to mental illness, when symptoms are florid and the patient is in potential danger, can be frightening and have overtones of violence. My family had to trust that I would be well treated, and I had to submit, to become captive in order to become well. For me, the outcomes were ultimately positive— medical treatment and medications have provided crucial, and thus far successful, tools for my stability—yet this remains a tragic, often dangerous, dilemma.

During those times in the hospitals, I had relied on standard survival mechanisms to deal with my fears— suppressing emotion, denying the severity of my experience. But I unraveled that December night in the darkness of my bedroom; the repression crumbling, the raw terror that has, at times, accompanied my mental condition re-emerged into my consciousness and memory. The ten years since my last hospitalization in 2002 had been harrowing, not only due to my struggle to recover, but also because I was constantly trying to outrun stigma and history. Always, in the back of my head, was the terror of losing control again—of my mind, yes, but also of my movements, my freedom, my choices. Although treatment of people with mental illness is hugely better these days, the reality remains that if you show severe enough symptoms, you may rapidly lose control of your destiny.

To live with a mental illness is to live in the shadow of history. A stigma roosts on your shoulder passed down through generations. Many times while writing this book, I considered using a pen name. Very few people knew of my diagnosis with manic depression. I hid it, never spoke of it, never told anyone who did not have specific need to know. I was ashamed, embarrassed, terrified of stigma and other peoples' assumptions. It did not occur to me that I was stigmatizing myself.

Many thinkers have theorized that internalizing stigma means participating in our own oppression. I read about the concept in college, wrote about it in impassioned essays, and missed it entirely in myself. Ironically, on that December night when my defenses came crashing down and I thought I might lose my mind again to the horror of our history, I found my voice; I found my people.

The unknown bones behind Western State do not belong to strangers, and I am not an "Other"—indeed, I am more likely to be your neighbor. I grew up in the comfort and safety of a middle-class subdivision in the Northern Virginia suburbs. My parents built a loving family that valued education, curiosity, service, and kindness. I went to public schools all the way through college, where I graduated Phi Beta Kappa at the University of Virginia. I was active in a high school church youth group that went on service trips to homeless shelters, retirement communities, and places like West Virginia and South Carolina where lower-income communities had been harmed by natural disasters.

I grew up idealistic and privileged, serious about social justice and peace and environmental protection, wide-eyed and sheltered, endlessly curious about the world beyond my experience. These days, I am still many of those things—also now married with a good job at a university, a garden, a quiet life. I am a friendly, kind person: you would like me. Mental illness does not exist somewhere outside of the human experience among monstrous, bad, frightening people. Though it may require treatment, there is nothing *wrong* with mental illness. It is simply one more way of being human.

So I dropped the idea of a pen name. I began instead to assemble the tools of compassionate resistance—my effort to refuse stigma and oppression while doing my best not to lash out in anger and blame at people who perpetuate them, including me.

The first tool of my resistance is naming. Writing under my own name means claiming myself as a human being. Choosing to name my disease "Manic Depression" means I claim it as my own. The current medical term "Bipolar Disorder" is too coldly clinical for me—it tells little of the disease. "Manic Depression," in contrast, is vivid, weighted with a bloody history and descriptively accurate.

"Bipolar" describes a range of mood disorders of varying degrees of intensity. I do not minimize any of those experiences—all mental illness is difficult, disruptive, and painful—but there are gradations of symptoms and huge variations in how people are treated based on those symptoms. Some go to their doctor for a diagnosis and a prescription; others face arrest and incarceration due to their behaviors and demographics. As for me, I resonate most with my friend Catherine's words: "Until you've been strapped down to a gurney, injected with drugs, and hospitalized against your will, you don't know. You just don't know."

My diagnosis is Bipolar I: the full-blown, full-spectrum, all-the-way-up-and-all-the-way-down form of the disease. Even in remission, I experience volatile moods and a sometimes unnervingly chaotic mind. I want full credit. I am manic depressive, and I have been out further into the strangeness of the brain than most people will ever need to go.

The second tool of resistance is truth telling. I cannot tell you what it's like to be a man or a person of color dealing with mental illness, but I can emphasize the discrepancies; I can try to clarify that in this book I am only telling my story. There is hope and possibility in my story, but the huge issues of justice and the need to heal and humanize the treatment of people with mental illness go far, far beyond my comparatively minor experiences.

What I can offer, however, is my best attempt to tell the truth about living inside my manic depressive mind. I wanted to provide access to mental illness for people who see it only as alien and frightening. As far as memory allowed, I tried to depict what I saw and thought and felt during the extremes of my disease and in the key times of my recovery without embellishment or interpretation. I also wanted to make my story available to readers who share my diagnosis, who might find some resonance or hope or even amusement. And I sought to give our doctors, friends, and families some small insight into what it's like to live with extreme states—even though the disease manifests in each individual with widely different behaviors, some similarities of experience often remain.

If I am lucky, perhaps others like medical personnel and law enforcement will catch some deeper insight into the humanity of people with mental illness. After all, one of the many impressive people in my story was a police-man who, instead of arresting me or forcing me into the emergency room, bowed with courtesy and kindness, of-fered me his arm, and walked me gently into the hospital. Humanity. Friendship. That's all we've really got.

And that, perhaps, is the ultimate goal of this story for me. I want a world with more room in it for difference and strangeness and for people to embrace and rejoice in opportunities for diverse friendships. I hope that telling the truth about what happened inside my mind will broaden the field of possibility, if only for just a small cir-cle of readers. The deadly, dehumanizing stigmatization of mental illness is rooted in a world that demands conform-ity—a culture and society based on domination and com-modification and a very, very narrow understanding of Nature and Love and God.

These are the Big Three concepts around which my life rotates. By the time this story began, in the year 2000, the three had become completely enmeshed with my work as a forest protection activist. The Presbyterian church that I attended with my family emphasized service and social justice. In college, at UVA's excellent Religious Studies department, I delved into Tibetan Buddhism, early Christian history, and especially Hindu mysticism. My personal beliefs became more syncretic; I began to attend Quaker meetings. After college, my long-term interest in environmentalism expanded into a rich love and learning about planetary ecology and my local bioregion. As I spent more and more time among Virginia's forests and mountains, my experiences of Nature, Love, and God wove together seamlessly; it was a time of deep meaning in my life.

My understanding of oppression also grew rapidly during these years as I witnessed the extent of the destruction of Earth and humanity caused by human greed and brokenness. I picked up the phrase "dominator society" from Riane Eisler's book *The Chalice and the Blade* during that time. Her definition, with its focus on relations between men and women seemed somewhat narrow, but the concept made sense to me: dominator society is one in which "human relations must fit into some kind of superior-inferior pecking order... [and] human hierarchies are ultimately backed up by force or the threat of force."[4] I was most concerned then, in those years leading up to 2000, with human-imagined hierarchies over the natural world. I see now that domination is all of a piece, whoever it is enacted by or upon.

This cultural world view of "power over" underpinned the dark history of psychiatry; it gave doctors justification to forcibly sterilize patients at Western State in the first half of the 20th century, to treat them as blank objects, experiment on them, bury them in nameless

---

[4] Riane Eisler, *The Chalice and The Blade* (San Francisco, CA: HarperCollins, 1987), 27 and xix.

graves. It is a familiar story—the same fate for whatever group is marked as undesirable by our dominator society; at its worst, this treatment amplifies into genocide, holocaust, slavery, war. Hence the need, always the need, for resistance.

My experiences with mania and depression—starting in 2000 and many years beyond—took me on dangerous roads, both inside and outside of my mind. I made terrible mistakes and put people I love through hell. Alongside that, woven all through, were extraordinary experiences of Nature and Love and God. Trying to reconcile my diagnosis of manic depression with that wild grace was agonizing—the most difficult part, on an existential level, of my recovery. I gnawed at myself. The fear in my head, rooted firmly in dominator society and its rejection of otherness, said, "It's all just a trick of haywire brain chemistry. Forget that it happened. Move on." And yet that grace was real—that love, that God. To hide away my ongoing embrace of the mystic and mythic—and its on-going embrace of me—would not only mean falling prey again to stigma and oppression, it would also be profoundly ungrateful. Truth telling opens up the range of possibilities in the world, opens up the atmosphere to a broader vision of Spirit, and unmasks dominator society for what it is: a sickness, a delusion, and perhaps, at last, a cry for help.

The third tool of compassionate resistance is being alive. This tool has stages and gradations, among them survival, healing, health, thrill and thriving and joy. Surviving this disease—even if you are barely hanging on—is a triumph. Hang on. For years, I saw my survival as a bitter thing; I wanted my old life back; I wanted to do more than grasp at threads of sanity with my raw fingertips. But that dogged determination to continue to exist takes real courage and real strength. Remember that and hang on.

Learning how to heal is like learning a craft—the apprenticeship may be long, taking time, patience, discipline, study, working with doctors and counselors, learning to trust your own mind. Health is built on habits of daily life—exercise, sleep, food, medication, meditation—finding what works for you and making that foundational until you learn the next thing that will make you better, stronger, brighter.

Thrill and thriving come with time: when you have conceived strategies to care for yourself and set them in motion daily; when you can, at least some of the time, cry without despairing and feel your heart lift without fearing mania's blade; when you are alive and plan to stay that way. In those moments, and in every stage and phase of being alive, you can be a bringer and giver of joy. Joy is grounded in fierce compassion, for yourself and for others. And joy is the heart of resistance.

Part I

Part of what happens when one goes crazy is that there's a grammatical shift. Thoughts come into the mind as firmly established truth.

There is no simile or metaphor. There's no tense but the present. The fantastic presents itself as fact.

– MARK VONNEGUT
Just Like Someone Without
A Mental Illness Only More So

ONE

Tongues in trees, books in the running brooks,
sermons in stones, and [God] in everything.

– WILLIAM SHAKESPEARE
As You Like It

The young woman lies on the grass between the tiny house and the garden. Strands of haze are knit across the hillside, reflecting brassy midday sun, and threaded all through the thick forest that surrounds the mountain farmstead. Beside her, the hand-crank washer drains slow down the hill. Overalls, a cotton dress, some underwear and socks drape the line. It is the end of May, hot and almost still, though in the forest, leaves and needles never cease to rustle and hush.

The young woman's body is also still, long limbs laid out on the earth, as she leans back on her elbows. Her eyes move, wandering the sky, the trees, the garden gate woven out of saplings, the herbs growing in thick tufts and tall thickets, bits of sculpture, faeries, fragments of mirrors set among stones. The earth thrums as bees wander in and out of flowers. She watches. One lights on her arm

15

where the skin is darkening in the sun, thin hairs burnt gold. The bee meanders, sniffing like a dog.

"What are you saying?" she murmurs, gazing at the bee with narrowed eyes. A yellow jacket settles on her leg, while another hovers, crowding close to her face. She doesn't move, just watches, intent, listening.

In her mind, the haze is thicker. It freights the humming creatures with meaning. She can almost, not quite, decipher their language. At first, this almost-knowing amused and delighted her, but that good humor is slowly fraying to frustration. She cannot capture their meaning. It lies so close but out of reach. Sudden flame-colored flares of insight have illuminated her mind the past few weeks—cosmic codes broken, riddles unraveled. She sees connections instantly, living in a constant flux of free association. ("Blessed bee!" she thinks, watching the insects and giggling at her riff on a Wiccan blessing.) But now inside that radiant storm, her brain is beginning to hurt, an anxious twisting behind her eye sockets, and in her gut, brief glints of nausea and panic. She can almost see the whole, almost hold a God's-eye view, but not quite. The effort is undoing her.

After a while, she gets up and moves back into the shade of the porch. She rummages inside the tiny house to find a glass for water and turns the spigot on the white plastic drum in the corner. The water comes from a spring on the opposite slope, fed by gravity through a filter. I am drinking the forest, she thinks, smiling, embracing the green living frenzy that throbs outside like fever.

On the porch, she sits again on the blue bench seat from an old truck that functions as a sofa—her bed and her perch for the past many days, how many days? She lost count after the first night, when her sleep had been interrupted time and again by the singing of the stars, so wildly white here against the deep space blackness, Milky Way breathing, here in the far mountains. The Unakas— the ghost mountains—bend over her here, near the border between Tennessee and North Carolina, lifting her up to press her eyes to the sky. All that night, the stars had moved above her and visions filled her mind with curling auroras and music, until all but the morning stars and the old moon faded into lemon and coral pale.

That first morning, the sun had risen into a formless day, vague and loose like the others all week. She sat on the porch and wrote, or wandered the slim paths through dense mountain understory, often followed by or following the little four-year-old girl named Laurel. The child moved smooth as a serpent through the forest, the farm, and streams. The mountain slopes and springs were her domain. She knew them and ruled them.

The young woman pauses in her writing to gaze across the porch where Laurel is perched, watching a bird and crooning to herself. Long corkscrew curls, a blue t-shirt with a print of a white dove of peace. The whole family has those curls—Gabriel, his wife Erin, Laurel and her older sister, Alarka—perhaps, the young woman thinks idly, that is the mark of faeries. She has a growing suspicion that when Gabe drove her up the long rutted driveway in their rattling pickup, she had crossed into the realm of Faerie. As the dogs came running to greet them, she'd heard his voice in her mind, speaking silently, saying, "We use these voices up here."

They had invited her in. A few days earlier, back in Kentucky, Laurel had turned from catching salamanders in the lake to place a green mesh net on the young woman's head, saying, "I'm so glad we caught you!" Along with Alarka, they had taken a canoe out on the lake. The girls clamored around her while the young woman sank the paddle into the water, half-hypnotized, leaning back into sunlight. She had smiled at the girls, saying, "We are ladies of the lake."

Now she is caught in a different kind of net, a web made of roots and words. She thinks that some story must want her here. Some nebulous narrative wants her to catch it—like Laurel had caught her—and tell the tale of Turtle Island, reborn and rising, of clues and tricks and riddles and heroes. She has all the pieces, but somehow they will not fit together. The story eludes her, threads ending always in frays and knots. The story writes her instead. She is being spun down into a taut filament and then re-woven into this place, into late-spring heat and gauzy haze around the trees. She wears a dress made of hemp fibers dyed dark purple—the color of bruise and shadowed eyes and shadows at dusk. Color of grief, color of royalty. Lady of the Lake now Queen of the Greenwood, trailed by wild girls with spiraling hair.

She told the story to Laurel and Alarka yesterday. They had laughed and gamboled with her, draped in blankets for robes—the three of them in the lower field at dusk, parading around like queens, playing dress up. But something had frightened her in the shadows there. Among the damp, blue-green grasses, danger seemed to well up from the ground, from the deep hole dug beside the compost heap, or from somewhere nearby, some darkness inside her. To protect them, she had sent the girls away and then sunk to her knees, weeping, something jagged and violent in her guts.

She tries to write about it now, on the shady porch. Her terrible dread—like the looming shadows of the Hindu goddesses of childhood diseases and the agony of standing helpless when a child dies. She herself had almost died at age eight, floated above the hospital bed, watched lifetimes of strangling grief begin on her parents' faces, and then rushed back, diving into her skin to protect them from that brutal hurt. The memory roosts on her shoulder. She turns away so that Laurel will not see.

Memories, stories, mythologies: they all come back to her now, and they weave into the grand narrative that she is attempting, that will not quite cohere. The story is spread out all around her on sheets of construction paper, on the backs of letters from the Forest Service, on old bills. It began as a letter to her boyfriend, Matthew, written on colored construction paper borrowed from Laurel's craft box, trying to explain what was happening to her. What had happened in those brief, epic days before she arrived at Gabe and Erin's farm. Her mystical ecstatic experiences along the mountain borderlands further north between Virginia and Kentucky, and along the lake shore at the camp, and in an Appalachian forest on Pine Mountain so deep and rich and old that it had taken possession of her. By now, word must have reached him. Someone must have told him what had happened, how she had offered herself on the mountaintop in sacrifice and been transformed.

She writes for hours, for days, begging blank paper from her hosts. In the midday heat, while Erin is at work and Alarka is at school, Gabriel stops by and sits on the porch steps with her. He is building a new home for his family, a stone house to extend the miniature wooden nest where they live now. Friends and family come by each day to help him set the foundation. She waves from the porch and keeps writing, self-conscious, wondering what they think of her. Does mystic light shine from her transfigured face? Do they know?

"What are you working on?" Gabe asks. The letter to Matthew has long since unraveled into something else. The grant proposal that she needs to write for work lies entirely forgotten in her backpack. "It's a children's book that adults can read, too. Read to each other. In bed." The sentences slip out sideways, and she frowns as she speaks. The words she says aloud aren't the words in her head. Gabe smiles encouragingly. She smiles back. In his company, she feels calmer, the frenzy receding, at ease with him. He has a stillness to him and speaks more in his silences than in his words, the sweetness of his wife and daughters and land shining around him.

She has just finished writing a cast list for the story; the names of her friends and traveling companions from the past few weeks bent and shaped into pseudonyms, pen names, stage names. But the strangest names are real ones: names of her beloved boyfriend, Matthew, whose name in Hebrew means "gift," and her dear friend Adam, who'd been with her on Pine Mountain during the peak of the wild Earth-renewing magic, whose name means "man, formed from the earth."

But that is not the truly strange part. They are polar opposites, these men; their names and birthdays perfectly reversed: Matthew Adam and Adam Matthew born on Midwinter and Midsummer, like two pagan twins of old, bearing Biblical names, Old and New Testaments, mythic ancestor and apostle. Her head spins, holy mysteries written on her bones. Half-lit memories that always escape her grasp.

When Gabe and Laurel aren't there, the young woman smokes, lying on her back, touching flame to dry cannabis flowers and breathing in the rough smoke. Her pipe is made from the wood of a lightning-struck cherry tree, carved by a friend to the shape of a Civil War bullet. This is another recent and painful obsession: The War that devastated her Virginia homeland. A few weeks earlier, she had discovered that her house stood on a Civil War battlefield, site of the last battle fought in the Shenandoah Valley. The high-speed insights rolling through her brain these days tell her that the repercussions of that conflict have passed on between generations, never resolved. Now, they are implicated, she believes, in the environmental destruction of Virginia and of Turtle Island—an indigenous name for North America. They are enmeshed in the very issues that are the center of her life. She writes about this new knowledge in her narrative; it forms a subplot sometimes, other times it drives the story. In her head, the battlefield violence is a percussive body memory that rattles her like shell shock.

The marijuana slows her down, eases her mind. It is cheap stuff. She can smoke it all day and still get her writing done. Not like the flower-flavored sweetness, dripping with Humboldt resin that she'd smoked in those days leading up to Kentucky and the Pine Mountain magic. When she'd first tried that stuff a year before, flames had roared in her brain, and she'd folded neatly backwards, fainting into the arms of a friend. Surfacing from that black out was like rising from the deeps, breaking the surface, gasping air into lungs that had not breathed in centuries.

Rising from the dead. That is what she is doing now. Resurrecting herself in words, written words that are becoming more like pictures, spiraling, interwoven, crosshatched, narrative deconstructing into names and sounds, rhyme, tricks and puns, page after page. She amuses herself, writes a title page for her story that reads like a sales pitch from a snake oil medicine show:

ONE BIG TURTLE! Or— It Had to Happen!
(It's really long, because so many of us wrote it!)
And— How Mary Jo Got Married
(But that's not all! Also Inside— the Mad Waltz 'Cross Mexico in the Waning Moon of May!)
Plus! A Rollercoaster Ride through Heaven & Hell with Seven Dancing Angels, My Sister's Eyes in the Mirror, Turtle Hips Holding Up the Temple, and Four Guardians, Locking Arms, in the Green Fire.
Now Boarding... the Dancing Turtles & their Merry Laughing Crew,
Bringing you poetry & play for these Jubilee Days.

She puts down her pen and watches Gabriel pick up a black snake from beside the laundry bucket. "We call her Grace," he says, holding the snake just below the head as it curls into a spiral around his forearm. Laurel laughs and claps. The young woman's eyes light up with wonder. She remembers old stories—snakes as consorts of the goddess and guardians of wisdom (wise because their whole bodies are constantly in contact with the Earth)—and her pen traces busily, drawing a spiraling snake, its shape scrolling around the edges of the page, the curves shifting to trace the outline of a turtle.

Turtle Island.

They never reject her, Gabriel and his beautiful family, even as she steadily loses her mind at their farmstead in the mountains. Even as she devolves into a quiet lunacy, declining their offers of food, forgetting to ask for a menstrual pad and instead bleeding into her wadded up bathing suit, stuffed between her legs. Even as she wanders away one night at the new moon, down the long rocky driveway, to sleep in the backseat of their car by the road, convinced that a friend will soon come by to pick her up, take her to Asheville for the meeting she was supposed to attend. Another evening, she writes marriage vows for Thomas Jefferson and Sally Hemings and presents them solemnly to Gabe and Erin as they sit together at their kitchen table. She writes them a guidebook as well—a manual for raising alchemical children—that she tucks into a watering can in the garden.

She becomes more childlike, moving further into fantasy. The whole world speaks to her in resonant intimacy, and she takes infinite care to interpret it to fit her universe, which grows steadily more complicated, more divorced from daily reality. One morning, she discovers the radio. She had gone looking for a book for Laurel but loses track of her errand. "Thistle and Shamrock" makes the young woman gleeful, certain that they are playing this joyous Celtic music just for her. She chats with the host, reminiscing about her time in Scotland, and an English friend that she met on the island of Iona, and the time they stayed up through the short northern night to watch the sunrise over the water on Midsummer Day, and how the mist rising off the ocean seemed to ripple and writhe like a dragon.

Alongside these giddy interludes are darker moments. Her unstable universe refuses to cohere, and it grinds on her. Invisible rules twist around her; she is often terribly confused. She cannot remember: Is she allowed in the house? Should she walk down the mountain into Asheville? It seems like she has been at the farm for weeks. Surely her hosts are wondering if she'll ever leave. She wants desperately to do the right thing, to honor the hospitality of her friends, and sometimes her whole body shakes with the anxiety of trying to understand. One day, she goes with the family to their favorite swimming hole, a beautiful blue-green cove on a nearby creek, but never gets in the water. Despite the heat of the day, she cannot remember if she is allowed to swim.

On another hot afternoon, after Erin arrives home from work, the young woman, confused and flushed, asks, "Do my parents know where I am and that I'm ok?"

Erin lays a gentle hand on her arm, "You can use our phone, honey."

She calls later, inside the cool house, and talks to her mother. She rambles, and at times bursts into inexplicable laughter, "I just wanted to say hi and to make sure you're not worried. I've been busy up here learning Gaelic and Sanskrit, backwards and blindfolded, in runes. It's hard work. I need some kindly mothers of invention to get me out and help me on to the next part of this dance." She hangs up without answering any questions, without leaving a phone number.

The final night, she pulls her sleeping bag onto the driveway and curls up, still sleepless, because she hears music playing just over the hill, hallucinates a festival concert bigger than Woodstock, dead musicians returned from the dark side of the moon. She watches the constellations gather in a corner of the sky, forming into a great starship. When she hears The Band sing "Pepote Rouge" years later, the lines "a golden spaceship with the mother of the earth, carved in stone, the queen of avatars" remind her of this night and her vision and her sense of self as Spirit and Goddess, and—though long since stable and mostly sane—she knows, with that quiet mad way of manic depressives, she knows that she had been right all along, that the dreamtime hallucinations and soiled chaos of prophecy had been true, true, true, in spite of it all.

When her family arrives, the next day just at dusk, she is lecturing the pine trees—a small plot planted in straight lines—telling them to diversify: monoculture is a bad idea. Erin brings the girls to sit beside her as the old green Town Car rumbles into view, awkwardly navigating the gravel drive. Her parents and brother step out to find her embraced by this family, Laurel nested in her lap, their soft arms around her. She watches from a veiled distance as her family greets her friends, feels a warm glow of gladness when she sees the strong way her brother smiles when he shakes hands with Gabriel. They must be nearly the same age, and her six foot two brother is almost, though not quite, as tall as Gabe. Someone gathers her things, carefully stowing the piled pages of writing in her backpack. She leaves calmly, neither happy nor sad to see her family, to leave the farm. It is simply time. Before she goes, Erin hugs her fiercely, saying, "You are always welcome here. Always."

◆

I lived on Gabe and Erin's porch the week after Memorial Day in the year 2000 as the May moon waned into darkness. Those five golden days marked the crest of my honeymoon with mania. At my friends' mountain farm, I began to unravel, speech and thought decaying into full-blown delusion and anxiety. In future manic episodes, the golden days were briefer, psychosis arriving rapid and staccato.

The phone call to my parents and my question to Erin loosed a cascade of events. She told Gabe, "That's a cry for help." He was wary at first, wondering if I would be safer at the farm where they could keep an eye on me. But they began to call our mutual friends, to ask if anything like this had happened before. People speculated. Psilocybin? Ecstasy? An acid trip gone bad? My boyfriend, Matthew, called the farm and offered to drive down and pick me up; he could leave that morning, arrive by supper time. "No," I remember saying, though I wanted to say yes. I felt so confused, unsure of the rules: "No... I don't think I'm supposed to leave yet."

Meanwhile, my parents—disturbed by my incoherent phone call—were also calling my friends, trying to find out where I was. Word spread. They reached Matthew who gave them the number at the farm. When my parents finally spoke to Gabe, he struck a bargain with them. He was concerned; he'd never met my parents and knew nothing of them. He didn't want me to be mistreated. My family and my friends lived very different lives, but they were all kind, loving people. When Gabe said, "Don't hospitalize her by force," my parents said, "Of course," and they meant it. In return, he gave them directions to the farm.

♦

The old green Town Car spills out of the farm's driveway. She watches through the car window—the cemetery up the road is strewn with flowers left over from Memorial Day. She feels safe with her family and begins to talk, to try to tell the whole story. She speaks the whole long ride home, from the Blue Ridge highlands down to Johnson City and then north on I-81, heading toward Washington, DC. For eight hours she talks, rapidly, rapturously, chants, chirps. "Compressed speech," the doctors call it.

Her parents and brother exist only on the edges of her awareness, shadowy figures, recipients of her words. She looks sidelong at her mother who sits beside her in the back seat and encourages her to eat something, anything. She prefers to talk. The tape recorder that her mother slips onto the seat beside her captures the blaze of words and noises. To her, it makes sense—an epic re-telling, an oral history—to her family, it is terrifying gibberish:

"*My old friends*'—she clicks her tongue twice, snaps her fingers—"*once whispered in my ear: they said, 'If you ever need us, we are here... Oooooo...*'—a long, loud exhalation—"*Little transistor radios, little transmitters, beating, beating, beating!*'—her voice rises to a high, frantic pitch—"*We all took a powder. And we all took a beating. Right? That was the thing, that we would share it. It was a bruise. And the 'lil, 'lil, lalee, la-la, lou-lou*'—sing-song now and childlike—"*Lady Luck got to make a choice. And I chose wild dancing, black caped crow, and I chose plant totems, friends*'—voice rising like a thunderous preacher—"*And plants are now calling the show, 'cause this has always been Turtle Island!*"

She rhymes words and phrases over and over, or links fragmented ideas by sound. She laughs and then sometimes speaks with great pain about her near-death experience from her ruptured appendix at age eight. She calls her world-traveling father "sky walker" and makes her family laugh—but it is a deep hurting sound—as they sit around her, taut with fear.

They stop at a gas station in southwest Virginia. Her mother shadows her to the bathroom where the young woman catches sight of herself in the mirror, back-dropped by cheap wood paneling and blue paint. She stares.

... And some piece of quiet sanity sitting cross-legged behind my brow woke, sat straight up, and peered through my eyes. I squinted at my reflection. Something, I thought, is not right.

It was the first time I'd seen myself in a week. I was sunburnt, hair streaked light and dark with grime and sun. My face had sharpened, hollowed at the cheeks as if to lend extra strength to the cheekbones—strength to bear the oceans of shadow beneath my eyes. My eyes. I stared, fixated and uneasy, into black pupils that seemed to leap with a bottomless fever. I looked feral, radiant, apocalyptic. A phoenix heated to the smoking point, hints of flame beginning to lick from my fingers...

Then the moment of clear vision bends from the heat, and she sees a strange and sculpted power in her reflection: barefoot, the long purple dress pocked with mud and menstrual blood, blessings showered by the gods, vision of self as sacrifice, offering, supplicant, oracle. Layered, longing moments from many lives: arms bound for the sacrificial fire; hands open in the mudra of benevolence with rough fingers tattooed in henna; arms uplifted in prophecy with serpents threading the muscles; and arms spread wide, ready for the crucifixion.

♦

Late in the night, the car pulled into a parking lot, asphalt dotted with straight rows of bushes in berms. No forest here, stars hidden by street lights. Red letters lit up the side of a brick building: Emergency. Emergency?

No.

No, I'm not going in there. No. I belong outside, in the wild, earth under my feet, leaf and bough and breeze. There is no oxygen in there. No.

My family was gentle, reasonable. It was not their fault. With his hand placed lightly on my arm, my brother tried to steer me, following as I examined the portraits of hospital donors on the waiting room walls, the rows of vinyl, rust-colored chairs. After weeks of living mostly-barefoot outside, the blue and brown synthetic carpet felt alien and uncomfortable. My suspicions grew. We got as far as the automatic doors into the emergency room. They whooshed open, and I turned around, "No, I'm not going that way." I marched back out, out into the living world, cricket-scented, star-scattered, out into the June night. It occurred to me, I remember, that there was no use running. The kind-eyed security man who watched nearby was not simply a bystander.

I sat in the grass in a parking lot berm. A doctor stood over me, hands on her hips, delivering a lecture about why I needed help. I was sick and needed to come inside and cooperate, she said. I ignored her, looked at the deep green of the grass. Dew sparkled on the blades in the light of the streetlamps. My brain said, "Fuck off," to the doctor. I may have said it out loud. She seemed uncertain then, almost afraid.

In the end, it was the gentlemanly security guard who won me over. He offered me his arm, bowing slightly, and I took it like a lady should, walking regally beside him to the hangman's dais, the waiting noose.

It was not their fault. But the memory of those next few minutes clenches like rough rope around my throat, bunching the blood in my brain, exploding my lungs. No one strung me up. No one crushed my windpipe, broke my neck, and left me swinging. But it felt that way; sometimes it feels that way still.

◆

The interior doors whoosh open, and she marches through, arm in arm with a silver-haired man with a faded blue tattoo of an anchor on his forearm. She walks with her head high, smiling and chatting with her companion. They might be walking into a ballroom, preparing for a grand dance. But her smile fades as she notes the hospital gurneys, the nurses in scrubs. The room is too white and too cold. She smells anxiety and bleach and turns to her companion with a questioning look, fingers clutching his arm. She trusts him. Some kindness in his face and those blue tattoos make him familiar. These others here—the strange figures in white and blue uniforms with their chilled, arrogant efficiency—know nothing of mountain creeks and moss-covered boulders and wild-flowers in golden sunlight. If the guard was not with her, she would have run.

Then a nurse approaches them. The young woman smiles warmly at first, but the nurse only tugs at her arm, urging her toward a curtained-off corner of the emergency room. She turns again to her gentleman friend. She is afraid now and whispers to him, "Why are they doing this?" He does not answer, but she can read pain on his face. He looks stricken. Then he lets go of her hand, lets the nurse take her.

The doctor who'd lectured her outside joins the nurse. Grasping the young woman's other arm, they lead her toward a gurney. Their faces are blank. They do not look at her. One of them reaches for her glasses and pulls them from her face.

"What are you doing?!" Her voice fills with panic and she blinks rapidly, trying to focus her eyes. They take her multi-colored knit bag with the cherry-wood pipe and golden-green cannabis buds. "Hey! That's mine! Please, give me my glasses, I can't see." Pleading, she fights their grip. All of the warmth has gone out of the world. Cold florescent lights. Cold white sheets.

Holding her arms, they push her backwards, onto the gurney, pin her down. Her face contorts. "Please!" she calls to her silver-haired friend who stands a little way off, watching with frightened eyes. "Why are they doing this?" The nurse glances sideways, yanks a curtain and the man disappears. The young woman struggles. "Give me my glasses! I can't see!"

♦

Working in tandem, the nurse and doctor yanked restraints around my ankles, my wrists, and my chest. They were blue, I remember thinking, the color of the sky. At the sight of them, I understood what was happening. I knew what would come next and hatred bloomed like a mushroom cloud in my chest. I could not move. I watched the doctor prep the needle, sucking clear liquid from a vial into the plastic tube. She never looked me in the eye. I hated her. I still do. My people had tried to help me keep my dignity, but she trapped me, strapped down to the gurney. That was a violation; the needle was the execution.

I was beyond terror: "NO!! You don't understand. Please!" Please. Don't take my memory. Please don't take my mind.

Don't take my memory. Please God. I was so certain and so frightened that they could tear it all away—the golden days at the farm, the mountaintop ecstasy, the mythological world inside my mind—take it and replace it with a sterile conformity, lifeless, bleached, cold.

Please God. Don't take my memory. Please don't take my mind. I wanted every moment, every vision, all the chaos and frenzy, the colors of a wild forest in flower, the mountain earth under my bare feet, the laughter, camaraderie, the breathless joy. And every exact flavor and smell and sensation, the springtime pollen, the names of my friends. Please God. Don't take my memory. Please don't take my mind. The needle slipped into my vein. I breathed once and disappeared.

TWO

To see a World in a Grain of Sand
And a heaven in a Wild Flower,
Hold Infinity in the palm of your hand
And Eternity in an hour.
 - WILLIAM BLAKE,
Auguries of Innocence

The forest was in full flower. I touched the unfolding lips of a pale umbrella magnolia blossom at the edge of Watts Creek before slipping my bare foot into the water.

"There's an endangered fish that lives here. The Blackside dace, I think."

"You don't *think*," I said, grinning over my shoulder at Loki. "You *know*."

He laughed, then pointed upstream. We stood still, ankle deep in the chilly water, gazing at the view before us—an angular, brown tangle of rhododendron arms lifted an arc of green leaves above the stream. Mounds of flowers crowned the arch, blooming bright white or blushed with pink.

"My God," I murmured.

"Just wait," Loki said.

Conversation faded as we waded into the forest, ducking draped magnolia leaves that looked more tropical than Appalachian. On the far side of the creek, someone handed me a joint that tasted like springtime and said, "Welcome home." Under foot, hemlock trees had laid down centuries of needles, creating a soft dense soil that sprang back beneath each footstep, the reverberations echoing like a knock on a hollow tree. Fallen trunks lay like toppled columns; the forest was a temple destroyed and rebuilt time and again. Blankets of green moss, turkey tail fungus, slime molds, and mushrooms bloomed damp and fleshy from the rotting fallen trees. In forest ecology, they are called nurse logs—their slow decay providing nutrients and water to myriad life forms, rebuilding the forest, sustaining the temple.

I breathed in sweet air and sweet smoke. Sighed in bliss. The people around me smiled, I smiled back. A sense of belonging, larger than anything I'd ever felt, reached out from the forest, wrapping me in the glory of humidity, leaf-green sunlight, and old, old trees.

This forest was true old growth—never logged—draped over the long ridge in eastern Kentucky called Pine Mountain. In the Appalachian range, such a large tract of old growth—2,350 acres—is miraculous. Grover and Oxie Blanton bought the place in 1928 and passed it on to their daughters with the understanding that it should never be logged. How it survived intact into the late 1920s, through the devastating timber booms of the late nineteenth and early twentieth centuries, I do not know. Since 1995, the State of Kentucky has purchased parcels from the Blanton family, creating the Blanton Forest State Nature Preserve. The place gives a glimpse of an ancient forest type— known by ecologists as the mixed mesophytic. Extraordinarily diverse, these were unglaciated forests, refuges for plants during the ice ages. When the glaciers receded, plants reseeded the surrounding lands from these harbors of biodiversity. This was the Mother Forest.

Before the blight, American chestnut trees grew thick and tall along Pine Mountain. At Blanton in the year 2000, we clambered over and under oak and beech, magnolia, hickory, walnut, basswood and buckeye, tulip tree, hemlock, and more. We arrived here—driving past clear-cut scars around Big Stone Gap in Virginia, twisting through the coal-dimmed roads of Harlan County, Kentucky—and walked out into The Forest. Hallowed ground. A brief fragment of what used to be.

Loki and I and our friend Adam made the trip together. We left Waynesboro, Virginia on May 19th, the morning after the full moon. I had finished planting my garden as the moon rose the night before. A kitchen garden, mostly herbs, a few vegetables. I dug in the dirt thinking of the Civil War soldiers who had crossed this ground. They had been haunting me for the last few weeks, ever since I'd discovered a historical marker describing the Battle of Waynesboro.

In early March of 1865, Confederate soldiers had been encamped on the land beneath my home, along the low ridge where Pine Avenue now runs just west of downtown. The Union troops (led by the infamous General George Armstrong Custer) attacked from the west, lobbing artillery that kept the Confederates lying flat in the rifle pits that lined the road outside my front porch. A smaller Union force slipped around the Southerners' poorly-protected left flank, passing through a thick stand of trees near the South River where I took my evening walks. The Northern soldiers charged the pinned-down Confederates who scattered downhill, through my backyard, to the river where some 1,500 of them surrendered. The Confederate mapmaker, Jed Hotchkiss, who witnessed the battle, called it "a perfect rout." The Army of the Valley was finished. The Union forces marched east toward Appomattox and the war's end.

We drove south in Adam's VW Vanagon, catching the Blue Ridge Parkway in Roanoke, stopping by Floyd to watch the Friday night bluegrass pickin' party at the General Store, and then traveling on to our destination—a small camp on the New River near Fries, Virginia. We arrived to hearty hellos and hugs, greeting colleagues and friends from the forest-protection world. In the kitchen, I gave a happy yelp and hugged one of the cooks, his dark hair pulled back into a curling ponytail.

"Gabe! I didn't know you'd be here!"

"We're cooking this weekend. Activists in Aprons," he pointed proudly to his frilly, blue-flowered apron, smiling.

"I love it! Where's Erin?"

"The girls have karate, but they'll all be up next week in Kentucky."

I stayed busy that weekend, networking, note taking, helping to keep things on schedule and on track. Virginia Wildlands, the non-profit where I worked, had organized the conference, which focused on protecting Southern forests—particularly on private lands—from destructive logging. There were discussions about regional coalitions, workshops on fundraising, and one on community organizing where an activist from Georgia said, "With all due respect to the vegans and vegetarians out there, we just have more luck getting local people to come to events when we have barbeque!" Still, there was time to kick back. Late on the night we arrived, Adam and I sat at a picnic table near the river. I was chatty, bursting with ideas to share.

"I started writing about the Civil War, Adam, and how the land gets imprinted with traumatic memories, how those memories still affect us and how we treat the land. I'd really like you to read it."

Adam nodded, "I'd like to."

"I've been thinking, too... you know, we keep doing the same thing in this movement. Fighting with government agencies, acting as doomsayers. We're not really reaching outside the circle. But we have so many talented people... musicians and orators and artists."

"Mmm-hmmm."

"We could put together one heck of a carnival, a traveling festival, with music and solar energy demonstrations and magic shows."

Adam grinned, "Yes." Looking down slope toward the river, his voice seemed to hiss a little in the darkness, "I've been thinking the same thing. A chataqua."

"An old time medicine show."

"Yes," again, the low hiss or perhaps it was just the wind in the river grass. "I wonder how many other people are dreaming this same dream?"

I smiled at him. Hanging out with Adam was a thrill. He was a leader in the movement and seemed like a celebrity to me. I had a sort of crush on him. Not the dreamy, moon-eyed kind, more like the academic crushes my friends and I used to joke about in college: admiration with a dash of hero worship for the professors whose words and ideas inspired us. And Adam had always been kind to me, supportive of my work, a mentor. He knew just about everyone in my activist circle; he and Matthew and Loki were fast friends.

But there was something unnerving in the air that evening, sitting in the night breeze by the river with him. Something very different from a crush. Since he'd arrived in Waynesboro, bearing a bouquet of St. John's Wort sent by his wife, Danielle—a lovely lady who I admired deeply—he had felt unusually familiar to me. Not the closeness of a slowly growing friendship but something deep and difficult, like he'd been dear and lost to me in some other life. The sense of connection disoriented me—especially the grief, profound yet untraceable, that was interwoven with it. What was going on? I watched Adam gaze at the river in the dim light and tried to talk myself out of the feelings. I had a known propensity for wild whorls of imagination; this was just another day dream... although, how odd, I thought, to concoct a dream so thick with pain.

On Saturday, the conference facilitator led the group through an activity. He split us by gender and assigned us to draw our vision of an ecologically sound world. The women drew beautiful, bucolic scenes—solar panels and industrial hemp, community gardens and compost piles and intact forests. The men drew an apocalyptic, visionary landscape. A giant volcano had reared up out of Virginia in the Tidewater region near Richmond. It was erupting, a stream of turtles flying into the air while others stomped, smiles on their faces, down the sides of the volcano. Forests too were spreading from the crater to cover Virginia. In one corner, a small, smiling turtle munched on a large orange-spotted mushroom—the Appalachian subspecies of *amanita muscaria*—an entheogen, psychoactive fungi eaten ritually to commune with the gods.

"You drew that, didn't you?"

"Why would you say that?" asked Loki, throwing a long arm around my shoulders.

"Because tripping turtles in a healthy, intact forest is your idea of heaven."

A mischievous grin. Loud Loki laughter. No answer.

When I met Loki, in 1996 in Charlottesville, Virginia, he had a huge snapping turtle that he'd rescued off the highway in the backseat of his car. The first night of our friendship, we drove out beyond the edge of the city's light pollution and trespassed by star shine across the fields of a horse farm. He released the turtle with a hushed splash into the sedges surrounding a stream. I had just finished college at the University of Virginia and was just beginning to learn about forests. Loki took me under his wing. At the time, he was one of a few forest activists in Virginia, working—usually as a volunteer—toward a vision of national forests as unlogged, unroaded havens for biodiversity. He had a particular fondness for reptiles and amphibians, a wild adoration of turtles, and was one of the kindest people I knew.

On Saturday night at the conference, in the tradition of forest-activist gatherings in the South, we had a square dance in the camp lodge. Breathless, sweaty, hilarious, none of us knew what we were doing, but we dragged each other through the steps and circles while the fiddler played and the caller laughed. I partnered with Gabe—at six foot six inches—for the Virginia reel, standing on tiptoe, not quite able to reach his hands when it was our turn to form the arch.

On Sunday, Loki, Adam, and I packed ourselves back into the blue Vanagon. We had four days before we had to be in Kentucky and no real plans. We meandered west on Route 58, picked up a hitchhiking Appalachian Trail thru hiker and gave him a lift to Damascus, then stopped at Beartree Lake for a break and a nap. I'd slept on the porch of the camp lodge over the weekend, where the bright waning moon had disrupted my sleep. I felt tired and strange—as though the gold dust of pollen in the air had dulled the circuits of my brain—and went for a walk alone, eager to get away from the crowded swimming beach of the man-made lake. I sat beside a stream in the woods and got high, sighing and leaning back against a tree as the THC eased into my mind. Here among forests, flowers, and flowing water, I could relax. The day-to-day world of the families lolling on the beach seemed alien and sad. I craved wild places where I could be unconstrained, wide open.

These sensations had grown inside me all spring—a new power that seemed to erase self-consciousness and self-doubt. I felt unseen hands guiding me. In March, as green began to slowly seep up the mountains, my boy-friend Matthew bought a small piece of land in the Blue Ridge Mountains—a little under eleven acres—from his late uncle's estate. Beside the Tye River, butting up against The Priest Wilderness Area, the place was breathtaking.

On our first visit, we crossed the river barefoot, left our shoes on the bank, and slid through the trees—cool damp soil, soft ferns, the switch of hemlock branches. We split up to explore; Matthew followed the river, while I turned toward the mountain. I walked slowly, curious, feeling as though something was leading me, step-by-step. Almost in a trance, I arrived at a wide, flat-topped stone that jutted out from the slope, draped with mats of moss, a tall maple sapling growing from its heart. Without paus-ing, I stepped out onto the stone as if walking on stage, and in a fluid, unthinking movement, I knelt. My knees fit precisely into two rounded grooves in the stone. My heart thundered with a wild joy. I stayed on my knees a long time. This was no accident. The forest had given me a place to pray.

After a time, Matthew called from down slope. He'd found a stand of pink moccasin flowers—also called lady slippers—and was on his knees taking pictures. I scurried down to join him. Flowers had brought Matthew and me together. We'd met at a National Forest campground west of Lexington, Virginia on a botany field trip in 1997. He was a long-time forest activist, a close friend of Loki's, and a mad Bob Dylan fan—three factors that caused me to trust him—but it was his love for wildflowers that caught me. He showed me the silky, heart-lobed leaves of wild yam, graceful blue-eyed grasses, the exotic plumage of passionflowers. He filmed and photographed them, flipping through dog-eared field guides to find their names, loving their fragility, their beauty. Our best days together were in the forest, tracking flowers and salamanders, or doing some kind of forest activism; those adventures gave grounding to an often challenging relationship.

Matthew was an amazing companion, eager to show me the wonders of our forests and the people who defended them, but our relationship had a jaggedness to it. He was a tough guy, and I was never entirely sure of where I stood. I was twenty-three when we first met—he was older—and his love of motorcycles, pit bulls, and cigarettes, along with a strong desire not to be tied down, both attracted and frightened me. At heart, he was deeply kind and protective, especially toward animals and the natural world, and sometimes more sensitive than he himself could bear. One night, he lay in my bed curled up in physical pain while describing the violent maltreatment of animals in fur farms. But human relationships were difficult—for both of us—and we walked together unsteadily along the borders between wild nature and the human community, sometimes helping each other keep balance, sometimes not.

In the spring of 2000, those challenges faded into the background as a sense of anticipation built around me. Something was about to happen, and it seemed that my friends and I were at the center of it. Something was finally going to change. I had spent four years immersed in forest-protection work. It was my whole world, and I was ready to make real progress—not just suing governmental agencies and fighting timber sales one at a time, not just struggling to create cooperation among the competing environmental groups in the region. Something more, reaching out beyond the narrow world of environmental activism. Something that would sweep the nation and encircle the globe, leading people to forsake the false perception of separation and instead rejoice at reality: we are bound to the Earth, our fate and health and happiness inseparable from the planet. We belong to the Earth. Amen and hallelujah!

In early spring, Matthew had showed me a story written by an old Earth First! friend. It captured what I'd been thinking and lent fire to my dreaming:

> We are all under the impression that it is the forests, the creatures, the spirits, and the wildlands that are disappearing from the universe and not us. Not so.

Thinking like that is like thinking that if you stand on the end of a limb and saw that limb from the tree, the tree will fall and you will remain standing. Bugs Bunny might be able to get away with that, but we can't. It is we who have fallen away from the real world, into a world where we may carry out our twisted sterile dreams without threatening the earth and its inhabitants...

Somewhere, not so far from here, in the real world, the ancient forests are still standing, the buffaloes roam the prairies, the sky is full of condors, the deer and the antelope play, and dodo birds wander the sandy beaches, bumping into things. Where there are still wildlands in our dreamworld, strong connections still exist. Bridges, tunnels, portals.[5]

I read it and thought, YES! Yes. American chestnut trees still grow in the real world, and passenger pigeons flood the sky. Carolina parakeets nibble on cockleburs and dazzle the forests with feathers of orange, red, and green. I could see it in my mind, but how, I wondered, could I reach through the portals and bring the worlds together again?

I dreamed inside these dreams all spring, gathering heat through the month of April. Every aspect of my life

---

[5] Buck Young, *An Historical Overview of the Whereabouts of Gnomes and Elves, Fauns and Faeries, Goblins, Ogres, Trolls and Bogies, Nymphs, Sprites, and Dryads, Past and Present.*

began to take on extra layers of meaning. Words and images and encounters, no matter how distant, seemed intensely personal, deeply connected to me. Divine messages appeared within simple interactions. On May 1st, I called up Loki to check on a timber sale appeal that we were filing together. He was in Ohio, visiting Adam and Danielle. At the close of the conversation, I remembered the date.

"Hey! By the way, Happy Beltane."

Loki was grumpy, "Yeah, great. Just what we need. Another fertility festival. More babies."

"Come on," I said, "Fertility's not always a bad thing."

"On an overpopulated planet?"

"What about fertility of imagination? Or fertility of a really good idea. Or an endangered species?"

"I don't think that's what Beltane's generally about, Christina."

"I know, but think about it. What would a fertility ritual look like in an age of overpopulation? If the goal was specifically not to make babies. That would be really interesting to figure out."

Loki laughed. "Good luck with that," he said, but not unkindly. I wrote a note for myself after we hung up and left it on my desk: "Design non-reproductive fertility ritual."

The springtime tides began to run faster and hotter as May progressed. On the 5th, I took a different route on my evening walk and discovered the historical marker for the Battle of Waynesboro. I stayed up all night writing about the War and old traumas written on the landscape. On the 7th, I turned twenty-six. I gave myself a few days off work as a present and spent the time haunting the library, researching the Civil War in the Shenandoah Valley.

My writing was expansive. I sought a grand narrative to explain why people fight so perversely in favor of things, like mountaintop removal coal mining or a polluting factory, that harm their health and family and quality of life. Looking backward into the darkness of Virginia's past—beyond the Civil War to slavery and the slave trade, tobacco farming, Jamestown, genocide of native peoples— I sought answers for today: Why do we cling to this culture of death and hatred? Why do we create our own ruin? And why this death grip on the idea of ownership and property rights—the supposed "right" to destroy?

As days passed, my ideas leap-frogged and my writing became not just an exploration of history but a plea for liberation. I had been to the Jubilee 2000 rally in Washington, D.C. a few weeks earlier, calling for debt forgiveness for impoverished nations. The rally took its name from the Hebrew tradition of Jubilee: every 50 years, debts were forgiven, captives set free, the land left fallow to rest and replenish. I wrote that it was time for a jubilee of the spirit. Time to make a fresh start, to acknowledge and free ourselves from our tragic past and move on.

My mind jumped sideways, connecting to a new plot. It was also time, I wrote, for a hemp jubilee. A plant that could replace trees as a fiber source for paper, a plant that could replace tobacco as a cash crop in the South. A plant that was illegal for no good reason must be set free: Hemp Jubilee!

I pulled all these stories and themes together—Civil War, American chestnuts, slavery, ancestral memory, industrial hemp, forests and extinction and always The Land—and titled the draft *A Patchwork Theology of Soil Liberation.* Patches of idea and story, straining at the connecting seams but related just enough for the stitches to hold. My brain had leaped fast and quick between all these concepts, but my thoughts and speech remained coherent, my insights were real.

On the 7th, my friend James stopped by with birthday gifts. He and his wife Ruby lived around the corner, and I spent almost as much time with them as with Matthew, perched at their kitchen table, watching Ruby paint, or sculpt, or make tiny things out of beads. They lived in a cozy house, full of the jeweled colors of her paintings. With their four kids and a constant flow of friends, there was always a pleasant racket of activity. I liked to sit back and watch, talk with Ruby, listen to James sing. He thought my nickname "Shewulf" was hilarious and wrote me a song called "Loba Diabla"—devil wolf—"the last wolf in the mountain range, the only one that still remains." On my birthday, he knocked at the door with a massive bouquet of purple zinnias, a beaded bumblebee that Ruby had made for me, and a beautiful pipe, carved out of cherry wood with a bamboo stem.

"The tree was struck by lightning when I was in high school. I saved a few pieces—it seemed like there was a special mojo to it."

"James, you didn't have to do that. Thank you so much!"

"Can you tell what it's supposed to be?" I shook my head as he touched the concentric rings carved around the upper half of the pipe. "I thought you'd recognize it. This is the shape of a Civil War bullet, a minié ball." I felt goosebumps on my arms. "They find them around here from time to time. Haven't you seen the display case at the library?"

I threw myself a birthday party the next weekend and baked a vegan German chocolate cake with the rune of Ing—symbolizing light, energy, and abundant growth—carved into the icing. And then the full moon came, and Adam arrived. We shared the last of the cake, then early the next morning went with Matthew to his land by the Tye River. We took a swim in the deep pools between the river's blue rocks. As the sun warmed the stones, I looked up at the sycamore leaves waving across the clear sky and thought up a poem about a new season coming, a season of friendship that was just now beginning to stretch out its leaves. We could launch a new era, heal the kinship between humans and other creatures, embrace friendship with the land. I felt whimsical and dreamy and empowered. We could do this. Back at home, we packed up and said goodbye to Matthew, then Adam and I set off, picking up Loki in Staunton and heading south.

After the conference in Fries, after our stop at Beartree Lake, Loki, Adam, and I found a place to camp on the border of the Feathercamp Roadless Area in the Jefferson National Forest. It was nearly dusk, so we just pulled the Vanagon a little way off a dirt road. I pitched my tent in the woods nearby while Loki built a fire. The dark gathered; there was food and whiskey. Adam had his blue guitar, bought for $35 in Mexico. He had read my *Patchwork Theology* piece, with its Civil War stories, earlier that day.

"Do you know the song 'Spoon River'?" he asked.

"No."

"Your story reminded me of it. All the grief and beauty. Your writing sounds like an A minor chord." He strummed the sweetly eerie notes and smiled at me, then sang the song—sad and sweet as the summer evening, about the brave soldiers who fought in that bitter Civil War and now sleep in their graves. A song about the deep bruise left behind in a heartsick community, mourning the loss of family and friends.

I felt lightheaded as I listened, on the brink of crying. The sorrow in the song tore at an old wound, bullet-punctured and purpled with a ragged, unhealed edge. Who was I? Ever since I learned about the Civil War battlefield underfoot back home, I had felt haunted. Did some ghost take up residence inside me? The song woke a strangely familiar ache, much like the vague aura of pain I felt around Adam. Wartime grief and loss, my beautiful homeland turned into fields of slaughter, bodies left behind, unburied, after the fight had moved on. And yet the song was soothing somehow, a plea for love, for one more beginning. Adam finished singing and the night wrapped in around us.

"There never was reason for hurt," I murmured.

"No," Adam said. "No."

I listened as my heart beat and the wood cracked in the fire. Adam had opened up a hole in my side and started it healing at the same time. I felt a little scared of him; it seemed too intimate an act for someone I only casually knew. Then the night's silence tore open. The owls came sudden and swift and very close, their throaty voices like an answer to Adam's song. He and Loki leaped to their feet, returning the calls of the barred owls, and for a few moments the two men and two owls sang to each other. The haunted night shook off the gloom and seemed to laugh out loud.

Soon after, the clouds that had thickened all afternoon dumped a sudden rainstorm on our fire. We ran for the Vanagon. The storm was quick but very heavy. When I returned to my tent, it was full of water, my sleeping bag soaked through. I had left the rain fly unzipped. I crept back to the van, where Loki slept in the pop-up overhead, and whispered to Adam. He gestured for me to climb in. The backseat of the Vanagon folded down into a twin sized bed. I lay down beside Adam, and he slung the blanket over me.

I woke in the morning with static in my head—hazy and tired, needing to step away for some time alone. I hung my camping gear to dry while Adam did his morning yoga, then wandered off through the chirping, humid woods. My head ached. I smoked a bowl, and it hurt a little less. When I returned to the camp, Loki had disappeared. Adam was cleaning out the van.

"Where should we go now?" I asked.

Adam straightened up. "Well, I talked to Sean at the conference, and he invited us up to their place. Roxanne's out of town. He said we can stay as long as we want."

"Oh, fantastic!" I said, brightening. Sean was my boss, and I had been to his home many times. "You will love it! Their place is up on the side of Clinch Mountain, in the forest. They have a sweet farm house and a huge vegetable garden. And there's a tiny house in the garden with a sauna and stained glass windows and a hot tub..."

Adam laughed as I rhapsodized. "Alright then, let's go there."

In memory, the time we spent on Clinch Mountain has a dreamlike quality. The beauty and peace of the place stretched those few days into a slow, sunlit idyll. Sean and I spent a little while working, charting out a fundraising plan and priority projects for the summer, but mostly we took time off and called it team building. Loki and Adam helped Sean harvest strawberries—rifling their hands through a bed of low green leaves in the garden. We pondered shortcake but ate the berries straight from the bucket instead, still warm from the sun and dripping red.

On May 24th, we hiked Clinch Mountain, walking barefoot up the steep trail. In the forest, we encountered millipedes striped with yellow and orange and smelling, Loki pointed out, like almond extract. "The smell warns predators away," he explained, "because they're excreting cyanide." We found two box turtles in quiet repose beneath the understory flowers. And on the summit, a single, perfect lady slipper orchid—moccasin flower—bloomed in plush pink. Crouched on my hands and knees, eye-level with the blossom's seductive lobe and fold, I wondered at how much the flower resembled male and female genitalia combined.

I mused on that, how people also contain both feminine and masculine energies, and that reminded me of other things, older things—mythologies and stories from around the world about the power of male and female essences joining together, sometimes in physical union, sometimes even in one body—androgynous deities like the Hindu god Ardhanarishwara, half-man and half-woman with one breast and a penis, or the Greek god Hermaphroditus, child of Hermes and Aphrodite, in whom male and female bodies are fused into one.

Sean interrupted my thought as I gazed at the flower. "Did you know—our side of the mountain is named after that flower? Moccasin Valley." He pointed out how the forest changed here at the ridgeline from leafy, rippling deciduous trees, dense dark soils, and wildflowers to drier forest with pines and shrubs dominating. "The rock on our side of the mountain is limestone. That's why our garden grows so well—the soil is naturally rich." He gestured across the ridgeline, at the valley spread out at our feet. "This side of the mountain and on down into the valley is sandstone. They call it Poor Valley—poor soil, poor folk. The Carter Family kin are all from that valley."

I nodded, fascinated, and pointed out that—speaking of the Carter Family—did they know that today was Bob Dylan's birthday? Loki laughed and rolled his eyes. My status as a devotee was well-known.

We went down the mountain a different way, and I dropped back, running my hands along the exposed rock faces, interbeds of limestone and sandstone. I pressed my body against the rock, cooling my overheated forehead on the mountain, and dreamed of geologic time: the ancient love affair between Earth and Sky; stories of earth mother and sky father; the fertility that grows from joining soil and falling rain; water running over rock and making mountains. The vast scope of the Earth's age made my head light and giddy. I stumbled through a thick grove of May apples, slipped down a rocky gulch as stones scuffed my ankles and bruised my bare feet, drawing blood.

When I arrived late back at the farm, Adam hollered from the house, "Go wash your ankles, Rose invited us to supper!" The soap in the shower was Dr. Bronner's All-One Hemp Rose Pure-Castile soap. Hemp Rose, supper at Rose's—the coincidence of names seemed significant. Indeed, everything suddenly seemed magnified in significance, as though the moccasin flower on the mountain top had pulled open a door inside my mind—and now again and even more so, *everything* had meaning, a personal meaning, specifically for me, beamed instantly into my brain, and deeply interwound and interwoven with every part of my life.

Rose was Sean's mother-in-law. Well into her nineties, she lived just down the hill from the farmhouse. She had baked sweet biscuits for shortcake, and we brought the last of the strawberries, stripped quickly from the beds that evening. She showed me around her little home, through the keepsakes of her youth, and tears slid from her eyes as she spoke about losing a daughter that year to breast cancer. Loki charmed her into laughter; Adam sang her songs. She showed us pictures of her husband, and her mouth smoothed into a warm arc, eyes soft. She loved him, oh how she loved him, and he was there with her still, she said, always with her. I wiped a few tears from my own eyes, and we all smiled at each other around the supper table. Being with Rose turned us all into family.

The space between Adam and me, however, grew more oddly painful. That sense of familiarity I felt when he arrived in Waynesboro became discomfiting at Sean and Roxanne's farm. He was mostly a stranger, and yet he felt like my twin, fused at the hip and familiar as my own voice. Perhaps it was all in my mind, I don't know. My mind was slowly drowning; everything had a message for me, from the trees twisting in the wind before a storm, to the black cat named Spider that curled up in my lap every time I sat down, to Adam's silvery eyes that seemed to laser into mine across the creaking porch swing, leaving me disoriented. The wind rose to meet the thunder, and I was lifted up on a funnel of air, looking down into a whirlwind of entwined lives.

I never said anything—how can one speak of such things without sounding crazy?—but it seemed like he knew, he must know. As we sat together editing the *Patchwork Theology* piece, the porch pitched and rolled around us, my mind curling with vertigo and confusion. At night, I had dreams of fire. In one, I knelt in a cave where blazing flames filled the entrance. I did not try to escape. Hermes, the Greek messenger god, appeared on winged feet, leading Adam and Loki, silhouetted against the fire. I woke and lay sleepless for hours. I could have leaped from my skin that night and danced ghostly and bodiless among the turtles and millipedes and moccasin flowers on the slopes of Clinch Mountain.

We left Sean and Roxanne's place on the Thursday before Memorial Day, crumbs from Rose's homemade doughnuts littering the Vanagon floor, and crossed from southwest Virginia into Harlan County, Kentucky. This year's annual Bloodroot Gathering—a conference led by the coalition for eastern forest protection that Adam had helped organize ten years ago—would be at a decrepit Boy Scout camp built around a lake at the foot of Pine Mountain. The Blanton Forest State Nature Preserve lay just beyond the border of the camp, on the far side of Watts Creek. Although dilapidated, the camp buildings were scattered within a stunning hemlock forest, the tall, deeply-green trees doubled in reflection on the lake. The warm air looked golden with pollen and humidity.

When we arrived, a skeleton crew was there already, cleaning and setting up meeting spaces for workshops, prepping food. Gabe and Erin were running the kitchen; their girls were running everywhere. People came out to greet us, saying, "You've got to go up that mountain—it's amazing." Loki and Adam took off immediately. I stayed below to sweep out cabins and try to give my overflowing brain a chance to quiet.

THREE

Loki and I crossed Watts Creek together on my first climb up Pine Mountain, but by the time I reached Knobby Rock, he had disappeared. This was not unusual. The first time we went hiking together without a group to lead, he had slipped away, silent on bare feet, only to reappear a few hours later. He found me effortlessly while I struggled with the map, trying to keep my bearings. I began to appreciate his approach, so when I was in the woods without the responsibility of guiding a hike, I too would go solo into the understory. It is easier to notice the small things in solitary stillness, moving slow on bare feet, so I fell back from the group walking through Blanton Forest.

Majestic wildflowers filled the forest in late May. I had never seen the drooping golden flowers of blue bead lily in bloom or the white spires of galax blossoms above their glossy oval leaves. Cohosh and striped trillium sprouted from the rich soils, and everywhere groves of May apple twirled like faerie umbrellas—a single pale blossom on the female plants swaying low. The forest was in heat, flowering and fruiting and fertilizing, wild and gorgeous and overwhelming.

Knobby Rock appeared suddenly at my feet. The dirt path ended at a broad plateau of bumpy stone, canted steeply sideways. It looked like a choppy ocean turned to stone, or a congregation of turtles, I thought, smiling. Adam was there, slipping easily into leadership mode to guide a group up the mountain.

He turned and smiled, reaching his arm out to hug me. "What do you think?"

I shook my head. "There are no words."

"Wait 'till you see what's up ahead."

We gazed out into the valley and the mountains beyond, a vast view, lovely even with the scars from strip mining and clearcuts. He pointed across the valley where jags of mist dangled over folds in the mountain face.

"Imagine," he said, in a different voice—soft but distinct, calling me to pay attention. "Every place where mist is rising, there's water flowing down below." I looked at him curiously, but he had turned to gather people to him.

Further up the mountain, the forest changed. Huckleberry, blueberry, and mountain laurel grew in the understory. More oaks and pine filled the canopy. Here and there, springs and seeps formed marshy patches, covered with moss and fern.

"A spring like that feeds Watts Creek," Adam said. "We found it yesterday."

When we reached the Maze, Adam gestured to me to go in first. A long jumble of sandstone boulders created a series of caves and crevasses to climb over and under and through. The rock was beautiful, sparkling with thick sand granules and small stones, but rough—slow going on bare feet. I fell back again, letting the group move past me while I admired the moss and green plants growing beneath the boulders. A single hemlock sapling reached up toward a strand of sunlight that fell through a break in the rocks. Everyone I encountered along the way had a look of awe, a hushed reverence.

At the far end of the Maze, I stepped out from the boulders, back into the damp, rich, amazingly green forest. Fallen, moss-covered trunks leaned against massive rock formations. I thought I saw Adam back among the trees; he'd moved away from the group and climbed up between two young Eastern hemlocks. Holding on with each hand and each foot, he hung between them like a spider's web. I continued slowly along the trail, wondering if what I'd just seen was real—the line between truth and imagination had thinned considerably in the past week—and yet, I had no trouble making sense of the scene. Adam must be up there catching adelgid in his teeth, saving the trees from those wooly aphids that had been sucking hemlock needles to a dry death up and down the east coast. Another pestilence like the chestnut blight that might wipe out a native forest species.

I forgot Adam as the group rounded the corner of a last rock wall and stepped suddenly into the Sand Cave, a shallow cave hollowed in the sandstone at least a hundred feet high. The golden rock walls were streaked with undersea colors—washes of blues and greens and browns. A huge stone slab stood like an altar in the heart of the cave. Spray-painted high up on the cave wall, in cursive letters of ruby red paint, was the name "Jonetta." It cracked against my head like lightning.

Another sign! My heart thundered. This was clearly written just for me. There could be no question. "Jonetta." Matthew's last name was Jones. "Jonetta": male and female energies joining, joined in that name, and painted here in this astonishing place for all to see. For *me* to see. Surely this was the turning point, the call to mark the beginning of a new age. My legs staggered back involuntarily, as though they might drop out from beneath me.

Someone said, or I think they said, "You should take that as your middle name."

"Yes," I think I said. "I know."

~ ~ ~

I, the fiery life of divine essence, am aflame beyond the beauty of the meadows, I gleam in the waters, and I burn in the sun, moon, and stars.... I awaken everything to life.

- Hildgard of Bingen, *Liber Divinorum*

Here her brain begins to cook and steam. On the mountain top, barefoot and believing, she is ecstatic. She takes long curling threads of religious practices from around the world and dances with them, spinning them together, red and gold, white and black, like a child weaving ribbons around a May Pole. She knows the answer to the riddle she had set herself back at Beltane, on the 1st of May: create a non-reproductive fertility ritual? Easy.

Take the usual ritual of the season—the Great Rite, marriage of goddess and god to bless fields and wombs, to bring forth crops and children—and turn it sideways. In fact, take it overseas, to India, and then go inward, to the belly and the brain and the spine. Mix in themes of alchemy and yoga: male and female energies moving through the body, embracing, entwining. And their union is fruitful, but instead of babies, it brings bliss, enlightenment, vision, and healing that can be shared with the broader community. Such union could bring renewal, too, she thinks, renewal for all the world. Health and healing between people and the planet—the season of friendship at last.

Sand Cave has emptied out. She is alone with the forest and with her revelation. She notices the skeleton of an American chestnut tree leaned up against the rock wall of the cave. This mountain must have been covered in chestnuts once, before the blight. She climbs up on this one, lays her cheek against the smooth silvery wood and finds herself crying. The mountain is lonely without these trees, the giants of the eastern forest. And she is lonely too, heartbroken at what humans have done, at the lost species, the extinctions.

She remembers Adam hung up between the hemlock trees like some crucified figure and is distraught. So many religious traditions include the story of a dying and rising god, a man sacrificed for the renewal of the Earth or the removal of sin. But she does not want this. She will not invoke a sexual rite—this is a non-reproductive fertility ritual after all—and she does not want a dying god, not this time, and certainly not her dear friend Adam. Human history has seen too many ritual deaths, too much blood sacrifice. If anyone must die, she will be the one.

For now, she offers her tears for these trees—the chestnut, the hemlock—a tiny repentance on behalf of her species. After a time, she stands up on the chestnut bole, and her feet slip on the damp wood. She falls, landing on her hand, feeling bruise slam through her palm, a thin crack opens in the bone. Such is the price of these things, she thinks, I am not afraid to sacrifice.

Cradling her hand, she moves through the cave, gazing up at the rainbow walls and the name in brilliant red. On the ground beneath "Jonetta," someone has left a cracked turtle shell. She picks it up. Inside are two broken millipede shells. She thinks of the vivid hike up Clinch Mountain with turtles, almond-scented millipedes, and the moccasin flower in bloom. In a ritual trance, she carries the empty shells toward Watts Creek. The stream flows beneath the sandstone boulders here; she must crawl and jump and contort to get to the water, careful of her hand, landing on thick mats of hemlock needles. She finds a place where the water drops into a tumbling cascade and releases the empty shells into the stream with a prayer. You cannot put new wine into old wineskins, she thinks. Flowing water is renewal. The turtle is a mythical symbol—Turtle Island, a stack of turtles holding up the Earth. The broken shells will become whole, bringing healing. She is helping to birth a new world.

Later, as she tries to find her way down the mountain, she becomes lost. She wrestles and slides through thick jig-saw arms of rhododendron. The plants grow so tall and intertwined that she often has to backtrack, finally slithering onto Knobby Rock scratched and bruised. The others are there. She blinks at them as though emerging from a dream, from another world. She is tired and sits to rest. An ant crawls onto her foot and tastes the blood from a cut between her toes. She waits while it drinks. She has offered herself to this place. Whatever it asks of her, she will not deny it.

At the base of the mountain, she discovers a red car in the camp parking lot that was not there before. A sign on the door reads "Hemp Jubilee." Awed, she kneels to touch it. She had written about just such a thing in her story, the *Patchwork Theology.* Now, it is beginning to come true! Her writing made manifest and tangible in the world. The renewal begins.

The Hemp Jubilee turns out to be a traveling store run by a young couple who make hemp clothing. Hanging from the porch of the camp dining hall are elegant long hemp dresses with slits up the side for dancing. One is royal purple. The young woman smiles and bows to the vendors, saying, "Thank you. Thank you for making this one for me." She buys the dress and puts it on.

When she stows her other clothes in the Vanagon, she finds Adam's blue guitar. She sits in the front seat with her feet propped on the open door and begins to play. She took lessons for a few months in high school with two girlfriends, mostly as an excuse to spend time together and, after the lessons, to walk along the railroad tracks smoking cigarettes and dreaming big dreams. She remembers only a few clumsy chords from that time. But today she plays as though someone else's fingers move through hers—easy and clean, rhythmic—channeling a new song.

She breathes lyrics that come unbidden to her mind. The camp caretaker stops by to listen.

"You sound good," he says.

"Thanks!" she replies, not pausing in the song, "We're going out on the road real soon."

Later, at one of the conference's discussion circles, she rises briefly to speak. Her friend Jerry stands with her, holding onto her hand, as she says to the group, "We must make the world safe for children. We must protect the innocent eyes." And she speaks the names of Gabe and Erin's daughters—Laurel and Alarka—along with the names of wild creatures, the box turtles in the forest, barred owls in the trees.

She spends the rest of the afternoon watching children catch frogs and salamanders in the lake. As she kneels to peer into the water, Laurel lays a net on her head, laughing: "I'm so glad that we caught you!" On her knees, the young woman bows her head to the little girl, humbled and honored. She has been anointed, crowned by this faery child with curling hair and dark eyes.

That evening proves difficult. She felt calm with the children, but adults make her skittish. She wonders if she can speak aloud about the mountaintop magic. Surely Adam and Loki must already know. They are her brothers. They understand her, surely they can read her mind.

On her second time up the mountain, the next day, another idea grows in her mind. Another thread of ritual, another interpretation. Climbing mountains, she thinks, is like yoga. The act of pilgrimage up the mountain takes effort and will, creates heat to enliven the kundalini serpent coiled at the base of the spine. The movement of the pilgrim up the mountain lifts the serpent, the body's female energy, up the spinal column to the skull. The male energy dwells there, in the top of the body, on the peak of the mountain. And it is there, on the mountaintop, where the male and female energies join.

As in yoga, their union brings transfiguration, and new energy descends from the brain into the body as enlightenment, purification, healing. Likewise, pilgrims descend the mountain and return into the world, bringing with them the transformative wisdom of the mountaintop, a great healing power. She wrote a paper speculating about this in college. Her Hinduism professor never told her if he thought she was right or wrong, though he did give her an "A" and grinned his elfish grin, saying, "You'll have to go to India to find out."

Then she remembers Adam talking about mist rising over flowing water. The rain that falls, the mist that rises between Mother Earth and Father Sky. The evaporation cycle! Is that the origin of yoga? Of course! The connections are everywhere, the stories and mythologies lie before her like a painter's palette. She needs only to choose the correct combination. Mix and match. She is recreating religion now. No problem.

She continues climbing, barefoot as always, through dense forest, crossing Knobby Rock, and on into the Maze. She feels quite pleased with herself. Through this pilgrimage, through the journey and the climb, she has found a way to make an offering of herself on this mountaintop, to heal and renew the Earth using internal heat and union—no sacrificial death and no giving birth. A non-reproductive fertility ritual. Loki will be so proud.

And it seems that others are proud too. Around her, she senses ghosts. Beloved, helpful ghosts. Her grandfather, who flickers above her on raven wings, protecting and guiding, and Matthew's uncle who owned the land by the Tye River and who was her gymnastics teacher as a child. He catches her when she loses her balance on the mountainside, sets her foot on solid rock and says, "There. Now you can't do anything wrong." And she is strengthened, running her fingers along the stones, joyful, guided, never alone.

When she arrives, sweaty and sun-drenched at the Sand Cave, Adam is there, on the great altar rock inside the cave. He appears to be doing yoga. She is pleased that he understands, that he has agreed without speaking to be part of this. She does not go near him but simply waits, breathing the life of the forest into her body, holding him with her mind, keeping them both safe while the magic rises through them and billows outward. Male and female. They are working together. Perhaps this is why he has

seemed so painfully familiar, so they could be ritual part-
ners in a yogic mountaintop fertility dance in which they
do not touch or speak or even come face to face.

She has never been able to articulate what happened in
this time on the mountain. Something golden and vast
and threaded with power. A great light and rush of wind.
Perhaps—and this is what she prays, later, when she begins to wonder if she made a terrible mistake by messing
with rituals that are not her own, begins to fear that she is
being punished for some sacrilege—perhaps, just perhaps,
there on Pine Mountain, a hole opened between the
worlds and a wild gust of healing wind, burnished with
flame, spilled across the threshold that stretched between
her and Adam. Perhaps, she prays, that healing is still carrying on, somewhere below the surface of the jittery, dangerous world. Or perhaps it was not enough, perhaps she
failed, perhaps that is why.

◆

I told Adam later that returning to the camp and the
gathering below felt like walking into a room full of mortals wearing the face of a sky god. He nodded sadly; I think
he said, "I know." I could not communicate what had happened. An aura like blazing arrows flared out from me.
People seemed to look at me strangely, and I felt punc-

tured, exhausted, and yet at the same time, exhilarated, wildly alive.

That night, the weak joint between those two extremes in my brain gave way. I felt it, like a boulder that cracks then crashes downhill in a landslide. I wept by the stone fireplace of the camp dining hall and was comforted by friends. A band was playing at the front of the hall, and people danced around me, stopping to lay hands upon me. I told Adam that I would have died if not for the kindness of those friends. I could not express what was wrong. I hurt with the wounds of the world—the lost chestnuts and dying hemlocks, the extinctions, the broken people. I broke publicly, my brain cleaving in two for all to see.

~ ~ ~

Dance, when you're broken open...
Dance when you're perfectly free.
– Rumi, "The Longing"

Late that night, the crowd thins out and she rises to her feet. She is finished weeping and feels an electric thrill in the night. Loki and Adam and others are drumming in the dining hall. She walks out to the porch and hears them chanting with the drums. They seem to say, *You are the one. You are the one.* Me? she thinks. Yes, it must be. She begins to dance, dance among the tables of brochures and petitions—campaigns to end forest destruction, to promote renewable energy, to clean up elections. She picks up the ideas, twirls them around her to build the framework for the healthy future that she is dancing into being.

Behind the lids of her eyes, she sees the intricate patterns of Mayan temple carvings and Celtic knotwork. She is weaving prayers for a new beginning, dancing with the drums. She sinks downward, down to black bedrock, deep and subterranean, the foundation stone of Turtle Island. From here we will rebuild, she thinks, and her dance braids together all the extremes of her mountain pilgrimages, all the learning of these past months, the yearning for healing, mending the rift between people and Earth, mending traumas to the land. And here at last, she finds the portal, reaches through, and dances the worlds together.

All night, along the shore of the lake, she dances alone in the dress of purple hemp, long after the drums fall silent and the camp falls asleep. She dances into deeper and wordless places, into the black void and through it. She dances as nameless, ancient gods and goddesses, the stars and planets, creatures extinct and alive. She is Siva-Natajara, the Hindu Lord of the Dance, whose dance destroys ignorance and creates new worlds. Around her in the night, the bullfrogs in the lake and barred owls in the forest call out to her, and she weaves them into the story that is the dance. Her heart is a super nova, radiating light.

The world takes form and reforms around her. At the cusp of dawn, she waltzes with the waning moon as it slides toward the glimmering lake, thinks of Adam's wife, Danielle, and they dance together, hand-in-hand; the young woman bows to her, thanking her for the healing of friendship.

♦

I woke by the fireplace in the dining hall, after a single brief hour of sleep. The early risers were arriving for breakfast. It was Memorial Day, the last day of camp. But I did not wake into a day of celebration for my miraculous night of dance. Instead, I woke to Adam asking if I had a way to get back to Virginia. He and Loki were traveling on to Ohio, without me. Disoriented by sleeplessness, I stared at him. What? Although we had made no plans to continue traveling together, he and Loki had been my companions, my safety net. How could they leave? I wanted to tell Adam everything. To talk about what I knew and what he too must know. Instead, distraught and exhausted, I struggled to understand. This didn't fit with the story I'd woven in my mind.

"There's a meeting in Asheville I'm supposed to go to later this week. I could catch a ride from there back to Virginia." We looked at each other. Knowing what the other was thinking.

"Gabe and Erin."

"You could stay there for a few days."

He went with me to find them in the kitchen and helped us hatch a plan. Then he and Loki hugged me goodbye. I stood in front of the dining hall, squinting into hot morning sun, and waved as the blue Vanagon pulled away, kicking up yellow dust. The raw glare hurt my head, left me bereft and feeble. None of this seemed right, but I was too tired to understand, too confused. My eyes ached, and I felt suddenly enormously lonely.

Later that day, I packed up my tent and drove south through the Appalachians with Erin and Gabe, heading for their mountain farm, for the cresting wave of mania.

FOUR

I woke out of dreamless blackness under a thin blue blanket in Fairfax Hospital on June 3rd, 2000. Sunlight slid in through the closed blinds, glowing off white walls and a pale blue plastic curtain drawn between my bed and the next. My mother sat at the foot of the bed, watching me. She had spread her red raincoat over me while I slept in the chilly room. My eyes fixed on her face—lovely and familiar—and now so pale as to be almost gray. I felt relieved, reassured by her presence. I remembered her and my father swapping nights at this same hospital when I was eight years old and nearly died of a ruptured appendix. I took a deep breath, then another.

They had driven eight hours to Tennessee to pick me up at Gabe and Erin's, then another eight to return to the D.C. suburbs where I grew up. Arriving at the hospital late in the night, my mother refused sleep to wait with me, to make sure I didn't wake up alone, in a manic state, terrified and furious to be hospitalized. They recognized the fragility of the moment, the potential for their relationship with me, and my trust for them, to shatter.

I could not put a name to the drawn look in my mother's eyes—lonely, lost, yet steely and hard. In times of crisis, my mother transforms fear into rapid, efficient action. She had experience as a nurse in the Navy during the Vietnam War. Extremely smart, extremely competent, I had never seen her panic. She may have cried in the last few days, but her eyes now were dry, flecked with a knife edge of despair, and something more, something she would later describe to me as terror. They had no diagnosis on that first morning, only their brief experience of a crazed and frantic daughter.

I woke into what seemed like remarkable clarity in the early afternoon. They had knocked me out with Ativan, an anti-anxiety drug. It must have been a big dose. I had evaporated instantly off the gurney and slept in pure black. We spoke cautiously, avoiding eye contact.

"Have you been here all night?"

"Yes. Dad went home to rest. He started having trouble with his heart again last week in New York." Her voice sounded strange and alien, flat as tundra. Was she angry? I felt the first fan of guilt open across my chest.

I had forgotten that my parents had been in New York City the previous week. While I lost my mind in the mountains, my father had led the U.S. delegation to the re-authorization of the Nuclear Non-Proliferation Treaty in his new role as U.S. Ambassador to the treaty. It was a crowning moment in his career as a life-time civil servant, a proud achievement for anyone, even more so for a man who grew up poor on a farm in Iowa. The event had followed years of travel to signatory nations, hopscotching across every continent. The work he loved.

"What's wrong?" I asked, guessing at the answer. Rheumatic fever had ripped through his family as a child. Left untreated on the Iowa farm, the disease had ravaged his heart and those of his siblings. One by one in their later years, they'd had heart valves replaced or repaired. Six years before, in 1994, my Aunt Betty had died of a valve malfunction while Dad was on a plane flying to North Korea, the first Westerner to visit their secret nuclear facilities. Prior to a heart surgery in 2001, one of my father's valves flopped slightly, and the chambers of his heart sometimes chattered discordantly.

"He's out of rhythm again. It makes him tired." Her voice eerily neutral.

"I know," I said. "I'm sorry."

As my mother and I talked, visions of Blanton forest and Gabe and Erin's farm, of Laurel, Alarka, Adam and Loki, seeped into my mind, streaks of color lighting up the bleak hospital room like sunrise flaming the underside of clouds. I rubbed my bruised toes against the thick, bleached sheets, felt the ache in my broken hand, and breathed with relief. I could still remember. It had all been real. Immediately, I wanted out. Out of this pale, sterile place, back into that whirl of color and connection, but some instinct told me to wait. Stay calm. Take time to clear up the misunderstanding that had brought me here.

In my memory of that waking, I was present and clear, grounded and sane. I could comprehend and communicate, but I slipped rapidly back into a self-centered universe. I had no wallet or luggage, yet to my delighted surprise, I could remember the numbers on my calling card. I began dialing up friends to let them know that I was ok. The conversations were confusing. I assumed that everyone knew I'd been wrongly imprisoned in this hospital, but no one seemed to know what to say.

I moved cautiously through the cold, fluorescent hospital corridors. The psychiatric ward was a weird cross between a prison and a hotel. Hospital workers changed the sheets on the beds, cleaned the bathrooms, and brought food trays to the cafeteria, but the nurses watched my every move. My belongings had been searched. No one could have sharp objects, and the doors to the ward were always locked. Each time the nurses re-locked the doors after admitting doctors and visitors, I felt fear jerk tight across my shoulders. Psychiatric wards have a bad reputation. I could not shake the constant, low-grade dread that they would not let me leave.

So I didn't pitch a fit, didn't try to escape. I played along, went to the group meetings and recreational therapy, drew pictures in the craft room, pretended to participate, but mostly I watched the windows, gazed at the sky and clouds and sunsets, counting down the moments until I could get out, back to my mountain forest epic, my radiant transformation, my friends. Everything else became peripheral.

After my Dad came to visit and I knew that he was ok, I pulled away emotionally from my family, both irritated that they had put me here and guilty about frightening them. They needed to understand—what had happened to me was strange, yes, and my behavior was unsettling, but it grew from an extraordinary religious experience, something that could never happen again. The conditions simply could not be duplicated. There was no cause for alarm.

I explained this again to the young, bearded psychiatrist. Tall and angular, he folded himself into a chair while I perched on the hospital bed.

"Don McLean," he introduced himself.

I laughed. How appropriate for me—a faerie queen, healer of the Universe—to have a famous psychiatrist. *Bye bye, Miss American Pie...* I sang to myself and played along with the game. He showed me the diagnosis written in my chart and explained that I had manic depression. It was treatable.

"I understand you're interested in natural healing, herbal medicine?"

I nodded, thinking sadly of my confiscated cherry bullet pipe, and the herbal healing of cannabis—*sativa, indica*—like the goddesses of India.

"Yes, I am."

"Well, lithium is the gold standard of treatment for manic depression, and it's an element on the periodic table. You can't get any more natural than that."

I smiled. I liked him. There was a kindness to him, and he spoke to me with palpable respect. But my mind closed at the word "lithium." I did not trust psychiatric drugs. I had friends who had been put on anti-depressants after a single visit to a doctor. The drugs were over-prescribed, I thought, probably unnecessary in the vast majority of cases. Perhaps a sign of weakness in those who took them.

"No, I'm sorry. I'm not taking lithium." I leaned forward to make myself clear. "I had a religious experience. Something divine happened on that mountaintop. There's no way that this combination of things could ever, *ever* happen again. I don't need medication."

McLean tried again. I had sent my folks an early draft of *A Patchwork Theology*. They had shown it to Dr. McLean, along with my manic scribblings from Gabe and Erin's porch. He held up the patchwork piece.

"This is really good, very insightful and well-written. I learned a lot." Then he smoothed down a page of the scribblings, "But this is hard to decipher. It doesn't make sense. Don't you want people to understand what you have to say?"

Exasperated, I told him, "*You* don't understand. It won't happen again."

Finally they let me go. After a few days of sleep and food, I was calm—a grayish mood cut with thin flickerings of agitation. The doctor, my parents, my brother, and I sat in a common room and put an agreement down on paper. I would be set free, but I would go to Charlottesville to stay with a friend for a while instead of going home alone to my apartment in Waynesboro; I would get plenty of rest and eat well and exercise; I would never get high again.

~ ~ ~

Manic-depressive illness magnifies common human experiences to larger-than-life proportions. Among its symptoms are exaggerations of normal sadness and joy [and] profoundly altered thinking... In more intense episodes, [the above changes] profoundly disrupt the lives of patients, their families, and society.
- Frederick K. Goodwin & Kay Redfield Jamison
Manic Depressive Illness: Bipolar Disorders and Recurrent Depression, 2nd edition

I left Fairfax Hospital on June 6th, a cool and drizzly day. I woke to rain dimpling the roof outside my hospital window and sighed with relief. For days, I'd had a hunch that, when the rain came, I would be released. My parents drove me to Waynesboro first to pick up clothes, overnight gear, and my car.

Heading west on I-66, I saw the new roadside signs for the Mosby Heritage Area, named for the Confederate officer John Mosby who had led a band of partisan rangers throughout Northern Virginia during the Civil War. I sat straight up, my gray mood lifted instantly. It was all true. It was still happening! The stories that I had brought to light in my writings and pilgrimages were still unfolding. The hospital had not taken my memory, and it had not stopped my miracle. I wanted to cheer.

My parents chaperoned me to Charlottesville where they dropped me off at my friend EQ's peaceful, airy house. I camped out there for a week on a fold-out couch surrounded by trailing house plants set in open windows. EQ and his late wife had been friends and mentors to me for years, strong supporters of my activism. EQ ran a small, private school where some of his students struggled with psychiatric issues, so he had some familiarity with my situation. When he'd heard about my hospitalization, EQ contacted my parents to ask if he could help.

I had been encouraged to rest and relax, and for a few days, I did. Floating ethereal through the quiet house, I wrote long letters to Loki and Adam, explaining that I was okay and lithium-free, but now felt like a bright red question mark had been stamped on my brain. My friends in Charlottesville treated me like I had become suddenly fragile and strange. Worst of all, I had an uncomfortable, unsettled sensation inside my skull, as though my eyes remained out of focus even with my glasses on. A new low-level anxiety skittered around me, nipping at my heels.

Sean had suggested that I take some time off work, so I set aside the unstarted grant proposal and unearthed my *Patchwork Theology* piece. I wanted to draw my healing focus closer to home, to Virginia and the early history of America. At the weekend, I went with Loki to Washington, D.C. for a conference on eastern forest protection. We stayed with an activist friend named Alvin. As we drove around the city, I told him what had happened to me in the past few weeks. The next morning, Alvin said, "You told me one of your secrets, come see one of mine," and took me to my first 12 Step meeting. We sat in the back of the room, and I squeezed his arm and whispered, "I'm proud of you."

On Monday, conference attendees dressed up in business attire and went to lobby on Capitol Hill for a bill to end logging in National Forests. I participated calmly, but beneath a well-mannered exterior, my mind had started again to whirl. Every inch of ground felt sacred underfoot, and in Washington, D.C., so much history, so many symbols loomed around me. And every symbol attracted meaning like a magnet, until there were layers and layers—all reaching out to my mind. I walked slowly, aware of the soil, of the trees and their deep roots growing under sidewalks and asphalt. With each footstep, I thought, I am waking the wild. I was a sacred messenger, calling forth the links between humans and the Earth. I slipped off my shoes and went barefoot on the Capitol lawn.

Later that day, on a whim, I stopped at Arlington National Cemetery to visit Robert E. Lee's house. I was curious about him. From my Civil War research for *A Patchwork Theology*, I had learned hazy bits of his story—that he'd been offered command of the Federal forces but turned it down to fight for Virginia; that he never owned slaves himself, but inherited them from his father-in-law and then set them free; and that, after his surrender at Appomattox, he encouraged his soldiers to go home and be good citizens of the United States. To me, he seemed a mournful, tragic figure.

My earliest awareness of Lee came from peering out the back window of my parents' car as a child, driving across Memorial Bridge into D.C. The Custis-Lee Mansion, called Arlington House when the Lee family lived there, seemed to glower from the hilltop behind me, grim and coppery orange in the setting sunlight, surrounded by the National Cemetery's acres of sad, pale headstones. Set in the midst of a vast graveyard, the house frightened me.

"Who lives there?" I was young, so my Dad tried to explain in simple terms.

"That was Robert E. Lee's house. He was a general for the South during the Civil War. The Northern army occupied the land and started burying soldiers who'd been killed in the war around his house."

"Why?" I was shocked.

"They were angry. They felt he'd betrayed the country and wanted to punish him for leaving the U.S. Army to fight for the South." I shivered and turned my gaze away.

Now, in 2000, I made my way up stone paths past the dead of many wars, noticing the huge, graceful trees keeping watch between the graves. I stopped at a Southern magnolia tree and stood on my toes to smell the honeyed sweetness of the plate-sized flower. Rain water spilled from the curved petals onto my shoulder. I was still wearing my lobbying clothes.

At the top of the hill, the mansion stood empty. The inside was surprisingly small, but massive columns lined the front portico, and the view was extraordinary. With awe, I realized that the house's direct line of sight crossed the Memorial Bridge to the Lincoln Memorial, then to the Washington Monument, and far in the distance, the Capitol. The National Park Service brochure in my hand explained that in 1955, Congress had made the Custis-Lee Mansion a memorial to Robert E. Lee. And so this alignment... my God... Had they meant to create this symbolism of healing and reconciliation, or was it only in my mind? Memorial Bridge literally bridged the divide between North and South, between Washington, D.C. and Virginia, between Lincoln's monument and the memorial to the hero of the Confederacy. All connected. Tears leaped suddenly to my eyes. It was too much for me. I had to step away.

All around the mansion, the Park Service was restoring the gardens where Lee's wife and daughters had grown flowers. I walked along small stone pathways between beds of herbs and roses. The Park Service brochure painted a romantic portrait of the General: "It was Lee's custom to gather roses in the garden each morning and place one beside the plate of each woman present at breakfast." I took another step and the genteel spell broke—a flat, gray slab of stone lay in the middle of the path, marking a Union officer's grave. Then another. And another. The graves encircled the Lees' gardens, and some officers had been laid to rest within it.

I followed the paths back behind the house into a grove of old oaks and black gum trees. Here, the Union army had erected the Tomb of the Civil War Unknowns, a tall box of pale marble, mottled green and black with moss. The inscription read:

Beneath This Stone Repose The Bones Of Two Thousand One Hundred And Eleven Unknown Soldiers Gathered After The War From The Fields Of Bull Run, And The Route To Rappahannock. Their Remains Could Not Be Identified. But Their Names And Deaths Are Recorded In The Archives Of Their Country, And Its Grateful Citizens Honor Them As Of Their Noble Army Of Martyrs. May They Rest In Peace. September A.D. 1866

I walked around the massive tomb. Two thousand one hundred and eleven men? The weather had turned damp, with a chilly drizzle. Their bones gathered after the war. The remains could not be identified. My feet were cold in my dress shoes. Uniforms rotted away, bones scattered. The stones of the path pressed painfully through the thin soles of my shoes. No doubt the remains of both Federals and Rebels lay intermingled within the tomb. Honored by its grateful citizens. Reconciled in death? I hugged my arms, shivering.

I was cold, hungry, and emotionally drained when I returned to the mansion and noticed a smaller house set behind it: the quarters for some of the enslaved household staff. Inside, the Park Service display included pictures and short summaries of their life stories. I had read that Lee's father-in-law, who owned Arlington House and its many slaves before his death, was considered a "good" slave owner. His will required manumission for all his slaves. I had read that Lee himself disapproved of slavery and never owned slaves himself, but the stories in the slave quarters proved much more complicated than those romanticized biographies. Even if the household slaves at Arlington House were considered "part of the family," even if Lee's wife taught the enslaved children to read during a time when that was illegal in Virginia, the cold brutality of ownership still cast a sickening pall. Lee may not have believed in slavery, but he didn't free the enslaved people owned by his family until five years after his father-in-law's death. Such is the nature of "property"—the owner can do as he pleases.

I slid my palms along the stone walls of the house, remembering. A few weeks earlier, before my mind broke open, I had visited a small plantation house in Charlotte County, Virginia as part of my job. Virginia Wildlands had coordinated a tour of a bad logging job there for a group of state elected officials. After the event, the landowners—two archeologists from Baltimore—showed me some of the artifacts that they'd unearthed at the site. My guide placed a tiny shoe on my open palm, found under the floorboards of the house.

"We think that this was the baby shoe of a slave child," he told me. "The shoe of a white child would probably have had holes for laces or buckles."

This slipper had only a simple slit for the baby's foot. I stood rooted to the spot. The child who had worn this shoe had been owned by another person. *Owned.* I could not speak. The tangible reality of slavery was here resting on my skin. A few days later, back in Waynesboro, I had discovered the Civil War battlefield beneath my home, and in my mind, pieces began clicking into place—how history is embedded in the land; how the land connects us to the traumas of the past; how ownership of land and the environmental destruction done in the name of "property rights" connects back to slavery, one of the nation's original traumas, psychological scars burned deep into the present day.

Slavery had destroyed so much: the lives of the men and women stolen from their homes in Africa, and also the claim to morality among Europeans. White Americans involved with slavery turned cruel and selfish, entangled in a ghastly hypocrisy—enslaving human beings while professing to believe in liberty and equality, despising a group of people while confessing faith in the teachings of Christ. In America, slavery fundamentally changed our ability to love and to trust. Could we recover from such a massive wound?

As I walked away from Arlington House, the drizzle thickened into rain. I wondered if Lee had felt this way when he left for the war in April 1861, never to return. Was he shaken by moral confusion, saddened by the circumstances that would lead him and his divided loyalties down such a destructive road? I felt sick at heart and yet had the strangest feeling that Lee would be on my side— that he *was* on my side in this quest: reconciling the past and the present would heal the rift between humanity and the land. I knew it. I knew I could do it. I knew the next stop on my journey.

~ ~ ~

If you want to sing with angels, you've got to dance with ghosts.

- Danny Dolinger, "Walking in Power"

During the next few weeks, I divided my time between work, family, and roadtrips to recruit ghosts in Lexington and Richmond, Virginia. For a brief interlude after the hospitalization—about twelve days—I kept my promise not to get high. But when a pipe passed by me at a party in mid-June, I took it. Sparks lit up my brain followed by a familiar spiral-shaped buzzing, like pollen-drunk insects on a hot day, and my thoughts sped up. I could feel the shift and hear it: the rattle and squeal of an old tape recorder on fast forward. At first, the experience frightened me, and I refused the pipe the next time it passed by and did not smoke again for several days. But the sweetness and sparkle were addictive, and the plant seemed to expand my vision so that I could see the connections between ideas and concepts more clearly and watch the patterns unfold in kaleidoscope colors.

During the drug-free interlude, my life seemed mostly normal, though perhaps more highly charged than usual. I did some work, helped out with a rally at the Forest Service office in Roanoke, Virginia, protesting the influence of private corporations on logging in the National Forests.

My mother came to visit me in Charlottesville, and we went to Monticello—Thomas Jefferson's home. After the tension of my hospitalization, her visit was a chance for us to reconnect. Together, we took the fascinating new Mulberry Row tour that focused on slavery at the plantation. In the museum bookstore, my Mom bought me a book of slave narratives, smiling at the cashier and explaining, "My daughter's writing a book." I glowed.

Even as I moved home to Waynesboro and began to engage again with my job, the life of the past remained more real to me than the present. Matthew and other friends, as well as my family, all exuded a concern and watchfulness that put me on edge. I kept them at a distance. I didn't want to worry them—and why should they worry? I was fine! But I couldn't give up this quest. The past called out for my help. I could heal these layers of broken history.

I traveled to Lexington on a cool summer evening both to pay my respects and to recruit; Lee was already on my side, so I simply whispered my greetings to him in the Chapel at Washington and Lee University. Thomas Jonathan "Stonewall" Jackson was trickier. I knew very little about him except tidbits that I'd read during my pre-manic research: Jackson lived in Lexington before the Civil War, taught at the nearby Virginia Military Institute, and was buried in the town's graveyard. He was, by all accounts, an eccentric man. He had protected the Shenandoah Valley—breadbasket of the Confederacy—from federal control with clever strategy and an army of fast-moving, often-barefoot, Valley boys. He loved to eat lemons. His wife, like Lee's, was named Mary. He too broke Virginia law by teaching enslaved people in his Sunday school class before the war. He had been killed by friendly fire in 1863 at age 39, leaving behind a two-year-old daughter.

I visited Jackson's grave in Lexington but found no trace of his presence. After reading a bit more about his life, I decided to seek him out in Richmond. I had a meeting there on the day after Midsummer, the perfect excuse for a pilgrimage.

~ ~ ~

Let us cross over the river and rest under the shade of the trees.
- Reputed last words of Thomas "Stonewall" Jackson

I rose before dawn on Midsummer Day. Mist filled the hollows of the Blue Ridge, and I thought briefly of Adam—"Wherever there's mist rising, there's water flowing down below." Today was his birthday. Adam Matthew had a summer solstice birthday; Matthew Adam was born on midwinter—polar opposites, these two men who loomed so large in my life.

I took the Blue Ridge Parkway south, passing through patches of fog and the beginnings of dawn, then turned east at the Tye River. The mist parted before me in layers, as though I was drawing back veils. I waded across the Tye barefoot, dressed again in the purple hemp dress and wearing a white jacket that my mother had given me. In it, I looked like a nurse, a Civil War nurse perhaps, a healer. I had pot in my pocket, mostly seeds. I planted some there on Matthew's land by the great flat rock that was my praying place, my altar. I knelt and gave thanks, asking for help and guidance, and always for the Great Healing, always. I laid the seeds in the dark, loose earth and sprinkled them with water. As I climbed up to my car from the river, the sun was rising. Two dogs were running up the road through the mist.

Richmond was not my favorite city. Before becoming the Capital city of the Confederacy, Richmond had been the capital of the slave trade. Slave ships sailed up the James River and unloaded their human cargo onto Richmond's auction blocks. During much of the Civil War, the city was under siege, filled with masses of refugees and wounded soldiers; there was starvation, with bread riots led by local women. Richmond remained a haunted place—grief and anger trembled just out of sight; I could feel them in the air like a palpable weight.

The heaviness reminded me of the shadow cast by the War in the Shenandoah Valley—the bitter memory that still lingered in the minds of some Valley residents of the time they called The Burning. In 1864, Union troops under Generals Sheridan and Custer burned farms and barns and grain mills in the Valley, destroying livestock and livelihood, cutting off the Confederate Army's best supply of food. Anger rippled even today, underscored by maudlin mythologies, and always there was this sense that ownership and property are paramount, and that ownership and property are under threat. The same themes from the 1860s, repeating and returning. It set my teeth on edge; it crumbled my heart; I was determined to make things right.

In Richmond, I went to the hospital first—Chimborazo Hospital, one of the largest Confederate war hospitals. The site perched on a hilltop named after a volcano in Ecuador. I wanted to visit the slave docks, the auction sites, but they were unmarked, and I did not know how to find them. The museum at Chimborazo was closed, so I walked the perimeter of the large field and imagined the hospital tents that filled the hilltop and the thousands of injured men brought here from the front to convalesce or die.

I thought of them as men, not soldiers. Men who bled and dreamed of home, just like the soldiers wearing blue, just like enslaved men and women and children—all filled with loss and longing and pain. I could hardly fathom the hurt and had to force myself to keep walking. Moving forward felt like pushing through stagnant water, thick and festering. But I was the Civil War nurse, and I walked on among the wounded and dying of this nation, bringing elixirs of healing. I scattered seeds on the grass.

Then I traveled further into the city, to Capitol Square, where I had gone many times to lobby elected officials. The square was empty in the hot afternoon. I walked around the grounds, planting cannabis seeds beside trees and in the flower beds. I stood for a long time by the fountains, ringed with wine-red roses all in bloom. Something called to me, and my feet remembered the night by the lake in Kentucky, when I danced until dawn and called forth a new world.

I read in Jackson's biography that his body lay in state beneath the dome at the Virginia State Capitol. The solemn, white Capitol building that Thomas Jefferson designed stood uphill from me, and I walked toward it slowly. Slowly up the stairs of the portico, lined with six columns, all of them glowing white in the summer sun. And there, I found Jackson. I knew that I would. He smiled and bowed. I was only a stand-in for a last dance with his Mary, but that was enough. It was the right thing to do. And the dance came as a relief to me, a lessening of my grief. We waltzed around and around the front portico of the Capitol, the broad marble stones, the graceful white building, built—no doubt—by enslaved workers.

Round and round. There was no one in sight, just me, in my purple dress, dancing with a ghost.

I stayed that night at the home of a friend. The friend was out of town, and the brick house filled with stillness around me, a blessed peace. My mind had grown jittery again. When I saw that the house was on Stonewall Jackson Avenue, I'd nearly wept. In the darkness, I rested on a couch by an open window. The June moon was waning, a lopsided orb gazing down on me. Breezes off the river flowed into the room and the gauzy, silvered curtains moved over me sweetly as a lover. I stretched and curled beneath the air, wakeful, staring wide eyed into the night.

I rose with the sun the next morning, showered, and dressed for work. At the mirror, I peered into the dark of my eyes, remembering suddenly the strange drive from Gabe and Erin's farm to the hospital in Virginia when my pupils filled with leaping flame. I took a deep breath. My eyes were calm, though sparks seemed to pop in the blackness. I would have to be careful.

I had a meeting that day in Richmond, a board of directors' retreat for a coalition of Virginia conservation groups. The organization's mission was to promote a broad range of environmental bills and issues in the Virginia General Assembly. In reality, the group was hobbled by infighting and controlled by a clique representing the most moneyed conservation groups in the state. This was my first board meeting. I had fought long and hard for a seat at the table. We needed help with forest protection measures on the state level, and they needed us.

"You've got to have grassroots support," I argued. "Your political connections and major donors aren't enough, and you're getting steamrolled in the General Assembly. You need small groups, closer to the people." They finally relented and opened the door wide enough for me to zip inside, and now here I was, sitting quietly in a formal conference room with people dressed in suits and high heels. I felt like an alien and instinctively kept still, watching and listening, while the handful of leaders bickered and failed to reach decisions. At some point, I did speak, reiterating my points: we need the public to support conservation work at the General Assembly. Working behind closed doors won't cut it. We need to build a wide constituency among ordinary people.

At lunch, I shared a table with the director of one of the more influential groups. He said, "She's right," talking about me. I sat across the table from him as he spoke, but he never looked at me, just said, "She's right," and shrugged.

Perhaps I had truly become a ghost, perhaps he couldn't see me. Whatever it was, the day began to wear on me, listening to these droning tedious gate keepers infatuated with their tiny pockets of power. My shoulders hurt; irritation and pressure built in my head. I squirmed in my straight-laced clothing, leaned my elbows on the polished wood table and rubbed my eyes. Finally, I murmured my excuses and slipped away an hour early—it was clear that nothing of consequence would happen in that group, not that day, perhaps never. I stalked away from the office building, stripping off my suit jacket, kicking off my shoes, ready to be gone from Richmond. The corruption in the state political system leached into everything that surrounded it, including this organization. I wanted to jump in cold water and scrub off the day.

Instead, I pulled onto the interstate, out of the city, heading west to the Shenandoah Valley, like Lee had done after the war, like Jackson had done in his flag-draped coffin. I-64 made a straight shot from the city to the Blue Ridge. I drove fast, eager to reach the Valley. Ringed by its ancient mountains, I knew that I would feel safer there. I got high while I drove, the frustration draining slowly from my shoulders.

FIVE

In the Valley at last, she comes to a halt at her front door. The marijuana has soothed her irritation but intensified her restlessness. The cooling evening calls her outside to shuffle her feet in the grass, whisper greetings to the ghostly soldiers, and stretch out on her back on the porch. She is tired, a little feverish, yet a taut energy buzzes inside her head. She feels dangerous and divine again, like on Pine Mountain and at Gabe and Erin's farm, but even more so. She is a prophecy fulfilled, and everything, everything, each waver of breeze through the walnut trees, each flicker of bird wing bears a message, a meaning, and they all speak to her. They show her patterns and implications far beyond what most mortals can discern.

The feeling grows in coming days. She takes a drive along the Blue Ridge Parkway the next morning, and every song on the radio has been arranged specifically for her to hear. A single word or line sets off a cascade of ideas in her mind. A gospel song about Mother Mary sends her

careening through mythology and history. Reaching beyond Lee and Jackson's wives—both named Mary—
beyond the Virgin Mary and Mary Magdalene, to the ancient goddess called Meri or Mari, whose name stretched
across Egypt and Palestine to India. She sees herself briefly
as a deity, hewn from marble.

Mari the goddess was sometimes joined in androgynous combinations with gods like Egypt's Ra or the Se-
mitic El. The moccasin flower on Clinch Mountain, the
Sand Cave ritual, joining male and female energies—it all
connects. Perhaps, she thinks, she has become a Mary, one
of them and thus all of them. Perhaps that is why all these
stories keep coming back around, whirling around her as
though she was a May pole.

She and Loki are traveling that night to southwest
Virginia, back to Sean's place on Clinch Mountain. Loki is
going to paint their barn while Sean and Roxanne and
Rose are out of town. She rides along with him, planning
to write and think in the quiet of the farm. She will try to
collect her widely scattered wits.

She had hoped that Matthew would come along,
thinking they might wander the mountain slopes looking
for wildflowers, but he'd said no. Sometimes he seems to
understand all the cosmic codes unfurling in her brain,
but most of the time, these days, he just seems frustrated
with her. She has written long-winded letters of explanation to him, riddled with giddy poetry. In them, she tries

but cannot fully explain why she is so strange, and how her mind has loosed itself and sees now through God's eyes. He shakes his head, points out a verse from the Bible: Exodus 22:18. He is not religious, per se, but he knows the Bible. The verse says, "Thou shalt not suffer a witch to live."

Shocked, she says, "What?!" then stutters in confusion. "Are... are you threatening me?"

"What?!" Now his voice is shocked, hurt. "Are you kidding? I'm trying to *warn* you." He shakes the book at her. "There are people out there who believe this!"

She stares at Matthew without comprehending. Why is he so angry? They have no cipher for one another, and her confusion grows.

She thinks of him sadly while driving south with Loki, but soon loses herself in the adventure of travel. They sing along with Bob Dylan's *Desire* album and stop to rescue an orange box turtle ambling across Rt. 58 west of Abingdon. She hops out to pick it up, carrying it across the road in the direction that it was heading.

"Put it behind that stone wall," Loki shouts from the car.

"Good idea!" She grins and thinks of Stonewall Jackson and the Shenandoah Valley. Stone walls are good at keeping things safe.

They take a quick side trip across the border into Tennessee to buy paint. She waits for Loki in the car and sees the state flag of Tennessee for the first time—three stars looped inside a blue circle. It must represent her and Loki and Adam. How nice of the world to recognize them for the contributions they made on Pine Mountain. Then her eyes begin to ache, that strange twisting sensation inside her skull. She leans her head against the car window, suddenly tired. It is very hot. She cannot talk about these insights, cannot put them into words. It is her job to understand how all the symbols and clues and stories fit together, and she must do it alone. Perhaps then she can rest.

She does not see much of Loki after they arrive at Sean's farm. He camps in the woods and comes by the house only to eat. She is happy to be alone. On the first night, she invents opium. A few years back, when she smoked real opium for the first (and only) time, she had remembered a deep, unerring love for narcotics that she'd accidentally developed as a child. Despite suffering from intense post-appendectomy pain at age eight, the surgeon had taken her off morphine because she liked it too much. She remembers, even now, feeling bereft and hopeless when the doctor stopped the pain shots, stealing away her only comfort.

The appendicitis returns to her mind regularly these days as she wanders through mythologies of living and dying. She'd come so close to death as a child that she'd had a near-death vision. Perched on a window sill that floated above her hospital bed, she had looked out onto golden fields of glowing grass, bending in the wind under a bright sky on the other side. She had not understood what it meant, and she did not want to die, only to stop hurting, to escape the little fever-wracked body lying on the bed below her. The grief on her parents' faces had called her back. But the morphine shots had allowed her to escape again, to return to the window sill, to have a brief instant of blissful death.

As an adult, smoking opium was not an end to pain but a gift of aching delight. When the sweet smoke enfolded her lungs, the whole world exploded into diamonds, their glittering prisms melting through her skin, and the simple act of breathing, the simple touch of air against her skin, made her gasp with pleasure. Here on Clinch Mountain, she has no access to real opium, so she invents it—makes it out of pot and myrrh. She keeps tincture of myrrh in her medicine kit for healing wounds. When she puts a few drops on a cannabis flower in her new pipe and sets fire to it, a blue flame glows above the orange embers and lingers even after the match is gone. She is fascinated. The smoke is sweet as incense. It is not like opium, not really. The world does not go crystalline and voluptuous, but the sweetness of the smoke reminds her of the flavor, and in her mind, that is all that matters. She smokes obsessively, just to watch the blue flame burn.

But tinctured pot turns out to be a terrible idea. It gives her vertigo and nausea and speeds up her already over-heated thoughts, pops holes in her brain, gashes in her memory. One night, she chants loudly for hours, calling out across the Atlantic to the Scottish green island of Iona where she spent a summer working and wandering the smooth hills and serpentine-strewn beaches.

Later that night, she accidentally brings down the porch swing where she and Adam edited her writing the month before. She pitches her legs forward and back, like a child on a swing set, until the chains come loose, and it crashes to the ground. In the morning, Loki looks at her quizzically and asks if she is alright before helping her hang the swing back up.

She sees him one other time that day, when she plays with a piece of his painting equipment. She pretends that it's a javelin and throws it across the yard. He sees her and yells at her to stop. He is a big man, and his booming voice looms over her. She scampers inside. There is a storm brewing, wind beginning to gust, and she mixes up her fear of Loki's anger with a child's fear of thunder. The billows of wind convince her that a tornado is coming. She hides in the bathroom, confused and cowering, disguising herself in Sean's hat and coat until the storm passes.

When Sean and his family arrive back at the farm, she keeps her distance. They look strange to her, and she is suspicious. She tries to sleep in her car that night but never closes her eyes. She has discovered music. Smoking her opium-flavored cannabis, she plays Bob Dylan albums over and over. They have become the story of her life, or her past lives, or perhaps they are her forgotten memories. She sees herself and Matthew, Loki, Adam and Danielle all whirled together, their lives and friendships like spirals of stars. She and Danielle stand back to back, directing the show. It is extraordinary how everything fits together. Late in the night, she looks out the window. The car is floating like a boat in the mist that has settled upon the mountain. Outside is Mosby, or one of his Rangers, on horseback, keeping watch.

The Civil War ghosts have stayed with her since her trip to Richmond. On the drive home, she led them in a full-scale charge up the Blue Ridge: an army of men wearing both blue and grey. She busted them all out of hell—a cosmic jail break—with a huge whoop of freedom, a reclaimed Rebel Yell, signifying liberation, friendship, brotherhood. Now, the soldiers watch over her and keep her safe.

Matthew's uncle has stayed close to her as well. In life, he not only owned the land by the Tye River and taught phys ed and gymnastics at her elementary school, he also studied the lives of Mosby and his men. Now, in her strange state of mind, he is a companion and a comfort, a bright spot of stability. Their friendship is part of her perpetual quest for healing of the land and of history. One day in Waynesboro, she caught sight of him walking around the old battlefield. She ran down a hill to greet him, and he caught her up into a long hug as though she was a child and he was not a ghost.

The day after her all-night sojourn in the Crown Victoria, she and Loki prepare to leave the Clinch Mountain farm. In the garden, she gathers her things and accidentally breaks her glasses. A screw pops out and a lens disappears into the grass. The sun is hot on the back of her neck as she searches frantically for the lens. Uncomfortable and sweating, she feels sick again, feels holes opening again in her brain. It can't be lost. It can't be. She pounds her fist against the ground and tries to stand. Reeling with dizziness and disorientation, she stumbles and hides behind the blueberry bushes, fearing her friends—they will be so angry that she broke her glasses. Then she notices the lens, sitting there, transparent, on her notebook. She is confused and cannot remember if she found it and put it there and then forgot, or if it fell there in the first place? She is so dizzy, it is so damn hot. And what are they doing to her car? The hood is up and Loki and Sean are bent over it. Loki pops the trunk, pulls out jumper cables.

Then, somehow, they are bumping along the rutted road down the mountain. Loki is driving, she is in the backseat, and now she is cold, shivery. She pulls the sleeping bag around her and feels suddenly, horribly ill—

nauseous, light headed—but more than that, she is terrified. The scar from her appendicitis surgery is pounding.
She was cut open once when her appendix first ruptured,
then cut open again a week later when infection festered
inside her. It was torture and terror for an eight-year-old,
and now that fear comes for her again. This time it has
jaws and a sackcloth that it wraps over her head, and fear
has strong hands to grip her windpipe, and fear wants to
bust through the thick scar on the right-hand side of her
abdomen. Fear wants to burst her intestines, to spill her
blood across the back bench seat. It wants to kill her over
and over and never stop.

Her panic is silent; she wrestles the knife edge of her
terror without saying a word. Looking out the back window at Clinch Mountain, she sees that cloud has settled in
over the hollow where Sean and Roxanne and Rose live.
She is suddenly wildly bereft, certain that she will never
see them again. The cloud has taken them away, and soon
she too will be gone, ruptured, and the grief will be unbearable. Thoughts of her family finally call her back. She
remembers the fear on their faces as they watched her
nearly die as a child, and so she tries to hang on, to
breathe and breathe deeply and to pray. She does not want
to hurt them. Slowly, slowly, fear lets her go. She curls up
in exhaustion on the backseat as the night darkens. They
arrive late at her apartment where Matthew waits to take
her in. In her memory, on the long drive home, she sits up

regularly, puts her hand to the roof of the car and makes a strange loud ululating call. But Loki, later, says, No, I thought you were asleep, you didn't make a sound.

She and Matthew sit facing each other over her kitchen table. All the lights are off in the house; two candles glow between them. Matt has tried multiple times to get her to sleep, but she will only lie down briefly before popping back out of bed. The compressed speech has started again—strange sounds and tones and laughter punctuate her words. She imagines them as gamblers, guessing riddles for high stakes. Matthew plays along, trying by humor and reason, by gentleness and guile, to get her to rest, but she is beyond him, in her own universe, and she wins every round. She take swigs from a bottle filled with water, then slams it on the table like an empty shot glass. She is the only one who laughs.

In the morning, her family arrives. Matthew is still with her—raw-eyed, exhausted, and distraught—keeping her distracted so she doesn't run away. Her parents slip in the door, eyeing her warily. She stands in the kitchen, leaning against the washing machine, holding an empty water glass up against the low ceiling. In her memory, she stands silently, regal and calm, like a statue of a goddess. But her mother brought a video camera. Caught on film, the young woman is talking—an epic, endless swirl of words that make no sense.

From there, the day dips and twists. Her parents make phone calls, researching ways to admit her to the hospital voluntarily, without restraints. She is restless, listens to the radio, decoding messages, convinced again that all the songs are meant for her. Later, she writes a long email that she sends to everyone in her address book—friends, colleagues, near strangers—full of childhood stories, the names of friends and figures from history. It is five pages long and steams with insanity. She links ideas to images to names to colors to sounds, leaping crazy distances from one thought to the next. A brain in free fall:

wink, blink, windkkk, wind-k-ink- those SILVER EYES
surprise. Link.
what did she say? GANDHI?
what spinning wheel is on fire?
what flag, knit India home? what I? what eye? WHAT? I?

On and on it goes. A chaos of unhinged thought flung out like a flag for all to see.

Her brother arrives sometime that afternoon, and the family goes to dinner together in the nearby city of Staunton. She stays quiet. She does not entirely trust them. After dinner, her brother walks with her around the old church on Beverley Street, founded in 1746, where the Virginia General Assembly met during the height of the Revolutionary War. They circle the church over and over as he tries to tell her something. It is something important, but she cannot follow what he is saying. She trusts him more than her parents, but she is chronically self-absorbed. Her mind is so preoccupied, so busy, so full, that the existence of other people blurs into the background. Her brain keeps telling stories and folding everything around her into the stories, every detail: the red bricks in the sidewalks, the gold and pink of the sunset clouds, the old gravestones and overgrown grass. The narratives in her head are so absorbing and all-encompassing that they demand everything from her. She is the heroine of every story, and it is a tremendous, extraordinary, and terrible responsibility.

Low grey clouds and drizzle move in the next morning. Matthew is there with her at the apartment when her family arrives. Together, they explain something about a commitment process. She does not understand, but she follows Matthew into the backseat of her parents' car. He is kind, tender. He holds her hand. She wonders if a "commitment process" means getting married. How nice that her family can be there. Will Matthew's sisters join them? She looks out the window where grey cloud drapes across the deep green Blue Ridge like mist over the Iona hills.

At the community services board, Matthew sits beside her as she fills out forms and questionnaires. The questions are strangely unrelated to marriage, and she seems to be the only one doing paperwork. She asks about this. Perhaps the staff person explains, perhaps not, but she realizes at last that they mean to put her back into a hospital, into another psychiatric ward. She stands up and says, "No. No way, not again." And then everything becomes confused. The social worker makes phone calls. She ends up alone in a cold, barren conference room—brown chairs, brown rug, white walls—with a grey-haired magistrate. Who is this man? She huddles with her arms folded tight around her, frightened and confused. Her vision is fogged; the world blurs. He asks questions, and she answers or does not answer; her words probably do not relate to his queries anyway. She speaks her own language, tries to tell him that she is fine, she is safe in her own home. She can care for herself and poses no threat to others.

But it is to no avail. The magistrate rules that she be involuntarily committed. A nurse, holding onto the young woman's arm, leads her from the brown conference room to the chill bright white of a hospital corridor—a different hospital this time but with the same bleached white sheets on the beds, cold air on her skin, cold tile underfoot. No. Oh no. No, not again. Misery sinks down her spine and into her belly. She cannot run—she knows what would happen.

They lead her to a room where lunch is waiting for her. It is the vegetarian option—a bowl of lettuce, nothing but lettuce—next to a hospital bed. She begins to weep, knowing that she has been trapped, again. The sobs become more jagged, gasping, until the nurses drug her up and leave her to sleep.

She wakes late in the evening in the dark room with her forehead pressed against the cold, white wall. A quiet voice in her head tells her, *This time, take the pills.* She trusts the voice and whispers to the wall, thinking that the nurses will hear her down the hall. "I'll take the lithium, please." No response. She tries again, "I'm ready. I'll take the lithium."

♦

Her answer comes the next morning, at 6am, when the presiding psychiatrist, Dr. Sesti, does his morning rounds—early, evaluating his patients' sanity and responsiveness before they have time to rub their eyes or visit the bathroom.

"But why not lithium?" she asks mournfully.

"It's too easy to overdose. People commit suicide on it." Dr. Sesti is brusque and rude. He cuts her off when she asks questions. He shows her a tiny white pill. "This is better. It's new. It's called Zyprexa."

Zyprexa, her mind adds the rhyme: "That'll fix ya!" She swallows the pill.

After a day or two on the drug, her mind begins to film over. The vivid thread of manic narrative that has played out over the past weeks goes slack. Zyprexa is an anti-psychotic drug, designed to pummel the manic brain into submission and do it fast. Her mercurial mind, her universe of manic stories, her fine-tuned, wild-eyed senses, all become a wash of dull colors and angry sound. She struggles against the change, flailing her arms under water as hot air chokes in her chest, drowning.

She is a caged animal, and the glass doors to the outside world become a burning temptation. The hospital ranks her as a flight risk, and she prays that it will become true. That Matthew or Loki or anyone will break the glass in her window and whisk her away into the night. No one comes. When Matthew visits in the evenings, he walks through the front doors and chats with the nurses.

She is allowed outside with Matthew and a nurse. They sit in the tiny garden beside the psychiatric wing of the hospital and watch the setting mid-summer sun fire the clouds. The garden blooms with black-eyed susans and sprays of lavender. Twining vines weave over an archway. Each night, she sits quietly with Matthew and cries. The world has become alien—the language of flowers and sunsets slips away from her as mania recedes. Even Matthew's caring is painful. They are never this gentle with each other in real life. He brings her pictures and talismans—a black and white photo of a black snake, a gold Sacajawea coin. She keeps them on her bedside table. They make her cry.

Her friend EQ from Charlottesville comes to visit one afternoon at supper time. He seems awkward, and she feels impatient with him. Her frustration with the hospitalization is growing, and she is primed for a fight. He sits with her in the psych ward's cafeteria. The vegetarian food is disgusting, she tells him. Tonight they give her limp, white-flour noodles with watery tomato sauce and a pile of lettuce. "They tell me I have to eat to get better. How the hell is this shit supposed to heal me?" She rants, feverish and raw. She is talking to the air, not to EQ; he is peripheral, like all the people around her—the nurses, her family, even Matthew. The only real person is the doctor, because only he can let her out. She notices out of the corner of her eye that EQ's eyes are bright red, bloodshot. Concern flits briefly through her mind. Why has he been crying?

She spends her days in group therapy, recreational therapy, sleep. There are three manic patients in the ward, and they do all their organized activities together. All three are on Zyprexa. Her roommate, Ellen, who has been there for a week, says just about everyone on the ward is taking it. "He's testing it on us," Ellen whispers. Dr. Sesti's office is full of pens and notepads and posters sporting the Zyprexa logo. "He likes having power over us," Ellen hisses from behind her hand. The young woman dislikes him instinctively. He looks like a toad to her, but not in a good way.

Sometimes she does yoga in the hospital corridor or simply wanders. She meets one white-haired man suffering from dementia who also walks the hallways; he sings, or hums, or makes loud noises, and she likes him for his musicality. He does not speak, but she sometimes accompanies his singing, tapping on a wall or a chair leg, keeping time for him. She thinks of Bob Dylan playing songs for Woody Guthrie in the hospital in New York. The humming man often wears a baseball cap, and she wonders idly if it contains a hidden camera, if she is being filmed and broadcast live around the globe. In the back of her mind, she still harbors suspicions of her own personal grandiosity. She is still on a quest to heal and save the world.

◆

During this five-day hospitalization, even as my head slowly quieted, I never stopped believing in my manic mythologies. But the extraordinary, almost catastrophic sense of Spirit, of being enveloped by the Divine, disappeared as the medication began to do its work. The drug's powerful ability to stomp out the fire of psychosis left charred shadows and ash behind. The experience was violent and heart-breaking.

Sesti discharged me on the 2nd of July. My parents and I walked out the sliding glass doors into blazing heat. The sun burned like an enemy. Matthew waited in the parking lot beside his red motorcycle, holding two helmets. Ordinarily, I would have smiled, but my skin flinched at the touch of summer heat, and the mid-morning sunlight hurt my head. We made plans to meet my parents for lunch in an hour. I climbed on the motorcycle behind Matthew, and we rode slowly out of the hospital parking lot, onto the back roads and up into the mountains. I leaned my head against Matthew's back, feeling ill and embarrassed—I had thought we were getting married. Only a week ago, I had been so breathtakingly alive here in the Blue Ridge, but now there was no freedom in the rush of wind, just a pinched fevered feeling all through my body. The world around me no longer reverberated with wonder. I rode through my beautiful homeland like an alien.

A week or two passed, and nothing changed. I moved in a fog, distanced from the world around me. My body hurt with a weird heaviness, a puffiness in my glands as though I was coming down with the flu. I was intensely lonely. The natural world that had been so vivid in my awareness, with its black crows and rainbow flowers, grew distant. I felt removed from the world of my friends and family. My usual comfort—marijuana—was off limits. My parents had organized a family meeting that included

Matthew and Dr. Sesti to discuss my care. As usual, Sesti was brusque. He seemed to be in a hurry. When my mother asked him about my drug use, he snapped, "Of course she has to stop doing that," then stood up to leave.

Dr. Sesti offered to continue as my psychiatrist once I was discharged. I shrugged. I didn't know or care. He recommended that I have a neuropsychological evaluation done by his colleague, Dr. Reece, at the hospital. "You'll find it useful," he said. So I went to the appointment hoping to learn something about myself. Perhaps it would explain the immense power I'd felt on Pine Mountain, or my strange, luminous time chasing Civil War ghosts. But the doctor had no interest in listening to me. Instead, I spent the afternoon with Rorschach blobs and endless questionnaires. A few days later, I went back for the results. Dr. Reece was young, with long hair pulled back in a ponytail. He was not gruff like Sesti; instead, he spoke like a graduate student, more interested in statistics than in the patient sitting in front of him.

"You test at normal levels on all the axes but one. You indicate psychosis in your tendency toward self-isolation and solitude."

I frowned at him without speaking. What are you talking about? I have plenty of friends. I just like spending time alone. And what the hell does it mean that I test "normal" on everything else? If I'm so normal, why the fuck did they lock me up?

"So that's it?" I said.

"That's it."

I walked out of his office into another scorching day. The sun glared, my head hurt, and it was not yet noon. There was nothing in the world that I wanted to do. The doctors had defeated me.

I began to see a counselor. A friend recommended him, and I agreed when I found out that he had blue eyes, which reminded me of Adam, and that seemed like reason enough to say yes. We never got far. Really, we never got anywhere. I went to sessions and talked about mania like a heartsick lover, or I cried. Usually I cried—sometimes for the entire hour. He listened but rarely had anything to say. Once he discovered that we shared a love for Rumi's poetry, he'd often quote something meant to give me hope, or peace, or something. But I couldn't feel the poetry's warm flame inside me, couldn't hear God's voice in the poet's words. I just wept and then went home.

On a hot day mid-way through July, I lay on the threadbare oriental rug in my living room, trying to escape my body. I had loved this apartment—the ground floor of an old house with tall windows and a side porch, the historic battleground underfoot—but now it closed in on me. I lay still and tried to let my mind go, let it roam free, returning to the mountaintop in Blanton Forest, taking flight above the valley. But this time my mind stayed helplessly pinned to my body. I had always treasured my ability to escape through imagination or drugs, but the psychiatric medication had changed that. I was trapped and immobile.

The Eden Express, by Mark Vonnegut, lay just beyond the fingers of my left hand. I had finished reading it about ten minutes before, lying on my back, and now the book lay where I had dropped it. *Eden Express* charts Vonnegut's journey through drug use to a hippie commune in British Columbia and on into madness. I had flipped through other books about manic depression in recent days and shrugged them off: so what if my symptoms bore a vague similarity to theirs? Something miraculous had happened to me! Something extraordinary. But Vonnegut's experiences communing with wild nature and mind-altering substances while building an idealistic community with his friends mimicked mine too closely. I could see myself reflected in his visions, his wild quests and strange thoughts. This horrified me.

My religious experience on Pine Mountain and my epic journey into the heart of Virginia's history were beginning to decay. My beautiful, brilliant days of intoxicating vision were breaking down into diagnostic check boxes, a list of manic symptoms: magical thinking, grandiosity and inflated self-esteem, breaks from reality, decreased need for sleep, rapid speech, euphoria—on and on it went—increased religiosity, identifying with divine entities, attempting to right the wrongs of the world. On and on.

I lay flat on my back, feeling myself sinking through the carpet, blackness filling my vision but without the blessing of oblivion. No relief. Vonnegut had recovered with mega-vitamin therapy and dietary changes,[6] and here I was sucking down prescription drugs. Self-loathing slithered through my chest. I was horrified by the idea of being dependent on pharmaceutical medications. Dr. Sesti told me that I would need to take them for the rest of my life. He said it casually, like it was no big deal.

After weeks of slow sinking, my descent into full-blown depression was sudden and dramatic. One Sunday, at the end of July, I stood at the sink washing dishes and waiting for my brother to arrive for a visit. Memories of the past several months filled my mind, and I began to feel a strange sensation of intense cold creeping through my body, as though I was going numb. Then suddenly, beneath my feet, the ground gave way. Like a cliff edge crumbling, the earth disappeared from underfoot, and I fell with it, running to try to stay upright as the ground slid faster and faster. Finally, pitching forward, I landed on my knees, dizzy and gagging on tears. I clutched my arms around my chest and leaned my forehead to the floor as impossibly violent sobs wracked my body.

---

[6] Vonnegut was initially diagnosed with schizophrenia. He wrote in his 2010 memoir, *Just Like Someone Without Mental Illness Only More So*, that his diagnosis was revised to manic depression following a psychotic break in the 1980s. Since that time, lithium has played a critical role in his on-going stability and success as a physician and author.

When my brother arrived, I had only just managed to stand. I leaned against him, crying again, "I don't know what to do." We went for a drive, took a walk in the woods around Maple Flats—one of my favorite forest places, filled with sunlight and water and green—but I couldn't feel it. My sense of connection with the natural world had broken. I was a stranger in the places that had meant the most to me—the forests and mountains and streams. My brother tried to reassure me, to convince me that I would feel better, that this was temporary, but his kindness could not touch my grief. Everything about me— my body, my mind—felt unbearable. I was trapped inside. I had no means of escape or release.

S I X

The force that through the green fuse drives the flower,
Drives my green age; that blasts the roots of trees
Is my destroyer.
                                                - DYLAN THOMAS

She craves mania like a junkie. In the morning, she wakes and lies in bed, listening to the neighbors upstairs get ready for work. Tears leak from the edges of her eyes. She stares past the ceiling at a golden circle of light; it is the color of the sun rising on Blanton Forest, on the Tye River, on moccasin flowers and turtles. Each day, she falls further from the circle, deeper into a dim gray static. The memories of Clinch Mountain wildflowers and the Sand Cave at Blanton are brutal with yearning. Her skin burns to feel damp soil under her bare feet, to dance again, sacred on the lake shore. She presses her thumb against the palm of her hand, clinging to the sharp ache where she cracked her hand against the dead chestnut on Pine Mountain. At least the pain is real. It proves that she was actually there on the mountaintop. She grieves as the bone heals, as the last tangible memory within her body fades. One more thing taken from her.

She moves slowly from the bed, grits her teeth and crawls into the day. Internally, the young woman has collapsed, become boneless and limp. The smallest tasks take enormous effort and large ones are impossible. In the middle of August, she has a major grant proposal due. The foundation had invited her organization to apply, and if they receive the money, it will fund operations for a year. But she cannot do it. She is helpless. All she wants is sleep, oblivion. Please—she thinks, over and over—please, just let me go.

Her mother says, "No. Come home. I will help you."

At her parents' house, she occupies the couch. She cannot move. Her mother sets the kitchen timer for ten minutes. "When it rings, get up and write for ten minutes, then you can lie back down." They do this ritual over and over. The timer rings and the young woman staggers to her feet, pecks out a sentence, perhaps a paragraph, then collapses again. Sometimes she does not move when the timer rings, and her mother pulls her upright. The young woman cries—her body made of loose skin and tears— "Why am I like this?"

None of them understand. The family reads books, tries to grasp what the disease is, how it will progress, what they can do. They nod in recognition at the symptom list for depression: lack of pleasure, feelings of worthlessness, loss of energy, difficulty focusing or taking interest in life. But cold words on white pages do not convey the brutality of this depression, the way it batters her. She is dying fast within her living skin. She is all but a ghost. The same voice comes from her mouth, she has the same eyes and face, but they are all pale, the colors blasted away. Even in the late summer heat, she is cold, waxen. The luscious green that had fired her body now desiccates. There is internal bleeding in her chest, and the hurt in her heart never stops. The pain and ache and pressure push against her throat so that she cannot speak. The words that do emerge from her mouth are not real. They have nothing to do with her.

Sometimes hints of truth materialize from her fingers. She writes poems and sends them to Adam and Loki, weeping on their shoulders from afar. She wants them to understand. She wants them to tell her it was real, to say, *Yes, I saw and felt the same things that you did—it's all true.* But their replies seem brief and awkward—they do not answer her need, and her need is vast.

Her mother returns with her to Waynesboro, stays for several days and comes back to visit regularly. Though her mother does not say so, the young woman knows that her family fears for her safety. But she is too tired to contemplate suicide. She dreams of oblivion, not death. An end to pain. An escape: just let me go. She misses cannabis.

When she smoked, the sharp edges of the world receded, the numinous arms of the cosmos slipped around her. She could float inside herself, safe and happy. But the doctor says, "No." Every time she sees him, Sesti asks if she is smoking, and she dully shakes her head.

At most of her appointments, the young woman does not meet with Sesti at all. His nurse practitioner sees many of his patients. Sesti approves the nurse's treatment plans and writes the prescriptions. The young woman is relieved not to have to face his ugliness, his sneering hostility. The nurse practitioner asks how she is feeling. The young woman shrugs. She has no idea. What does "normal" feel like when you have a mental illness? Perhaps this is as good as it gets. To the nurse, she says, "Ok," and shrugs again, her hands open and helpless. She does not ask for help.

They keep her on Zyprexa. She accepts the pills without comment, swallows them daily, morning and evening. She never reads the drug information sheet from the pharmacy, just swallows the pills. Sometime in September, at her parents' urging, she tells the nurse practitioner how terrible she feels. They start her on an anti-depressant. It does not touch the iron weight of despair. After a month, they prescribe a different drug called Effexor. She becomes so exhausted that her mother comes to stay again, to help her get up in the morning, to drive her to work meetings because she cannot keep her eyes open. The doctor says that the sleepiness is a good sign—the pills are acting on her brain chemistry. Eventually the exhaustion lifts. She does not feel better, not really, but the drug seems to help her function. She wakes up more easily. Her skin does not feel so unbearably sensitive to air and sun.

Nevertheless, her life moves on without her. Summer shifts into a gray, cold autumn. The daylight grows pinched between long nights, and pale light hangs from the sun at low angles in the sky. She works, spends time with friends and with Matthew, goes to yoga, meets with the counselor, but she is not really there. Depression sways over her like a dark ocean, crushing her with pressure, shifting and rolling her with its tides. She cannot lift it or move it or push against it with her hands.

At her job, she tries hard to remain a viable activist in the forest protection movement, but the last six months have shattered her confidence. Shame drapes across her shoulders—it is greasy and corrosive and stinks so badly that surely everyone must notice it. She always feels uncomfortable, always embarrassed. At conferences and meetings, she wonders who has heard rumors about her strange behavior. Who knows about the hospitalizations, the medications, the diagnosis? She rarely speaks. When she does, her face flushes and sweat prickles sharp and hot across her back. Sometimes the anxiety overwhelms her, and she hides in the ladies' room, rests her head in her hands, trying to stop the shaking, to slow her furious heart.

In late November, she finds a brief respite. She and Loki have driven to a conference in Tennessee. He is the easiest person in her life at this time. He has seen her through her strangest days yet never treats her differently—none of the arms' length awkwardness and misunderstandings about her diagnosis that make her other interpersonal interactions so exhausting. On the way home from the conference, Loki pulls off the interstate and navigates the mountain roads to Gabe and Erin's farm. Six inches of snow have already fallen in the high mountains, and the air is frozen. Erin has taken Laurel and Alarka to visit family in Arizona. Gabriel welcomes them into the tiny house and stokes the wood stove. They have adopted two young cats since the young woman was here in May, and the kittens climb across shoulders and laps trailing tiny, sharp claws and purring. After the preliminary small talk, Gabe turns his dark eyes to the young woman and asks how she is.

She nods and shrugs as her eyes fill with tears, "I'm ok." She takes a breath and then blurts out from a raw throat, "Was there really a black snake named Grace?" These are perhaps the first real words she has spoken all season, and Gabe's response is perhaps the first healing she has received since the earth crumbled beneath her feet. He looks startled, then understanding fills his eyes. He nods slowly,

"Yes." She feels relief like he has reached an arm around her shoulders and said, *It's ok, we know, it's ok.*

For a few hours this night, she can relax. The friendship of these two men who know her story, know where she has been, creates a shelter. Inside it, she is briefly safe. She unrolls her sleeping bag in the girls' room upstairs. The mountains outside wrap around her, and for the first time in months, she trusts herself to the forest and the stars. They hold her. For one night, she sleeps a deep and blessed sleep.

She lacks the strength to maintain that brief flicker of grace in the flat, bleak winter in Waynesboro. She begins to despair. The golden mountaintop light is now a mere pin-prick in the sky above her, and she is always falling—always—further and further away. She is furious at herself for the visions and self-aggrandizement, for thinking she could change the world by walking up mountains and heal history by befriending ghosts. Yet she cannot stop believing, even as the evidence piles up that it was all delusion. She yearns for that manic certainty, the feeling of sacred wisdom overflowing her heart, the firm unshakeable faith in her own power and worth. Is she being punished for trying to walk with the gods? Did she do something terribly wrong?

She writes a long letter to Adam, full of questions that beg for help. She keeps thinking that somehow, if she can verify what happened in Blanton Forest, decode it, find that her mystic understanding was true, then everything will be true. The world will be changed and God will return to her in the leaping spirit of Nature and she will be embraced again by life. She will be well and whole; the manic depressive diagnosis will be erased. Adam seems like the cipher to all of it. He was there on the mountaintop when her entire life changed. Questions pour out of her in the letter: *What did you think? What did you see? Did it happen to you?*

For a long time, there is no response. Adam writes back two months later in the very beginning of spring saying, *Yes, it was real, something happened to me too*, but he does not give the details that she craves, and besides, by then it is too late. She has fallen too far; his words have little meaning. They only underscore what she has lost. She envies him desperately, angered that he could have experienced that same golden magic and escaped unharmed. She misses him, too. That feeling of closeness—of being known in that strangely intimate way, having a twin to her heart—has passed. She feels disconnected from everyone but misses Adam most of all.

As the winter darkens, she isolates herself further. She is growing desperate. Every person that she sees—every one—she envies. Every life looks better than hers. Every person appears more capable, more alive. Their eyes sparkle. They seem happy and confident. Everyone. Everyone but her. Their conversations and friendships light them up. They walk around in public as though it was an easy thing to go grocery shopping or pay the electric bill, while she must use brute force to get herself out of the house. The envy is a horrible, grating feeling—bitter as bile—and it goes on, intensifying, week after week. She wants to be anyone but herself.

Sometime around the end of the year 2000, she gets high again—it is either that or seriously consider suicide. While driving, she has started pondering tractor trailers, especially on two lane roads—how easy it would be to jerk the wheel into their path at just the right moment. Imagining the horrific violence of the crash appeals to her self-loathing. But she cannot do it. Her friend James is a truck driver—she cannot risk hurting a driver, cannot make someone else responsible for her death. Because she will never actually do it, she allows herself to fantasize about driving headlong into a big rig. She works hard to keep the more accessible options—the pills and razors and carbon monoxide—far from her mind.

Cannabis no longer offers a full-body escape into beauty and freedom; the THC works differently combined with anti-psychotic and anti-depressant medications. Still, it takes the edge off her anxiety and provides distraction, gives her a break from the obsessive cycling between hating herself and craving mania. It allows her to interact more comfortably with other people.

Around the same time, at her parents' urging, she begins to look for a place to live in Charlottesville, about half-an-hour's drive on the eastern side of the Blue Ridge. She had lived there for seven years before moving to Waynesboro and has more friends there. She can work in a shared office and have more contact with other people. In Waynesboro, she has been trying to work alone from her living-room desk, and her circle consists mostly of Matthew and her two friends, James and Ruby. They love her, but they too are lobbying for her to move.

In February, she finds a place. Her mother comes to help her pack, and Matthew gathers friends to move the boxes and furniture across the mountain. Her new apartment is the upper story of a large house in the Belmont neighborhood of Charlottesville. This is the fourth house in this neighborhood where she has lived over the years, and the familiarity of the surroundings comforts her. She knows people in the community, and her housemate—who owns the place—is kind and respects the young woman's privacy. She moves her desk and files into an office shared by EQ's school.

Her desperation recedes in Charlottesville, but at the same time her depression grows worse—a heaviness in her limbs, a smoky gloom that follows her everywhere. Every pleasure—from spending time with friends to walking in the woods—remains distant and raw. Her skin stings as though fevered. Laughter chokes her. She cannot remember how it felt to walk barefoot in the forest, to believe.

Mornings are hell. In the evening, after work and a long walk, she sometimes feels a slight lift in her mood. But by morning, inevitably, she slides backward into a deeper darkness. Waking is a horror show. She opens her eyes and remembers that she does not want to exist. The outside world presses in against her: terrifying and hostile. It is inconceivable that she could get out of bed and walk out the door into another day. Sometimes it takes hours for her to rise, crying and staggering. The pain is blinding, endless.

She smokes pot with increasing regularity, clinging to it for some kind of comfort. Most days, she retreats to her car at lunch time and gets high in the parking lot. On the worst days, she leans her head against the steering wheel, gritting her teeth against rattling sobs. Incessantly, rhythmically, she lifts and lowers her forehead against the steering wheel, craving the punishment of physical pain. Smoking pot gives her short breaks in the self-hate, brief moments in which her mind can unclench. After work, she walks in the park by the Rivanna River, pausing on a deserted trail to light another bowl. She begins to cling to the drug to get through the day.

The marijuana is unpredictable; it helps distance her from the unbearable intensity in her mind but sometimes leaves her anxious, confused. As for legal drugs, she continues to drive across the mountain to see Dr. Sesti or his nurse practitioner. She remains on Zyprexa and the antidepressant Effexor. Although her mood shows no sign of improving, she does not ask for help.

"How do you feel?"

"I don't know. Ok. I guess."

"Do you feel any better?"

"I don't know."

By some miracle, she continues to work, but she is merely going through the motions. Intellectually, she believes in her work, but her heart no longer leaps and flares with activist energy. And then there is the political climate. On a grim January day, she went with friends to D.C. to protest the inauguration of George W. Bush. The gray sky poured with icy rain, numbing her fingers on the protest sign ("Selected, Not Elected"). After the parade, her group walked, dispirited, past men in cowboy hats escorting women in fur coats along the city streets to inauguration balls. Her sodden friends looked heartbroken.

She remembered a day in October 1999 when they had all sat together in the audience as President Clinton announced a plan to protect National Forest roadless areas, a campaign they had worked on for years. Clinton had given the speech on a mountain peak in Virginia called Reddish Knob, surrounded by the russet panorama of the George Washington National Forest. She'd felt such joyful optimism that day in the mountain wind, a rush of possibilities, as she looked out across the landscape of her home. Now she and her friends trudge through the D.C. rain as Bush takes office by Supreme Court decision—he has already promised to dismantle the Clinton Roadless Rule at the earliest opportunity.

Throughout the winter and spring of 2001, she makes lobbying trips to Richmond and D.C. Anxiety wrenches at her every step, but she has to do it. She has to keep her job in order to keep her health insurance. Psychiatric medications are expensive, and Zyprexa is the most expensive on the market. Everywhere she goes, her fellow activists are grim and downcast; Bush's election means that many battles fought and won will now have to be fought again.

The bright spot of the late winter is—strange to say—her paternal grandmother's passing. At age 92 and suffering with debilitating Alzheimer's disease, death comes as release and relief. The young woman's extended family gathers in Iowa for what becomes a kind of reunion. They visit the former family farm. She meets cousins that she hasn't seen since childhood. She feels a safety among family, an acceptance that sparks a small warmth inside her chest. One cousin even shares her diagnosis of manic depression, and an aunt took anti-depressants for years. Knowing this makes her feel less alone.

Once she returns to Virginia, the small light inside her goes out again. She cannot sustain hope or happiness, and she brings home another layer of self-hatred. Neither of her recent apartments have had full-length mirrors, so the reflection of her body in the Iowa hotel room caught her off guard. She had always been slender and lanky. Now she is dimpled, bulging. The chunky body in the mirror belongs to a stranger. She doesn't understand—she walks almost every day, tries to eat well. She does not think to read the prescribing information for Zyprexa with its warnings of metabolic change and rapid weight gain. Sesti and his nurse practitioner never mention it.

In early April, she goes with EQ's school kids on a heartbreaking field trip. They visit a paper mill, a coal-fired power plant, and a mountaintop removal mine in West Virginia. Seeing the mine feels like having the last piece of hope in her heart dug up and charred to ashes. She had been shocked a few years before to learn about this form of mining, but she had never seen it in person: mountains cut down in layers to scrape out the coal, explosives packed into bore holes in the rock and then detonated—blowing stone and dust into the air and lungs of the neighbors—then the loose remains of the mountain scooped up by massive machines and dumped into surrounding valleys. She is frightened by it, the arrogance of taking down a mountain, the very bedrock of what God has made, her sacred mountains. She thinks briefly of Pine Mountain and despairs. Here, fully manifest, is the heartlessness that pummels her every morning when she wakes.

In the Appalachians, spring is just beginning. The mountaintop mine—this ultimate destruction of nature—gashes open the soft beauty of new green. The contrast overwhelms her, turns her stomach. She returns home beaten, paralyzed by the desecration. As April blooms, the warming season reminds her of the year before, the spring of 2000 and its leaping clarity. Now her world feels hopelessly broken, her activist work useless—how can they ever hope to stop those massive machines? Her body slack and ugly; her heart and mind fogged. She cannot connect with God or joy. She is sick and alone.

From there, she enters a precipitous tail spin. For some time, her anti-depressant, Effexor, has seemed ineffective. She thinks it may be making the depression worse. Mid-month, she decides, spontaneously, to stop taking it. The drug is an SNRI, a serotonin-norepinephrine reuptake inhibitor. Stopping it suddenly leads to drastic rebound effects as her brain chemistry struggles to readjust. She goes into withdrawal fast, in the space of a few days—like bringing a sledgehammer down on her own head. Her brain feels riddled with holes. Vertigo punches her repeatedly, leaving her swaying, nauseous, unable to focus her eyes. She smokes pot to try to make it stop and that makes it so much worse.

One day, she goes walking in the park by the Rivanna River, on a hot, spring afternoon, full of bees circling flowers. At a curve in the path, she loses her way. She has walked these trails a hundred times, but suddenly she is confused and dizzy, the frenzy of spring wrapping around her throat. She staggers sideways, loses her balance, and falls into the bushes. She is a jigsaw puzzle coming undone, pieces falling away leaving gaping holes behind. The doctor has not warned her about this. In 2001, the drug companies are still fighting about whether discontinuing a SNRI or SSRI really causes the debilitating symptoms that patients report.

She goes back on Effexor. The worst of the withdrawal symptoms quickly subside, but she continues to feel wretched. Exhausted and angry, she sets up an emergency meeting with her nurse practitioner. "These meds are not working," she says. "I need something else." The nurse takes her to talk with Dr. Sesti. They find him walking along the hospital corridor, chatting with another doctor. Sesti takes out his prescription pad and scrawls slanting black lines on the green paper. He says, "Alright, you didn't like the Zyprexa. Try this." And he hands her the prescription—tosses it at her, really—and walks away. Stunned, she scowls after his receding form, but she is also hopeful. Perhaps this will make her well. Sesti gives her no guidance, and the nurse practitioner offers nothing but the basic dosage information. She is left with a slip of green paper that might as well be a death warrant.

Within a few days of starting the new medication, a whirling darkness closes in around her. The world outside appears only as streaks of color against a sky turned to sickness, the virulent greenish-black seen when a twister descends on earth. The new drug plows into the chemical chaos of her brain, severing the slim lines of control that she has struggled to hold all year. This is not mania, not really, though she is possessed with a restless anxiety that wants to chew through her skin. No, this is depression turned deadly, for she is suddenly, desperately, suicidal.

The anniversaries of last spring's climb toward mania—the May 1st festival of Beltane, her birthday on the 7th—pass unnoticed. Something has changed; it is no longer important to try and make sense of anything. Nothing matters. She is immobile, barely holding on. For three weeks, she exists inside a writhing tornado, blasted into blindness, hands knotted together to keep hold of her life; her knuckles bleach white with the strain.

May 13th is Mother's Day, sunshine and clear blue sky. She visits her parents and brother for the weekend. For most of the morning, she has been lying on the couch. Here with her family, she has let down her guard and is beginning to unspool. She cries repeatedly and finally goes upstairs to be alone. She stands in front of the mirror in her childhood bathroom, and her sobs are vicious. She wants to punch her reflection, ram her head through the mirror, and then peel the glass shards off the wall, tear them through her skin, her veins and arteries, down to the bone. With her blood in full flood, all the vileness inside her will be released. It will be over. There is only a shaving razor in the bathtub, but there are straight razors in the medicine closet in the hall. She pounds her fists against the bathroom counter, sinks to her knees breathing hard. Wordless, furious, she tries to vomit, but her throat chokes shut.

Finally, she forces herself to her feet, then down the stairs and out into the backyard where her family is talking together on the porch. She sits down in the grass, beside a cluster of lily of the valley, their sweet flowers open to the spring air. She is crying again, or perhaps she stays silent, rocks her body back and forth like a child, or simply sits still. It takes an eternity to speak the words.

"I think I need to go to the hospital." Their heads swivel toward her as one. They are not sure if they heard her correctly. She speaks with more force.

"I need to go to the hospital." She does not have to explain why. They move into motion, their relief palpable in the air. For months they have lived in fear, not knowing how to help her, and now they do. Her mother has stayed in touch with Dr. Don McLean. She calls his emergency line, and he calls the hospital, finds a room for her, admits her by phone under his care. It all happens very fast. She goes blank now, silent and numb, frightened, her heart hammering. She packs a bag, remembers to take a warm sweatshirt because hospitals are always cold.

There is no traumatic admission this time—no restraints, no needles, nothing involuntary. She does not even have to enter the emergency room, just fills out a form in a quiet office, hands over her insurance card, and takes the elevator to the psychiatric ward. She is assigned to the same room where she had been forcibly detained the June before, the same room where Dr. McLean first urged her to take lithium. She wants nothing more than to lie down, but a nurse carrying a clipboard waits for her.

"I just need to ask a few questions." The nurse's smile is warm. They sit together in a meeting room and talk about her diagnosis, the medications, the past year. It hurts to talk, but there is relief too. The young woman unfolds the story in a thin voice. Finally, they come to the reason for her presence at the hospital. The nurse puts down the clipboard and gazes gently at the young woman.

"Did you have a plan?"

"Not yet. Almost. Yes." she pauses to breathe, "I was planning to make a plan."

The nurse nods, "You're going to be ok."

Late in the evening, she lies in bed in the familiar room with her arms wrapped around herself, shaking. She does not believe the nurse—it is impossible that she will ever be ok—but she is grateful to be here. Here, at least, it is possible that she will survive.

After breakfast the next morning, Dr. McLean arrives to see her. He has reviewed the notes from her intake interview and seats himself beside the hospital bed, flipping through the pages. With little introduction, he says the only words that might win her trust:

"I was looking at the medications that you've been prescribed this past year..." He clears his throat, "I don't usually speak ill of others in my profession, but I have to say, it was a very irresponsible course of treatment."

She turns wondering eyes to him.

"Lithium is the gold standard for treating manic depressive illness. It's been time tested since the 1940s. It should be our first line of treatment, but you were being prescribed some of the newest medications on the market. They simply don't have a track record."

"I had a terrible doctor. He was evil." Her voice is flat and heavy. She notices that the side of Dr. McLean's mouth may be twitching with half of a smile. She continues. "He said that lithium was too dangerous. People overdose."

"People can overdose on any medication. Lithium works."

She nods slowly.

McLean continues, "I'd like to start you on lithium and discontinue the other meds. I'd like you to stay on Effexor for now since it seems to have helped you in the past. Ok?"

She does not argue. "Ok."

SEVEN

One year later, the same hospital room in Fairfax, same doctor, lithium proffered again. It was as though the universe was trying to shake me awake: *Go back and start over. Get it right this time.* Depression still lay vast and dim over me—the constant ache in my chest, frequent tears—but there was relief in being at the hospital. Every ten minutes or so, a nurse peeked around the door, verified my continued existence and moved on. I had not realized how much desperation had reigned over my life the past many months, or how long I had huddled in rattling anxiety, uncertain that I could continue to survive. Being on suicide watch at the hospital provided a strange easing of that tension. I could let someone else worry about whether I stayed alive.

I had lobbying visits arranged with half of Virginia's Congressional delegation for the following week in D.C. I called my boss, Sean, with shaky hands.

"I'm so sorry, Sean. So sorry. I can't go." My voice sounded small and faint in my ears.

"Don't worry, Christina. Really. Do. Not. Worry. Just take care of yourself. We can find folks to cover. We need you to get well." He was so kind. I put down the phone with tears on my face and curled up on the hospital bed.

My brother brought me a copy of *The Story of B,* a novel by Daniel Quinn about seeking environmental sanity. The book begins in a hospital, where the narrator is trying to regain his memory. I hid myself inside the book, spending as much time as possible reading, either lying on the hospital bed or sitting in an empty common room. It allowed me to stop thinking, to live elsewhere. My room stayed quiet since my Vietnamese roommate spoke almost no English. When her doctor came to see her, they talked through a translator. My roommate suffered from postpartum depression. Her husband came to visit every evening; he was clearly crazy about her, and it created warmth in the chilly room. She and I smiled at each other and didn't speak.

I remember only a handful of details about this time in the hospital. There were the usual activities—random conversation with strangers in group therapy; recreational therapy, which involved kickball in the hallway; art therapy, where I sadly drew a picture of the old Abbey on Iona in Scotland, wishing I could go there and live a different life. Mostly I remember the green sweatshirt that I brought along to stay warm in the chilly rooms and the relief of reading and escaping, of not having to think or do or try. I let go of the façade that I could handle things on my own and finally landed heavily on the dark, mossy stones at the bottom of that long, long fall away from the golden mountaintop light. I lay there, still and silent and broken.

On one of Dr. McLean's visits, he mentioned that, in his opinion, lithium was under-prescribed for manic depressive illness.

"Why?" I asked.

"Like I said, lithium is an element on the periodic table. Lithium carbonate, the drug that you're taking, occurs naturally—you can basically dig it up out of the ground. There's no way to patent lithium, so pharmaceutical companies don't market it." I thought of Sesti's office filled with Zyprexa paraphernalia and realized with sudden intense relief that I never had to see him again. McLean continued, "So we have all these new drugs, without strong track records, being heavily promoted—advertising campaigns, free samples for doctors to give out—"

"Lithium has to fend for itself."

"Right. And it is a complicated medicine. You have to have regular blood tests to determine the right dosage, and there are side effects—some people simply can't tolerate lithium, but again, that's true with any drug. When lithium works, it works extremely well."

Lithium worked for me. It took time. Weeks, months, but it worked. I noticed the changes in small shifts. First, I realized—even before I left the hospital—that the wrenching static of anxiety in my head was quieting. As the weeks went by, I began to feel carved out, emptied and hollow, but not in a bad way. It seemed as though lithium was healing some of the horrific feelings of the past year, and there was nothing to replace them—just an empty space inside me. But somehow, within that emptiness, I did not feel lost or desperate. Instead, I had a sense of vastness—like the space between stars—with no emotion except perhaps a faint glimmering of peace in the silence. I tried not to think or focus on my own life. A rank ocean of grief lapped at my heels. I did not dare glance at it for fear of being pulled back in.

The board of directors at Virginia Wildlands offered me a two month unpaid leave, generously allowing me to keep my health insurance benefits intact. I would come back to work in August. For now, I had time. Time to rest and see where the hollowness would lead me. I lived at my parents' house in my old bedroom. I had always loved the yellow walls that lit up with light in the late afternoon sun. I felt like a child kept home sick from school. For the first few weeks, I stayed in bed as much as I could, allowing myself to get lost in books. For the most part, I read the battered science fiction and fantasy novels still on my bedroom bookshelves. In worlds filled with dragons and starships, my extreme experiences from the past year did not seem so alien. I could hand myself over to fiction, where time travel and telepathy and communing with extraordinary powers were commonplace.

On any given day, I would wake up, find the book next to my bed, read for a few hours, get up and find breakfast, read through the afternoon, take a nap, and spend time with my parents in the evening. My one commitment to the doctor and to my family was to get outside and walk every day. Exercise and oxygen and sunlight were the best things for my body and my brain, they told me—to help my moods, to energize endorphins, and to deal with the weight I'd packed on via Zyprexa and depression.

Matthew and I talked on the phone regularly, but he never came to visit. I don't remember contact with other friends. I think of this as a time when I simply disappeared, cocooning myself into the safe quiet of my childhood home. I thought about leaving my job and relocating to Fairfax—making a clean break from my old life and rebuilding something new. I think my parents were quietly rooting for this option, but they held back their opinions and allowed me to find my own way.

Sometime in mid-summer, I took a trip back to Charlottesville to gather some belongings. My mother came with me. I didn't want to spend much time in town, didn't want to run into my friends or my housemate. By this point, I had almost made up my mind to move back to

Fairfax, but the phone rang just as I was preparing to leave. It was Loki.

"Christina! I've been trying to reach you for weeks—I didn't have your parents' number. Are you back?"

"No, I just stopped in. I'm heading out this afternoon."

"Well, when are you coming back?"

I smiled, "I don't know, brother. I haven't been doing very well."

"I know." He sounded sad. "I'm very sorry."

"I'm thinking..." I sighed. I didn't want to have this conversation, but Loki was like family, one of my best friends. "I'm thinking about quitting at Virginia Wildlands and moving back to Fairfax. I don't really want to, but god, Loki, I've been having such a hard time."

"I didn't realize things were that bad."

"No, you wouldn't have. I haven't told anyone."

There was a long pause on the line. When Loki spoke, his voice was sober and slow, emphasizing the words. "I really hope, Christina—I really, truly hope that you won't go. Things have gotten so much better since you and Sean started working on Virginia forest issues. We need you. We really *need* you here."

I was taken aback and touched. I'd never heard Loki talk this way. Images of old trees and moccasin flowers, turtles and millipedes and mountain streams flashed in my mind. Did they need me too? I felt a flicker in my heart for the first time in such a long time, a memory of connection.

"I'll think about it, Loki, I really will. I miss you a lot."

"Well, I miss you too. Come over when you're back in town."

That phone call cinched the deal for me. Moving back to Fairfax would have been easy. I could have walked a slow, relaxed path in the safe circle of my family and eventually—hopefully—found my way back to independence. But returning to Charlottesville and to forest work meant holding on—holding on to my sense of identity and purpose. In addition, the truth was that despite the hospitals and medications, I could not shake those ecstatic manic experiences. They stayed with me, always, just below the surface.

I had tried, since getting out of the hospital, not to think about mania and mountains and ghosts—to just shut them out of my mind—because whenever my thoughts strayed there, my heart twisted with yearning. The complexity of my emotions was exhausting: a mix of hope, shame, and deep sadness. Loki reminded me of my connection with Nature—bare feet on the forest floor, purpose and passion in activism. He called me back to it, but he could not give it to me. All these things remained at a distance, just a glimmer and a hope.

I finally moved back to Charlottesville in August and returned to work at Virginia Wildlands. Within a few weeks, Matthew and I took up again. When I was considering staying in Fairfax, it had seemed like he and I might simply go our separate ways. We were both tired; the relationship and my illness had become emotionally draining. But back in Charlottesville, we began spending time together again, slowly easing back into our old routines—both good and bad.

I stayed in the relationship because of a combination of love and deep loneliness. Matthew was dear to me, and I was grateful to him. During the awful hospitalization in Waynesboro last summer, he had reached out far beyond his comfort level to help me. Matthew also symbolized a kind of safety net to me; over the course of the year and the illness, I had grown scared and anxious around people. Despite our difficulties, Matthew was a familiar companion who knew my struggles—I did not have to explain myself to him.

The days eased into a slow normalcy as I settled into Charlottesville and work. With lithium in my blood, I was better, so much better, though I still struggled with ongoing, low-grade depression—not near the intensity of the past year, but a lingering, grinding sense of loss and loneliness. I felt disconnected from others—no one could really understand the places I had been—and still, despite moments of hope, I remained terribly disconnected from the things that had once filled me. God and Spirit and Nature lay far off.

And yet, I was better. There were even days when my heart felt truly glad. I remember September 11, 2001 for all the terrible reasons but also because that morning—before the planes hit the towers—marked the first time I could remember feeling really good, lighthearted, happy. I woke early that day and hopped out of bed—a remarkable thing in and of itself. I went out for a run in the park and listened to the brand new Bob Dylan album, *'Love and Theft,"* while preparing for work. I slipped off my shoes on the walk to the office and went barefoot, smiling at the crystal blue of the sky. I arrived at work moments before the second plane hit the tower. My office mates and I spent the rest of the day staring at the television screen in horror.

I had a meeting that afternoon with a representative of a foundation that funded my organization. Her plane had left Boston, heading for D.C., shortly after two of the hijacked planes. She flew over black smoke rising from the World Trade Center just before the airspace over New York City was closed, then passed over more black smoke hovering above the Pentagon just before all flights were grounded. The passengers sat in terrified silence; the flight crew made no announcements—no one knew what had happened.

Her plane landed safely at Dulles airport near D.C., but her flight to Charlottesville was canceled. She rented a car at the airport and arrived at my office right on time. I hugged her and asked if she was alright, if she wanted to just go to her hotel and rest. "As long as I'm here, we might as well meet," she said and tried to smile. "It will give me something else to think about." Her face was grey and bloodless; her hands shook.

My tangled moods paled in comparison to the chaotic waves that spread outward across the country from 9-11. For days, I watched and listened to the news, trying to make myself believe that it was all real. I cried seeing the fences in NYC where people posted photos of loved ones, hoping that they might be alive in some hospital. Cried at the rubble, the firefighters, stories of heroic deeds, and yet I felt personally detached. The reality seemed far away from me as the nation cracked open in grief and fury. I feared for the future, knowing there would be war, but I don't know if I fully grasped the enormity of the events. My own trauma stayed wrapped around me, a blanket that muffled the world outside. I was already grieving when the 9-11 attacks took place; my sense of reality had already been upended. As the nation struggled to make sense of horrendous violence, I kept my head down, doing my best to stay on my feet, to keep moving.

My friend Catherine helped me. She was the only person that I knew with manic depression. Her illness had been diagnosed in college following a dramatic manic episode, and Catherine had endured numerous hospitalizations and rock-bottom depressions before stabilizing. I'd met her six years before in Scotland when we both worked for the Iona Community. A dancer, artist, and deeply spiritual woman, Catherine also had a wild streak, and we formed an easy bond. One evening on Iona, a purple sunset lit up the sky. The two of us looked up into those colors and spontaneously took off running west; we stopped on the rocks at the ocean's edge and howled at the sun going down.

By 2000, she'd been living with a diagnosis of manic depression for over a decade and living in Charlottesville for a few months. I'd never seen Catherine manic or deeply depressed, and we'd talked very little about her experience with the disease. But when I was diagnosed, she reached out and kept reaching. She came to see me in Waynesboro during the fall of 2000. Her visit felt like a single ray of light in that dark time. Although her recovery had on-going bumps and challenges, she was doing very well, exploring her life with joy, creativity, and authority. I could look at her and see the possibility of recovery, even though that possibility seemed hopelessly remote for me. During the autumn of 2001, we met regularly for dinner or a walk. She listened to the perpetual heartsick exhaustion in my voice and said, "Christina, I am so sorry. I understand." It helped.

Over the course of that fall, I recognized how much my role in forest protection had shifted. I had become a participant rather than a leader. I went to meetings that other people organized, assisted with events rather than leading them, and politely applauded from my seat rather than standing on stage.

Something had changed fundamentally over the past year. Depression and the diagnosis of mental illness had transformed me, and I hid myself like a battered animal. Even though my mood had stabilized and improved, I still found myself wracked with debilitating shyness, a kind of social anxiety that made it difficult to be relaxed interacting with people who I didn't already know. I went from working enthusiastically with new people on projects and events, taking leadership roles, giving speeches and interviews, to fumbling with even the simplest conversations. My voice seemed to be knotted at the base of my neck, tight and hard. I could no longer speak my truth, because the truth was terrifying, the truth was stigmatizing, the truth made no sense.

The loss of voice and self felt like a betrayal, along with the loss of heart and health and God. Red streaks of anger snaked under my skin that fall. I wanted my old life back, wanted to care and feel and work again with passion and fire. I wanted to be *me* again, not this balled up, sniffling, sorrowful, fat, gray shipwreck of a person. I could not stop looking backward, wishing for the past.

I had been an activist in the forest protection movement for nearly four years when the mania hit in 2000. Before that, I had led recycling efforts as a student at the

University of Virginia; I worked in homeless shelters and on home-building projects all through high school. Service work fueled my life.

The summer after graduating from college, I was driving home to Charlottesville when I caught a glimpse of the Blue Ridge Mountains in panorama; they had seemed to call out to me, saying, "Stay!" My plan had been to move to London in the fall, but I realized in that instant how much I wished to learn the mountains' streams and trails, the names of their trees and flowers and creatures. Soon after, I discovered a group of students in Charlottesville who were fighting against logging on Virginia's National Forests. I decided to stay and threw myself into the work.

We linked up with a loose group of doe-eyed oddballs from across the state—vegetarian rednecks, barefoot bow hunters, off-the-grid back-to-the-land types, vegan punks, peaceniks. They were delightful people; in the years to come, I met networks of these folks across the country. Forest protection—trying to save outposts of wild nature—was a community, a circle of work and play that centered on potlucks, campfires, and beautiful places. By the time my mania began, I could have traveled to any state in the South or Midwest and had a friendly place to stay with a bed or a fold out couch, a back lot to pitch a tent, or an old bus in a farm field, cozy with blankets.

Within half-a-year after graduating from UVA in 1996, forest work had become my whole life. I was good at it. I could write and speak, use laws and science and weave in poetry. I could organize events, put together conferences, recruit volunteers. The state and federal forest agencies in Virginia, the timber industry representatives, the clean-cut political environmentalists (who regularly snubbed our more raggedy crew), they all knew me. They worked with us sometimes, and fought with us often.

I was pretty, polite, and a pain in the ass, with a charming sweetness to soften my often acid edge. Even the angry loggers and bitter lobbyists found it hard to be mean to me, at least in person. I debated the State Forester and the chief lobbyist of the Virginia Forestry Association and led citizen lobbyists to meet with their state and federal elected officials. I even received death threats—the true mark of a successful activist. From time to time, the FBI called me, stopped by the office, wanting to "chat" about the activities of certain radical friends. I managed to avoid them. They managed not to solve the death threats.

I fell in love with the activists, with their desire for change, their commitment to living lightly on the Earth. Spent nights strategizing at someone's kitchen table by candlelight because the batteries were running low off the solar panels, drinking flame black coffee, dreaming a shared dream. Rose early to walk in the woods, attend a hearing, a meeting, a conference, a protest. So many gatherings—like the one at Blanton Forest—that were focused partly on strategy and education, partly on music and laughter, partly on disappearing into wild forests. And so many beautiful places, secret places that only the locals knew—the waterfalls and deep springs, places where rare plants grew high on the ridges, where an underground river reappeared suddenly, where rock formations spired and pirouetted above a magnolia forest. Places to swim naked and solitary. Places to be humbled, to grow small and silent and sacred.

In 1998, I quit my day job in the UVA library and lived off my savings to volunteer full-time with the forest movement. I learned to be nimble, to troubleshoot, to raise money, write press releases, legal appeals, OpEds, anything. I had a team and a network, media contacts, a powerful address book. I spun webs, thought in terms of connections—who could help who? Within the absurdly divided and divisive environmentalist community in Virginia (how could so few people find so much to fight about?), I could bring people together, at least make them talk, take small strides.

By the end of the '90s, it truly felt that we stood on the verge of a breakthrough, of societal change, tipping point for the world community, to live lighter on the land, solar-power in the cities and suburbs, the sustainable future. We had God on our side, my circle of forest activists. The

God that embraces tall graceful trunks and makes love to the deep soils with rain and fog and sun. When President Clinton stood on Reddish Knob and announced the roadless rule in October of 1999, it had seemed only a matter of time.

But by the fall of 2001, almost all of that had collapsed. The selection of George W. Bush yanked the rug out from under forest protection efforts, and the 9-11 attacks further muted interest and funding for environmental causes. My life and my strength had also toppled. I spent very little time in the forest. I no longer trusted myself. Feeling deep connection to anything—Nature or God or another person—seemed very dangerous. And it was painful, tremendously so, to open myself up. Staying shut up inside, severed from my connections, was painful too, but it seemed safer. Lithium granted me stability, and I clung to that—at least the raging anxiety of the previous autumn was gone, replaced by low-level depression and that terrible shyness.

I stayed on Effexor—though in hindsight, I don't think the anti-depressant ever did much good. I found out from later studies that anti-depressants may not be particularly effective against bipolar depression. But I didn't rock the boat. I was better. The possibility of recovering joy and stability on a long-term basis seemed unthinkable.

What did occur to me, sometime in October, was the possibility that getting high might lift my spirits and restore some of my confidence. I started thinking that since I no longer felt out of control, it would be ok to smoke again. At least once. Just to try it out. When I first breathed the rusty smoke into my lungs, I felt the safe arms of an old friend around me. The smoke supported me, lifted and eased and excited me. And suddenly I could do it again!

The plant took down my mile-high inhibitions and let me back outside under the open sky. I could melt again into the forest, feel the rush of Nature moving with my bloodstream and heartbeat. I went alone to Matthew's land by the Tye River and wandered on bare feet again through the water and across the damp earth, feeling life pulsing through my skin. When my father had open-heart surgery in late October to replace his floppy heart valve— an event that might previously have filled me with dread and terror—I was calm and upbeat, helpful, glad to be present with my family. For a time, cannabis proved to be an excellent anti-depressant. For a very short time.

In November, I gleefully invested a few hundred dollars in several ounces of pot—two bulging, sweet-smelling bags—more than I would usually smoke in a year. I no longer needed to ration and could smoke whenever I wanted. I started taking a bud or two with me everywhere I went, even to my parents' house, where I would stop my car briefly, up the street out of sight, and take a quick puff. I had a small, metal pipe that let me smoke a tiny hit at a time, one deep breath of smoke, just enough. I loved having cannabis back in my life; we quickly became inseparable friends. The heaviness in my life grew brighter and easier. Things like walks in the park, drives in the countryside, meanders in the mountains, transformed into adventures again.

November began mellow and golden. In my lighter mood, work grew increasingly interesting and fun. I spoke up more in strategy sessions, laughed more easily. On the 15th of November, I met Matthew and EQ in Washington, D.C. for a Bob Dylan show. I shivered when he played "Searching for a Soldier's Grave," remembering the thousands of unknown bones in the white marble tomb at Arlington House.

Hearing Bob's voice brought back more memories of mania: staying up all night at Sean and Roxanne's home, draining my car battery playing Dylan songs, and looking out the window to see one of Mosby's riders keeping watch in the mist. At a quiet moment in the show, just after the applause died down and before the next song began, I yelled out, "Thank you!" to the band.

After the show ended, I felt loose and adventurous and decided to take a late-night roadtrip up the Shenandoah Valley rather than heading straight home. I stopped in Woodstock and pulled my car into a cemetery behind the military academy, near the single plinth that marked the graves of more unknown Civil War soldiers. I slept in the car for a few hours and then, on a whim, drove south to Appomattox Courthouse, scene of Robert E. Lee's surrender to Ulysses S. Grant—the beginning of the end of the Civil War. I was suddenly back in the groove of the Civil War nurse-healer. I pulled out my cannabis seeds to plant in the warm dust.

My solo road trips increased with my drug use. The annual Leonid meteor storm—one of the most active in decades—peaked on the weekend of November 17th. I slipped out of Matthew's house in the earliest hours of the morning and drove through the darkness to the Blue Ridge Parkway. I lay on the grass beside a small cemetery near Love Gap and opened my eyes to the sky. For hours, the meteors sparked in the night. Silver spikes and curves, popping like fireworks, falling embers trailing white flame. I drove home dazed and giddy as red dawn light climbed the horizon.

The Dylan concert, the memories of mania and war, the sleepless nights combined with the marijuana to trip a wire in my brain. The world around me grew increasingly intense. The stories in my mind began to hum with the themes of earlier manias, particularly my Great Healing Quest—healing between people and the land, healing between the present and the past, healing the scars of war. But these things did not taste like mania to me. They seemed noble and important; they called to me as though they were my purpose on this Earth, the meaning in my life. And so I smoked more pot, needing it to deepen my insights and open my mind. Without cannabis, I might again lose this connection; I might fall back into the dismal sickness that had curdled my mind.

EIGHT

In its early stages, mania feels like a miracle. The blood in your body turns bright gold, and for a time, everything is weightless, effortless. The flow of existence carries you in loving arms and shows you the exact right thing to do at every moment. Your intuition is sharp and fine as an archer's arrow. Air slips across your skin in a fine caress; walking feels like dancing. Brief as a firefly's flicker, the world is exquisite, and all is destiny.

Then the colors grow more vivid and begin to move. The pulse beat of the earth becomes visible, and you begin to see things—patterns and intersections, tangible metaphors—like a journey on LSD or psilocybin, except it never stops; you never come down. Instead, the stories in your mind become obsessions, fraught with a fevered anxiety as you try to keep up with your careening senses. Everything speaks in codes that only you can decipher. Fears jostle up against your throat; the thickening complexity of the world around you overwhelms your capacity to comprehend.

Then the tunnel vision folds in. Nothing matters but your own mind. The people you love, your work, your life are blotted out by some giddy, pulsing, internal hurricane, and you move through it, at the center of your own universe, stumbling, still seeking, trying to understand, trying to make sense out of massive sensory overload.

But now your skin grows raw—the constant flaying of hurricane-force wind draws blood—and the flames behind your eyes melt the world into a fevered wash. Now frantic, skittering, breaking open, now a husk, a shell, a ghost burdened with an unyielding mind, expanded and distorted, sleepless, raving, unbound.

◆

Inside the brief splash of early, golden mania in the fall of 2001, I traveled to my parents' house for Thanksgiving. My father was recovering well from the open-heart surgery. The valve replacement was successful, but the beat of his heart would not cooperate. It continued to skip in and out of rhythm. I laid my hand over the long purple scar and tried to send healing beats through his mending sternum into his heart. I remembered the humming man during my second hospitalization, how I would drum along on table tops to keep time with his songs.

My Dad took my hand and smiled at me, saying, "Hey, it was worth a try."

That weekend, I had a strange and vivid dream. I floated in the air, wrapped in velvet blackness. My eyes were open, but I could see only inky dark. Then a small light flared below me, and I saw an empty stage in an empty theater. The light grew brighter as the trap door in the stage opened and a small round platform rose from it, rotating slowly. A man stood on the platform, and I smiled, knowing him though I could not yet see his face. Then he looked up, and a smile lit his face as he recognized me. I woke into the quiet darkness of my childhood bedroom. By morning, I felt silly—dreaming about celebrities seemed adolescent and foolish—yet I smiled softly many times that day, remembering running into Bob Dylan as an old friend in my dreams.

On the Sunday after Thanksgiving, my friend EQ and his girlfriend Meghan arrived at my parents' house. I had hired Meghan—a professional photographer—to take some casual portraits of my family for a Christmas present. EQ brought me a copy of the latest *Rolling Stone* magazine. I gasped and rocked back on my heels when he handed it to me. The cover featured Dylan, in black and white, holding a harmonica and gazing into the camera. After my dream, and in my state of mind, this gift from EQ seemed full of portent.

Earlier in November, Matthew had brought home a newspaper clipping and handed it to me, grinning. In the interview, Dylan referenced the Civil War and commiserated with Lee and Sherman—one general from each side—about dealing with people who try to sell your secrets. He said, "I have the same feeling about them that Sherman and Lee had about people hanging around their tents. They're spies."

Mania's sticky metaphors made it easy to concoct a connection out of these things—my dream of Bob, the magazine, this mention of the War. In years to come, in writings and song, Dylan spoke more about the Civil War. Apparently, he did have a fascination with the War; so did I; so do many people, but in the late fall in 2001, the idea that he and I might share the same ghosts made him a collaborator in my mind, a partner in purpose.

Bob became a tangible, imagined presence in my life over the course of the coming mania. He rode with me as a traveling companion on my disjointed and chaotic quests for cosmic healing. A part of my mind knew full-well that I was creating an imaginary friend, while another part said, *So what?* His imagined presence helped me, helped to stabilize and provide a degree of continuity to my life during this time of gigantic unraveling. And if his fame spoke to my manic grandiosity, all the better. I already had some of America's most famous Civil War generals as friends.

On the Monday after Thanksgiving, I set out for Richmond. I had meetings there in the morning about lobbying plans for the upcoming General Assembly session. Instead of heading straight back to Charlottesville that afternoon, I made a snap decision to drive south to Jamestown. Another road trip, another quest.

In Virginia history, all roads lead back to Jamestown, the first permanent English settlement in the New World and original birthplace of what would become the United States. With my mystical fascination with healing Virginia's traumatic past, I had known for a long time that I would have to return to Jamestown.

Twice in the past, I had been to the Jamestown settlement site—once as a child on a family trip and once in 1997 for a conference. Just out of college, I had worked for an unusual think tank, housed at the University of Virginia Medical School and run by psychiatrists who applied the insights of their profession to large-group psychology. They studied the behaviors and patterns that feed conflicts and hatreds between countries and ethnic groups. The director, Dr. Vamik Volkan, held a prominent position in conflict resolution circles. A cornerstone of his theory was that traumatic historical events—past wars, past humiliations, past abuse experienced by large groups of people—are replayed and transmitted through the generations on a societal level until those traumas can be resolved.

As part of my job, I had written a successful grant proposal for the organization to host a "Preparing for 2007" conference. The grants funded events that would lay the groundwork for the upcoming commemoration of the 400th anniversary of Jamestown's settlement: May 13, 1607, when the English ships arrived on the banks of the Powhatan River. We proposed to trace the repercussions of Jamestown's traumas through the centuries into modern times. Most other "Preparing for 2007" grants funded blandly patriotic school projects or museum exhibits. Ours paid for a day-long conference in Charlottesville with a keynote address titled, "Preparing for 2007: The Hidden Transmission of Destructive Aggression from Jamestown to the Present."

Rev. Benjamin Campbell, an Episcopal priest from Richmond, gave the speech, identifying disturbingly consistent patterns of thinking from Jamestown—where the English colony's enslavement of African people and extermination of native people began—to the Civil War, to Jim Crow, to Virginia's "massive resistance" against school desegregation, and onward to today's drastic socioeconomic inequalities. He blew the romanticized notions of Jamestown that I had learned in elementary school out of the water, stating:

The first 60 years of the Jamestown settlement were a disaster. The human events in Tidewater Virginia were deeply tragic, a grisly companion to other great tragedies in human history. There were massacre, natural disaster, mass starvation, slavery, plague, cannibalism, arbitrary murder of people by their leaders, rape, theft, physical torture, and the sudden and pitiless destruction of a culture which had existed for at least a millennium.[7]

The same sanitized version of Jamestown that I had received from my education was a significant part of the problem, Rev. Campbell said. By romanticizing the violent traumas and oppressions enacted on indigenous people, on enslaved people, on poor people, Virginians (and by extension all Americans since the country's history began in Virginia) participate in a vast denial of our traumatic past. Failing to recognize that reality means, according to Campbell, failing to enact forgiveness of ourselves and others, and failing to create a more just and gentle future.

I sat in awe, drinking in his words. Campbell's ideas explained so much of what seemed intractable and horrific to me about my home state and my nation. And I saw how his theory could extend seamlessly into my environmental work. The traumas and oppressions and violence do not occur only between people but also on the landscape,

---

[7] Rev. Benjamin Campbell, "The Hidden Legacy of Jamestown: The Transmission of Destructive Aggression in Virginia's History," *Mind & Human Interaction* 9, no. 1 (1998): 18.

shaping our attitudes toward ownership and cultivation and wilderness. The traumas of the past are written on the land, and the land suffers.

These were the fundamental ideas in *A Patchwork Theology of Soil Liberation*, the multi-faceted piece of writing that I had started back in 2000, on the brink of my first mania. In his 1997 talk, Rev. Campbell theorized that by using "psycho-spiritual historical analysis," one could dig into the past and reveal the "instinctive and unconscious" transmission of trauma through generations. In my writing in 2000, I had tried to rise to that challenge, to undertake that type of analysis, and then had plunged into my own mental carnage.

I visited Jamestown in 2001 on a balmy afternoon, carrying the *Rolling Stone* magazine with Bob Dylan on the cover in my bag. I wandered around the archeological digs and stopped to gaze at the statue of Pocahontas in front of the rebuilt 17th century church. Little remained of 1607 Jamestown. The Europeans had denuded the peninsula of forest within the first year of their arrival, and the river had shifted the shape of the land.

After a while, I took off my shoes and ambled across the grass along the banks of the James River. Humidity and pollen glazed the day. My feet scuffed against thick layers of history. Parts of the original Jamestown fort remained buried beneath this ground; the first enslaved Africans set foot here sometime around 1619; earthworks built by Confederate troops during the Civil War stood nearby; and who knows how many bones—English, African, Powhatan—lay somewhere underground. I sat down with Bob beside the river and dipped my toes in the sunlit water. Leaning back on my elbows on the warm grass, I let myself doze and dream.

But it is not quite a dream. In the shadow space between true sleep and full wakefulness, I slip into the water. Ghost-like, my feet do not touch the silty riverbed, and I glide deeper and deeper, away from the sun, crossing under the ocean, back to England, back to the islands where this all began. The statue of Pocahontas at Jamestown matches a statue at Gravesend, England, where Powhatan's daughter died and was buried. Saint-like, the hands of both sculptures are outstretched at her sides, her palms turned outward in a gesture of blessing or welcome. Did she truly welcome the newcomers into her world, sadly overestimating the kindness of these strangers? Thinking perhaps that her people would always outnumber these cruel Christians, or that both groups would someday grow to accept and help one another?

In the deep ocean, I pass Pocahontas' ghost returning to Virginia, to her native land. A fatal illness had cut short her journey home in 1617, so now we trade places, building bridges of friendship. Our fingers touch in the barest of greetings as the currents bear us onward. She emerges onto the shore at Jamestown and slips away into the woods. I surface on the far side of the Atlantic, stepping out onto an island of green, the vast jagged coast of Cornwall, my mother's family's ancestral home. Voices call out, welcoming me back.

Sometime later, I returned slowly to wakefulness, still staring into the river at the hypnotic bend and curve of sunlight inside the gently rocking waves. I took out my journal and jotted down my thoughts: "I would like to have turned back the three ships from these shores in 1607, to turn away the great peril and pestilence that these Europeans carried. But now our homelands are so intertwined, there is no going back. We have no hope but friendship to make peace between all times, spaces, faces, species." I lay back against the sun-warmed grass and spoke to Bob on the cover of *Rolling Stone*. "Friendship, Bob," I said. "That's all we've got."

Over the next several weeks, I slid smoothly between sanity and the incessant tugs of delusion. The pages of my December calendar were filled with activities—meetings, travel, conference calls—but my mind was occupied elsewhere. Pocahontas took me captive. It all led back to her, of course, to Jamestown and the mythology of that place and time. The denial that burned in my nation's veins, fed by myths of a welcoming Indian princess, as well as false tales of genteel slaveowners, and the "Lost Cause" of the South in the Civil War. Oh yes, tragedies were thick on the ground in the Old Dominion—I couldn't take a step without falling into another huge Virginia heartbreak—but these were not the same tragedies perpetuated in our make-believe patriotism, our imaginary history. The real tragedies stank of purposeless violence that eviscerated the concepts of kindness and charity taught by the Savior Christ our Christian founders purported to worship. The real tragedies were genocide, slavery, heartless greed, and sacrificial war. They destroyed the possibility of any moral foundation to the United States of America.

These thoughts ground at me—sandpaper on my brain, on the nubs of my bones. I lived in a tidal wash of guilt, anger, and bewildering grief. I fed myself on more Native American stories, exploring a history that I had never been taught. I found myself flushed with the fury of the 20th century and the Indian schools where children were kidnapped off reservations, taken far from their families, and enculturated with white "values." I read about the American Indian Movement (AIM), Wounded Knee, the Trail of Broken Treaties—all these stories I had never known—and their courage to fight and protest, even while the government lashed back viciously. The story of John Trudell floored me. He was a high-profile, highly-active AIM leader. At one protest in 1979, he burned an American flag outside FBI headquarters in Washington, D.C. Twelve hours later, his pregnant wife, three children, and mother-in-law were killed in a highly-suspicious fire at their home.

Matthew had played me tapes of John Trudell's music and speeches the first time I spent the night at his place. I returned to Trudell's words—finding a comfort there in his courage, his ability to dig truth out of despair: "We are all indigenous to this planet," he said. "We are all Tribal People. Our physical components are made up of the components of Earth itself; that's the reality."

I sat on the floor in my spare room, listening to Trudell's spoken words. Turned up loud on the stereo, I played music by Robbie Robertson, the masterful guitar player for The Band in the '60s and '70s whose mother came from the Mohawk tribe. His keening guitar wove in and out of Native American chants, drums, and flutes. I twisted joints and burned incense, gazing into the distance, trying to open my mind far enough to find the answers. THC was kicking again in my neurotransmitters, and my sense of grandiosity was growing. There was nothing wrong in the deep way that I engaged and immersed myself in history, the powerful extent to which I *felt,* but I obsessed over solutions, certain that I alone could find a way out. Surely it was my responsibility, surely I could piece it all together and heal the broken world.

My family gathered in Maine for Christmas at my grandmother's house. A few times a day, I would slip outside to smoke—just a little puff—or get high in my bedroom, blowing silver smoke out the window into the cold winter night.

My mother looked at me intently as we passed in the hall, "Have you been smoking?"

"No. Why?"

"Because you smell like smoke."

"Really? Huh. You know, I wore this jacket out to see a band a few days ago. Really smoky place. Maybe that's what you're smelling."

She glared at me but did not press the issue.

On that trip, I began to write about past manias. Looking backward, recapturing memories. I had tried to write before but always the pain of remembering shut off my voice. Now, with cannabis in my blood, I could suddenly find words and meanings to explain those strange days. But my interpretations began to go sideways, slipping into the mythic grandiosity that had seemed to herald my past free-falls into madness. For the last month, my questing had a humble edge to it, the pilgrim seeking peace and reconciliation with the land. Now my writing had the cadence of a preacher; I cast myself in the role of a savior. I was treading onto dangerous ground.

I spent New Year's with Matthew. We stayed up late watching *One Flew Over the Cuckoo's Nest*. He couldn't believe that I'd never seen it before. To me, the movie seemed vaguely silly, with characters who struck me as stereotypes. Oh well. I planned to be done with psychiatric wards and mental hospitals.

The first days of 2002 degenerated quickly. I stayed high almost all the time now, even as I drove to Richmond early in the morning on the seventh of January to meet with Delegates about my organization's General Assembly bill. I smoked in the car, just enough to loosen my mind and light me up with the possibilities. I had chosen my outfit carefully—green trousers made from hemp and a pale dressy top that came from Adam's wife.

The regular General Assembly session started on the 8th, so things were still quiet on Capitol Square. My first meeting was with our champion, a Delegate from northern Virginia who would introduce the bill. The legislation was simple—it required loggers to notify the Virginia Department of Forestry of plans to log within three days of starting the job. Unfortunately, the attitude in the Virginia timber industry was that any regulation was bad regulation. The timber industry, thank you very much, could police itself.

Our champion was a genius. He quietly pulled aside a young, newly-elected Delegate from Southside Virginia who was known as a strong supporter of the timber industry. The three of us huddled in the hall; my Delegate didn't introduce us, just floated the idea of extending the reporting deadline to 10 days. We both said, "Yeah, ok, that sounds reasonable." And just like that, we had a deal.

My Delegate sent us off together to the clerk's office to get the changes made to the legislation. We chatted. He was married with young children, brand new to politics. This was his first day ever in the General Assembly—we had to ask directions to the clerk's office. He wore a sweater instead of the standard suit and tie. I smiled as we rode the elevator to the clerk's office in the basement: "Did anyone ever tell you that you look like Robbie Robertson?"

"Who?"

Our champion's rapid garnering of support for an environmental bill from a timber-oriented Delegate made for much less controversial legislation. We still had to work hard over the next few weeks, but resistance to the bill was limited.

After my meetings finished that morning, I took a tour of the Virginia Capitol building before returning to Charlottesville. It had been a good morning, and I was feeling energetic and happy. Two guards stood beside a metal detector just inside the door. I said hello—they were friendly—and handed over my bag. The small blue purse, made of hemp, held just a few items: wallet, car keys, a pen and notepad. The guard unzipped the top, and I stopped breathing. I had forgotten to remove the prescription bottle in which I carried my cannabis. Two good sized buds were inside the orange plastic cylinder, and my tiny pipe was stowed in the front pocket. The guard glanced down at my purse.

I smiled my best smile at him and sweetened my voice with a friendly drawl, "You must be fixing to get busy with the session starting back up."

"That's right," he chuckled and looked up at me. "The calm before the storm." He was chatty. "The delegates and senators have a separate entrance, so we don't have to deal with them." He glanced back down at my bag. "We do have all sorts of lobbyists coming through."

"Oh my." I nodded sympathetically, all my attention focused on the guard, willing him to look at me. "That must not be a whole lot of fun."

The other guard chimed in, "They don't much like having to get their bags searched." The two men laughed. The hair rose on the back of my neck as the first guard ran his finger along the prescription bottle in my purse. My mouth dropped open, searching for some excuse, some explanation, but he was looking at his colleague, still laughing.

"Sooo," my voice poured smooth as honey, "what should I see while I'm here?" I gestured down the empty corridor. My smile was intoxicating. "I've been coming to Richmond for years, but I've never been inside the Capitol."

The guard grinned. He zipped my purse closed without looking at it again and handed it back to me. "What I'd do is take one of the guided tours. They're free and really good."

"Really?" Relief amplified my enthusiasm. "Oh, that's fantastic!"

The other guard explained, "Just go around the corner to the information desk. They'll set you up."

"Thank you so much!" I wanted to hug them. Smiling back at my new friends as I walked down the hall, I chirped, "Have a wonderful day!" They waved after me.

I kept a diary of these trips to Richmond. Every few days, I would send off email updates to Adam and Loki, reporting what I'd discovered on these forays into the capital city. I wrote about details and symbols that struck me as meaningful, like the alignment of Robert E. Lee's statue inside the Capitol with a sculpture of Stonewall Jackson outside. I described in detail the polished, black limestone that tiled the Capitol floor in which 400 million-year-old fossils were clearly visible.

In the diary, my tour guide received a paragraph of her own—an elegant elderly lady, she practically purred when she told me that Lee had "glowing dark eyes... he was said to be a very attractive man." But I wrote nothing—nothing, not a word—in those journal entries about my close brush with catastrophe going through security at the Capitol entrance. Nothing about the guard tracing his finger over my illegal drugs while I stood there, smiling sweetly, a glance away from arrest and humiliation and losing my job and who knows what else. With mania curling my perception, it seemed like no big deal.

Later in the week, after another day lobbying in Richmond, I went to dinner with two of my colleagues. My mind and body felt restless, anxious, and uncomfortable. The noisy restaurant rankled at my nerves. One of my colleagues kept interrupting his wife who had joined us for dinner. I snapped at him: "Would you please let her finish?" Everyone turned to look at me in surprise. Stepping out into the cool night air was a relief. The Virginia January was unusually warm, with highs in the 60s and 70s. The night felt as unsettled as I did. I decided not to go home.

NINE

I take I-95 south; I want to go to Southside, the region of Virginia south of the James River, the heart of timber country. My trajectory will take me down the interstate toward Petersburg, but then I catch sight of a sign pointing off an exit ramp: "Lee's Retreat." Virginia tourism officials had laid a trail of signs marking the 1865 path of Lee's retreating army. After a long winter of siege warfare around Richmond, the men were starving. Grant's Union army broke through the lines in early April, and Lee's troops fled south and then west, fighting as they went and desperately seeking food. I pull off the highway and follow the signs. I have to. I have no choice.

Historical markers along the route depict the rapid tightening of a noose around the Confederate troops: promised train loads of rations that failed to appear, the battle of Sayler's Creek when almost a quarter of Lee's army was forced to surrender. Union generals Sheridan and Custer—fresh from the Battle of Waynesboro in my old neighborhood in the Shenandoah Valley—captured and burned three train loads of Confederate provisions. The Army of Northern Virginia's final, famished surrender at Appomattox Courthouse followed a battle in which Union troops surrounded Lee's forces on three sides.

My obsession with the Civil War has caught fire again, flames fanned by my time in Richmond, by this night flight. I chat with Bob Dylan on the cover of *Rolling Stone*. He sits with me up front. I glance in the rearview and see General Lee sitting in the back, gazing out the window, looking weary. Days later, my mother will express her fear for my safety on that journey through the deep night.

"I was fine, Mom. I had Bob Dylan riding shotgun and Robert E. Lee in the back seat. They're both gentlemen."

I pull into Appomattox Courthouse late and stop near a Civil War cemetery for a nap. Waking in the early hours, I search the map for the next leg of the journey. Yes. I can travel north and west back across the James River and catch Rt. 56 at Wingina. The road will bring me to Matthew's land beside the Tye River close to dawn. Perfect. I set off and immediately startle a cluster of deer off the roadway. After that, I crawl down the two lane, careful to avoid hitting one of the skittish creatures. No cars pass. My headlights are the only light in the world.

On the dark bridge over the James River, I turn out the lights, put the car in park, and step out into the night.

I am invisible. I cannot see my hand or leg or arm in the night's perfect blackness. Only the faintest glint of starshine drifts on the river's ripples below. I lean against the railing, gazing down, and swoon with love for my tragic, gorgeous home state. This grand old river, marked on the first maps of the region as the Powhatan River, knits Virginia together. South and east of me, at its mouth, lie Jamestown and the myths of Pocahontas. To the north and west, my beloved Blue Ridge, where I am going now, going home.

I drive past Matthew's land in the rising light, up to the crest of the Blue Ridge to watch the sun rise from the town of Montebello. Growing giddy in the fresh sunlight, I fly up and back down the mountain on wings of music, listening to songs by my favorite Earth First! troubadours—Robert Hoyt and Danny Dolinger: "Jack Road" and "Red River," "Ghost of a Chance" and "Walking in Power." No weariness touches me now despite my restless night. I am alive and alight with the joy of place and movement and song. Open my wings. Fly with the music.

At last, with sunlight flickering through the trees, I wade across the Tye River, carrying my sleeping bag, pillow, and a satchel containing Bob Dylan's face. I struggle up to the flat white kneeling rock and lay out a pallet in the dry leaves. I am suddenly exhausted. My head has unexpectedly started to pound, and my skin prickles like fever. I curl up with sunlight on my face, slipping instantly into sleep.

♦

Back in Richmond a few days later, I run into the Delegate from the timber industry who I met that first day—the one who looks like Robbie Robertson. I am walking into the building as he is walking out; we recognize each other as we pass. He looks different in a suit and tie—haggard and stressed. He juggles multiple gift baskets from lobbyists.

"How's it going?" I am glad to see him.

"Oh, it's ok…" He lowers his voice and rolls his eyes, "It's crazy in there."

"Wait a minute—I've got something for you." I fumble through my bag, pull out the photocopied page from an old songbook with the words and music to "The Night They Drove Old Dixie Down," one of The Band's classics. James made a copy of it for me back in Waynesboro. I'd been carrying it around, knowing that I'd run into the Delegate one of these days. I point out that the song was written by Robbie Robertson. The Delegate looks at me strangely for a moment, then breaks out laughing. The stress eases, and he looks like a nice guy again instead of a politician. He thanks me.

♦

I spend a few days out of each week in Richmond. I am still on the board of the coalition of Virginia conservation groups that lobbies the General Assembly. They ask me to speak about the logging notification bill at a citizens' lobby day. I stand at the podium and give my 10 minute talk, explaining the issue, and then hand out talking points for people to share with their elected officials. Afterward, several attendees approach me:

"Thank you. I never knew about logging problems in Virginia."

"That was an inspiring talk."

"I think I can get my legislator on board."

♦

I am shaking. The ground below me seems to move. My ears reel from canon fire and rifle shot. Petersburg battlefield. The Crater. The site is so close to Richmond; I had to come. I had to witness one of the most grim and infamous scenes in the War. A bungled attempt by Union troops to blast their way behind the Confederate defenses of Petersburg's train lines. 8,000 pounds of gunpowder exploded beneath a Confederate fort. Poorly trained and confused Union troops rushed in, tried to use the crater as a rifle pit instead of pushing on around it to break the

Confederate lines—they were slaughtered by Rebel troops shooting down on them from above. Ghastly.

Then the Union generals sent in U.S. Colored Troops who made the furthest advance behind the lines before being repelled by a Confederate counterattack. Hand-to-hand combat, bayonets, bare fists. Many of the black soldiers who surrendered were not taken prisoner; Confederate soldiers killed them on the spot, breaking the rules of warfare. The battle changed nothing, except adding one more cruel offense against humanity to the Civil War's long and bitter list.

I stand in the center of the low and rolling depressions in the earth—all that is left of the Crater, now covered with pleasant green grass—clenching my fists. *What the fuck is wrong with us? What is wrong with humans?* Standing there, remembering the carnage, is like being gut punched over and over. Sick and dizzy. *What the fuck is wrong with me?* Am I becoming some kind of historical masochist—addicted to the pain of the past? The last shreds of my grandiose thinking—believing that I can heal this, set this right—are fraying now. Our history is too toxic for me—beyond my aid. Too freaking awful.

I walk to a display of the old train line near the battlefield. Two short-barreled cannons stand beside the railroad tracks. In my demented mind's eye, they are Lee and Grant, kneeling with bowed heads before me. I lay hands on their heads. I have no more absolution to give.

"You have got to stop this." I say it like a prayer, "Please. This has got to stop."

♦

The geese fly over, wild against the night. I hear them like blazing trumpets, calling to me, calling for the ocean, and I call back, crying, "Take me with you!" Let me go with you. Let me cross over the river with you, take our rest in the shade of the trees. I am ready, so ready. Please let me go!

Across the river, I see another world. A peaceful place that treasures turtles and health and love. I stand like a prophet, trying to speak the new world into existence, but no one can hear, no one understands, because my words have turned to gibberish, my voice shatters like gusts of wind.

The geese are gone, but now in the pitch-dark night, I hear the front door open, footsteps on the stairs. And suddenly my friend Darrin is kneeling next to me, taking my hand, trying to calm me. He is a good friend and co-worker. We share an office. I have known him for years.

"It's ok," he says. "You're ok." I don't understand, why is he here? Of course I'm ok.

"What are you doing here?"

"Your housemate called. She heard you screaming."

"Screaming?" I am confused, almost amused. "No, I wasn't screaming. It was the geese. Didn't you hear them? I was calling to the geese."

◆

I have more lobbying to do, this time in D.C. My mother goes with me, partly to keep an eye on me, partly to help out. She likes to support our work and makes a fantastic, powerful, citizen lobbyist. We finish on Capitol Hill in the afternoon and make a quick side trip. I tell her that I've done enough research into the Confederate side of history for a while. I need to spend time with the Union; I need to visit Abraham Lincoln. So we go to Ford's Theater. She explores the museum cases displaying Lincoln's blood-stained coat and John Wilkes Booth's derringer, and I slip into the theater.

The space is dusky and unlit, rows of empty seats curving up to the stage. Red, white, and blue bunting marks the Presidential Box where Booth shot Lincoln. I sit in the back row for a long time, considering the space and the tragedy and its implications. Before I leave, I stand and sing, pitching my voice toward the President's box, a line from *Spoon River*, the song Adam played for me at a fateful campfire two years ago: "The Union's preserved, if you listen, you'll hear all the bells!" I want to kneel and pray, but instead I start to cry and leave the theater, my head suddenly aching; the cracks in my heart are brutal and endless.

♦

Matthew is angry as an explosion—a sudden flash of light and sound. He is sick of my chaos and fever. I have been underfoot and bitchy with him all night. I started picking fights as soon as he arrived home from work. Now we are lying in bed, and I have just called him an asshole. He downshifts his fury into icy calm.

"That's it," he says and picks me up, carries me down stairs, grabs my stuff, and sets me down on the porch. I hear him close the door and lock it.

It is late. Very late. I don't try to get back in the house. Fuck him. Instead, I climb in my car, turn on the heat. Where to go? Returning to my place in Charlottesville doesn't cross my mind. The Blue Ridge Parkway might be nice. There's an out-of-town friend visiting my pal, Jon, in Amherst, Virginia—about an hour's drive. I'll be there in time for the sunrise. Maybe bring them doughnuts.

The Parkway is pitch black, no lights anywhere, and the moon has already set. I drive slowly, very slowly, watching for spooked deer or other critters scurrying across the road. My car feels like a boat, wallowing through waves of darkness. I listen to Dylan songs, feeling my life weave together again with the words. I remember my mania at Sean and Roxanne's on Clinch Mountain, staying up all night, running down the car battery, listening to Bob and feeling like I feel now, like I live inside the songs—their characters inhabit my world, the stories are my story.

I wind through the mountains; the road braids the forests like a serpent. Then from the corner of my eye, I see a flash of fur, tawny gold, a cat, with spots, I think, and with a tail, a long tail. It runs in front of the car, then darts away beyond the driver's side bumper. I follow it with my eye and there, in the dark by the roadside, I see a monkey, black with dark eyes and a white stripe of fur like a mohawk on its head. My gosh, a monkey in the Blue Ridge... my loopy brain giggles, thinks perhaps it's a Pawmunkey— the name of a Tidewater Indian tribe—and the cat with its long, flowing tail—a baby cougar! What a strange night, wild animals on the loose like hallucinations in the darkness.

Crawling down the Blue Ridge Parkway, it takes me hours to make the drive. The night rocks me in its arms but holds my eyelids open, keeps me awake. I don't run off the road; I don't hit a deer. Instead, I pull up at Jon's house just before dawn. I sit on a lawn chair in his yard, wrapped in my coat, watching the sun come up. Jon lives on the side of a mountain in a solar-powered house that gazes into the forested Blue Ridge. The sun rises from the heart of the valley. I am dazed and awed, watching the stars fade into lemon-sweet dawn.

A half-hour later, Jon sees me in his yard.

"Hey! What are you doing here?" He lets me in, clearly concerned, and gives me a hug. "How did you get out here?"

"I drove. Drove all night. Matt threw me out, so I came to see you guys!" I am suddenly giddy, giggly. I cuddle up next to our visiting friend on the couch and—so I am told—try to kiss him. I tell inappropriate jokes. Jon knows about my previous exploits with mania. They confer quietly and decide to take me back to Waynesboro. Jon drives my car while I sit in the back, chattering about Blue Ridge monkeys. They take me to James and Ruby's place. At some point, someone calls my parents, and a few hours later, they appear. I am startled to see them, but mostly pleased; it is nice to introduce my friends to my family. But I am not happy to have to go with my parents back to their place in northern Virginia. That was not in my plan.

◆

I sit with my parents on the couch in Dr. McLean's office. They are concerned that I am getting high again. I lie to their faces. The room seems intensely hot. I have burning sensations across my skin; sharp knives prod my hips and belly.

"I'm not smoking pot. I didn't get enough sleep for a few nights and things got strange. I'm fine."

McLean stares at me, frowning. The knives poke harder.

"I'm taking my lithium, I swear. Check my blood levels!"

"Yes. I will." He writes a prescription for the blood test. "Can you stay in town until we get the results back?" He looks at my parents, not at me. They nod.

♦

Back at my parents' house, I take a walk. The evening is chilly, and my body slowly cools. The knives recede. Above me, a mass of crows flies across the sky. A black river. Sunset has turned the dusk to gold and pink—soft inner petals of roses tossed across the sky. The crows flow through them like a tide of ink. I stand in the middle of the road, head tilted back to watch the glorious sight, arms outstretched like the statue of Pocahantas at Jamestown. My breath steams in the January air. The blood of the crows is in my blood. Their voices call to me.

♦

I play *Music for The Native Americans* for my parents—Robbie Robertson again—"Isn't it beautiful?" I ask. And I write out the lyrics to "Ghost Dance," all of them, all the names, the tribes, calling them. I type them into an email and send it to everyone I know, every address in my email account.

In my bedroom late that evening, I write to Adam and Loki again, as always, telling them where I am and that I cannot leave. *I feel like an animal caught in a leg hold trap*, I write. *I'm going a little crazy here. Please, if you can, please send help before I chew off my paw.*

♦

The effort of holding myself together is growing. I watch myself very carefully—making sure that I don't say anything too weird, that I forestall my increasing tendency to get very angry very quickly. One evening with my parents, I hear my father snap at my mother. I am sitting on their family room floor, and turn on him suddenly, my voice cold and hard and almost threatening. I snarl at him: "Take the knife out of your words!"

♦

After a few more days, my family lets me go back home to Charlottesville. My lithium levels are good, normal, in the therapeutic range. And I am calm again, briefly, but I cannot stay away from the pipe and the bag of cannabis—why would I want to?—and I fly off again, into the clouds, the mountains, the underworld. I sit out back behind James and Ruby's place and explain my plan to use cannabis as my sole anti-depressant.

"I don't think that's such a good idea, Christina." Ruby knows a lot about these things. She has good friends in the world of counseling and psychiatry who she has consulted about me. "Pot can really mess with your other medications. Make them ineffective. Even if your lithium levels are ok, pot can displace lithium in your bloodstream."

"Huh," I say. "That's interesting. That's good to know."

She looks at me with concern. Ruby can read me like a book; she knows I am brushing her off.

I sleep on their couch frequently. James plays guitar in the other room. One night, he goes downstairs to his regular practice space in the basement and plays "The Weight," another song by The Band, plays it loud so it seems to echo through the house. I curl up and stare at the pulsing orange flames in their woodstove. It pumps out huge heat into the house, hot enough that I don't need a blanket when the nights turn cold.

One gray morning, James and I ride up to the Blue Ridge Parkway. He brings a guitar, and we sit at a scenic overlook, wrapped in mist. As he starts to sing, the fog lifts. We are suddenly bathed in sunlight, gazing down into the Rockfish Valley. I laugh out loud. Then he finishes the song, and the fog swirls back down around us. Now I am giddy:

"Look, James! My God—the fog! You have a magic voice!"

♦

Late one night, in Charlottesville, I arrive home to an empty house. I feel like a stranger, a soldier come home from war. My key fits the lock, so I enter. With cold fingers, I feel my way blindly down the dark hallway. The fire in the woodstove has burned low, a faint glow in the grate. My old coat is a soldier's jacket, but I am not just any soldier. I am a stooped and aged Robert E. Lee. Wife and children lost and gone, only Traveler, the old war horse, tethered outside, and this small island of warmth beside the stove.

I build up the fire, spread my coat out on the floor, and fall asleep there, whispering the names of my soldiers, discarded, dead, like dry leaves gone to flame; their ghosts haunt me, unforgotten, and their widows, their children. I cry myself to sleep. Hours later, in the greenish pre-dawn light, I wake, and now I am Lee's daughter, but somehow I have become blind and deaf and cannot speak, cannot reach out to comfort him. Then with the dawn, I wake again, and I have lost them. Lost them all.

In a gray early haze, I wander into empty streets, shell of a city, the buildings lean over me, curved in, all hollow. People pass and speak to me, but I cannot hear. I try to speak with my hands, but they looked sidelong at me, half-curious, half-disturbed.

That night, I am Lee again, or maybe some other soldier, and all there is for the agony is morphine. All I can do is lace cannabis with myrrh again and breathe the cool narcotic smoke into my wounds. The only release, the only end to the pain. The only drug that can touch the crazy psychic pain. Seeking, seeking, is it death or rebirth, release, *moksha*? Is it father or daughter? Am I even alive?

◆

The trees and sidewalk are black and white, pale and shadow. Here on the streets, among people, surely I am only a wisp of smoke on the edge of their vision, an agonized ghost. But alone again in the quiet of my room, my hands can open and close, they can move the bud into the pipe, the flame onto the dry flower.

◆

February comes, and the pain begins to crush me. I am beyond hope or despair. Overwhelming sensations fill my chest until I cannot breathe. Something massive, nameless, pushes against my throat, expands. What happens if my heart explodes? Please God, let the pressure release. Please. This god-awful pressure that is yet somehow divine. I am possessed by God and destroyed by God. A flame of joy within the agony. I cannot hold it, cannot take it, cannot bear it much longer.

♦

February 2nd: St. Brighid's Day, my favorite saint, my favorite goddess. Brigid, Brighid, Brigantia, Bride. She safeguards the poets, blacksmiths, healers, and prophets. Springs are holy to her, so I take a pilgrimage, seeking relief. I drive south to Lexington, then west through Goshen Pass. As I approach Warm Springs, Virginia, the creeks send up whorls of steam into the winter morning. Two round houses cover the springs of the Jefferson Pools—one for men, the other for women. I ease myself, groaning, into the warm waters, rest my feet against the rocky stream bottom and float, feeling my exhaustion ease.

But even in the buoyant warmth, frantic despair still pounds against my skin. The bath house is empty early on a Saturday morning, so I can moan and shake without receiving strange glances. I climb out as other women arrive. On the far side of the building, an outflow pipe dumps water back into the stream. I crawl under the falling water and let it hammer my body, my skull. I ask God or Goddess for cleansing and deliverance. Another baptism, a brief respite, a moment of relief.

♦

Ghosts darken my windows. I see them waking and sleeping. In the trees one morning, crows fill every branch in the yard; they shift and rustle their wings but keep silent. When the birds take to their wings, I try to follow, but the car will not start. Darrin tells me later, "The battery's dead. You left the overhead light on." He drives me to a potluck across town, but I can hardly function. I almost start yelling at the host. The house feels unbearably warm; my armpits sweat and my hands itch and I want to scream. Every fucking inch of me wants to scream and kick and maybe punch these asshole idiots smiling politely at me as I sit here chewing off my paw.

"Darrin, I need to leave."

He tries to look after me, but he has no idea what he's up against. After the last mass email that I sent, Darrin unplugged my computer and hid the power cord. Now I am starting to yell when I get around people. It's not what I want, but I can't seem to help it. Anger wells up unexpectedly; it's red and bitter hot, boiling in my belly. I can-not hold myself back. I don't know what words erupt from me, just that they hurt like coughing up vomit. Eventually, I stop going to work, stop going out.

♦

At home, I can be quiet. At home, I can get high. I can entertain myself. I can play god. I build Brighid beds in honor of the goddess. On her feast day, devotees craft Brighid beds to welcome the goddess into a home and give her a place to rest. I build mine like an act of ritual. I take two cots and pile them with strange belongings. Each item has precise meaning, placed in exactly the right spot, next to the exact right item. The objects will interact and fuse into radiant power, just as a uranium pile with the right combination of materials will result in nuclear fis-sion. And so there are pictures and clothing, bits of wood and stone, tissues stained with menstrual blood, a shoe, a pillow. I light candles around the cots, burn incense.

The heaps on the beds begin to represent me. After a while, I forget that they were built for the goddess. Over time, they start to frighten me. Am I there inside those heaps, suffocating? The beds are a chrysalis dissolving my skin. What alien being will I become?

♦

I feel dread in unexpected places. Sometimes it seems a certainty that I am dying, and I stare into my eyes in the mirror, terrified of the cancers eating through my organs. Other times, I wish for death. When the yearnings of the heart-sick soldier ghosts grow too much, I wish I could die with them, die *for* them. I wish, oh God, I wish I could be morphine for their wounds, curl cooling fingers around the hot, fierce pain inside their souls.

♦

Music helps. I listen to The Band obsessively until I accidentally destroy the CD when a burning hot cannabis seed leaps from my pipe onto the plastic. I find an aged videotape of *The Last Waltz*—a movie of The Band's last concert—and watch it over and over. Every morning, I wait until my housemate goes to work, pop the tape in her VCR, and watch it on the big screen. The tape quality is terrible; the musicians' faces stretch and contort, but their songs come through clearly. I am fascinated and jubilant, laughing, singing along, sometimes moved to tears.

I hear codes in the words and music. They sometimes make perfect sense, and I know, I am certain, that they connect to me, they are about me. My story is their story. My story is everyone's story. My friend Meghan looks remarkably like Joni Mitchell. Rick Danko and Robbie

Robertson play "Old Time Religion," and it links with something Loki wrote, using that phrase to describe tree-huggers dancing around campfires. And all those hand gestures, odd lighting, and camera angles seem to be telling me something, something I can't quite figure out. So tiring, so exhausting, to be entrusted with such a need to understand.

◆

I make one pot of miso soup and another of oatmeal and live off of that for days. "Miso soup for breakfast? Again?" I giggle at this joke, daily. Somehow it reminds me of Gabe and Erin's girls, or maybe some Bloodroot event, or maybe breakfast with the Zappa family. Didn't I used to know them?

◆

EQ and Meghan invite me over for dinner. They are both dear friends of mine, but tonight I am on fire. The room is scalding hot. The pressure of human contact is crushing. I feel feral, bar my teeth, leave early. Meghan calls my parents.

"Something's really wrong with Christina."

They are not surprised to hear it; word has come back to them from Darrin that I am weaving off the level, but they have their own trials. My father's heart problems are worsening. He has to go into the hospital to try another procedure to get his heart back in rhythm. They check him in, then my mom drives south to Charlottesville to find me.

♦

I have started sleeping in my living room. The Brighid beds in the bedroom now feel dark and dangerous. I do not like to wake up and look at them. Instead, I roll out Robert E. Lee's coat on top of my camping bedroll and try to sleep on the floor. Spread out beside my pillow, I have my smoking supplies, a box of incense, matches. The wood floor is sticky where I have spilled myrrh, and the room smells like a garish mixture of scented resins and smoke. My brain feels seasick again. My stomach surges with anxiety, so I do not eat. I live in a hot fever dream, holes punching again through the soft matter of my mind.

♦

When my mother arrives, I am not surprised to see her. I get in the car without question and curl up in the sleeping bag that she grabs from the house. There is a pillow and room on the back seat to stretch out. I am asleep before my mother finishes sweeping my room for drugs.

♦

The hospital is hazy, familiar, an orange hallway and intake office. The walls shimmer like waves of heat above summer asphalt. They sign me in and send me up the same elevator that I took the year before, assign me to the same room in the same psych ward. I fall asleep quickly. Late, late, late in the night, I wake wide-eyed into sheer pitch darkness. Having my eyes open or closed makes no difference.

A lucid dream. In the dark, a bat hangs upside down. A huge bat, the kind they call flying foxes, a fruit bat. Its eyes radiate a kaleidoscope of light and color, and I realize that it is me. I am the bat. All my memories and secrets, all the beauty and wisdom of these wild, tragic, manic years are here, held in my throat, precious jewels. They are safe with me, unforgotten. I can relax. Finally. Let go, sleep. I will not forget.

Inside the dream, an old teacher appears. He taught theater at a summer arts institute when I was in high school, using shamanic journeys and drums to lure us deeper into our characters and ourselves. He smiles at me, says, "You'll be ok. You're doing great. We've got to get you off of your father's heartline. It will give you both more room." In the dream, I understand what he means, and it gives me comfort. I have no idea that my dad is in the same hospital, hoping to settle his heartbeat into regular time, just a few floors away. I fall further into sleep thinking of Gabriel and Erin, Laurel and Alarka, remembering the farm in May 2000, the hot spring sunlight, those brief days of radiant joy.

♦

If it is possible to overdose on cannabis and myrrh tincture, I have done it. My heartbeat and blood pressure are erratic. Daybreak pitches me into chaos. The toxicology report shows "THC - POSITIVE" in bright red, flashing letters. The room dips and swerves around me like nausea, like fever, and Dr. McLean shakes his clipboard in front of my face so that I cannot look away.

"Drug induced psychosis, Christina. That's your diagnosis. I'm not putting down mania this time."

He speaks each word slowly, exaggerating his enunciation: "Drug. Induced. Psychosis." I try to focus my eyes: Psychosis? Oh shit.

♦

The anti-psychotic drug is called Risperdol but to me it sounds like "whisper dolls." I have a frightening image in my mind of blank-eyed china dolls. I do not want to turn into one of those. Do not want to be vacuous, stuffed into a closet or mute on display on some parlor shelf. I refuse. No, I won't take it. The nurse holding out the pills is Nurse Ratched from *One Flew Over the Cukoos Nest* come to life. All the other nurses I've encountered have been kind. Nurse Ratched is mean. She has puffy blond hair and wears too much perfume. I refuse the drugs again. She becomes angry at me. Visibly. Her voice threatens violence. She yells. I am amazed. She is like a caricature. Is this some kind of psych ward joke? Is she acting out a part?

The room gets hot. I don't tell her that the shadows move in the corner, and voices echo that she can't hear. I put the pill in my mouth and don't swallow. She calls a helper, and they force it down. I think of Matthew and watching Jack Nicholson on New Year's Eve and almost smile—Matthew will understand; he would've punched the bitch in the face.

◆

I call the boy Crazy Horse and myself Sitting Bull. We sit in front of the nurse's station cross-legged on the floor. We talk quietly, sometimes in code, and make plans to meet up at a hotel nearby when I am released and then take off for the coast. He talks about stealing a car. I say, "No, no, we can take mine. We just have to go to Charlottesville and get it to start." He is younger than me, brought here from a nearby homeless shelter. He has been on and off of heroin several times. "I can relate," I say. "Morphine kept me alive during the war."

Later that day, he is discharged, but I am not released. I desperately want to go, to get away from this place. I open the emergency exit door and look longingly at the stairs, but an alarm has started to blare. I remember the blue restraints strapped across my chest and arms and ankles, a needle coming to steal my soul. I hurry back to my room and huddle on the bed. Days go by.

♦

On Valentine's Day, I realize that I forgot my mother's birthday. She was born on the 13th. That means I was in the psych ward and my father in the cardiac unit on her birthday. Guilt leaps like a vivid bruise onto my breast bone. The nursing staff hand us white carnations to celebrate the holiday. My parents bring me a card from EQ, and I feel a touch of loving friendship—a brief warm flash in the cold hospital, a tiny light in the fast-falling darkness. I smile, but my heart has turned sad and bleak. I have been in the hospital for five days.

♦

There is nothing here for me. No phone calls out to friends this time. No books to escape into. The usual psych ward nonsense is a blank amble. I am numb, bored, sick. I walk incessantly through the halls trying to get something akin to exercise. I read and quietly discard newspaper articles in the quiet room. I dully play kickball and make the same stupid drawings in art therapy.

My brain aches. There are sobs stuffed deep in my lungs. Anti-psychotic drugs are violent. I would rather have a padded room, I think. And a drum kit. I could pound it out, scream, throw myself against the walls, and then they could dose me with Ativan and let me sleep for days. Sleep until the THC levels drop in my bloodstream. Sleep until lithium regains its thoughtful, measured presence in my neural pathways. That would be so much better than these anti-psychotic chemicals that slam shut all pleasure centers and pummel the vivid wildness of a manic brain into dull, cold gray in the space of a few days. I am clumsy, thick as oatmeal.

♦

My brother arrives early for visiting hours. We sit in the cafeteria of the psychiatric ward. The table is made of blue-gray plastic. He has written me a letter and brought me a print-out of a scientific study from Australia. The study is specific to my case; it describes how marijuana use can interfere with lithium.

"You can read the letter later," he tells me. "For now, let me just describe what it says." He draws a deep breath and looks at me, hard and sad.

"You have to stop using drugs. You have to stop getting high." I expected this, but the next line takes my breath away: "If you can't stop for yourself, stop for Mom and Dad. You are killing them."

His choice of words stuns me: *You are killing them.* My brother does not talk this way. I feel as though he's reached across the table and shaken me, hard. *Wake up, stop being selfish, stop being an asshole.* Except in kind words, because he is kind, which is why I cannot turn away from this. I cannot ignore or deny it. Because he is my brother, and he is kind, and I am killing my family.

TEN

McLean gives me two choices. He will either transfer me from the psychiatric ward to the in-patient drug rehab unit—he emphasizes the words "in-patient"— or I can leave the hospital and go immediately into an out-patient program in Charlottesville. I am relieved. I sign the discharge papers like articles of surrender. I am blank and very tired and have to stop using drugs and have to stop going crazy and have to learn to take care of myself in this hard human world. The February sun hurts my eyes as I walk away from the hospital. My stomach cringes with anxiety; my heart stays numb.

A few days later, I returned to Charlottesville and went straight into the month-long rehab program. I felt exhausted and heartsick—another rapid descent into depression had begun—and the rehab program itself was unpleasant. Compassion did not seem to be on the agenda, and the counselors came across as rude and hostile. Their main goal was to make sure we understood that we had a problem with drugs and/or alcohol. Their primary tool seemed to be encouraging us to feel bad about ourselves.

By this point, I had pretty much accepted that I had a problem, so I didn't resist. I was scared of myself and scared of what I'd done to my family. Part of what frightened me was the way I kept going back to using cannabis. I would start smoking again spontaneously, without giving a thought to consequences. And then I'd keep getting high, and keep getting high, and keep getting high—obsessively, not really noticing what I was doing—until the chemicals overloaded my system, and my mind went up in flames.

The rehab program did give me one great and life-saving gift; it mandated that we go to multiple 12 Step meetings each week. And so, one late-February afternoon, I stood at the door of a classroom in a church basement, my hands shaking on the doorknob. I was late. The large building stood empty at noon on a weekday, and I had stumbled around lost looking for the meeting. I finally found the room and creaked open the door. Heads turned to watch me walk in. The room was poorly-heated; folks sat in their jackets, rubbing their hands together to stay warm.

I cried at that first meeting. The rehab center had told us to speak up in meetings, so I introduced myself. When I said the words "manic depression," my throat kinked and tears rose fast; my voice sputtered and choked and I had to stop. After the meeting a kind man, silver-haired and clean for decades, smiled at me gently and said, "I think it's harder for people with a dual-diagnosis."

I had no idea what he meant at the time, but the term quickly became familiar. A "dual-diagnosis" referred to a diagnosis of both mental illness and drug addiction. Throughout the 12 Step rooms, many people had used drugs to try and handle mental conditions, to cope with depression or calm anxiety or accelerate the dangerous glory of mania.

Despite my dual-diagnosis, I remained frightened during the first several weeks that people in meetings would laugh at me and throw me out. I was a wan and sad-eyed pothead. In years past, I had heard the mantra, *"Pot's not addictive!"* so many times that I thought of it as commonly-accepted fact. The idea of being a marijuana addict seemed absurd. I had not ventured into harder drugs—only cannabis and occasional hallucinogens—nor did I particularly like to drink. But the 12 Step program worked on the concept that it's not what you use, it's how you use it, and I had used pot like an addict: obsessively, compulsively, ignoring the needs of others, harming myself.

For weeks, I remained irrationally frightened of being rejected by people in meetings. But it never came up. No one ever asked me what I had used, nor did they name the drugs they had used. People told their stories, described the harrowing places that drugs had taken them, and shared the challenges of staying clean. They spoke non-specifically of "my drug(s) of choice" and that was all. I felt hugely grateful. In meetings, no one ever asked for proof that I belonged.

Only my sponsor pushed me on that question. I met Sarah at my first meeting. The rehab program encouraged us to get a sponsor as soon as possible, so I asked her timidly soon after. I liked her. She had her act together and showed genuine kindness and concern for others. We set a time to talk outside the meetings.

Her first question was, "What makes you think you're an addict?" And I panicked. Would she tell me that I didn't qualify? I desperately wanted in with this group of people. I didn't see any other options. After the events of the last few months, I was scared of myself, my brain, my drug use. Nightmarish scenes from the recent hospitalization remained luridly spattered across my memory. I had gone from an occasional toke back in October to smoking daily, hourly, sometimes around the clock—while never noticing that I had become psychotic.

The rain fell thick on the windshield of my sponsor's car as I told her my story, trying to answer her question, to explain why I thought I was an addict. I stumbled over the words, remembering the winter of 2001 when I got high to survive—sitting in my car at lunch, smoking while I cried and hit my forehead against the steering wheel. I started to describe other examples, but Sarah stopped me.

She wasn't testing me. She just wanted to know my attitude toward the first of the Twelve Steps: *We admitted that we were powerless over our addiction, that our lives had become unmanageable.*

Sarah smiled, "I'm not going to kick you out. I can't kick you out! I just want to see where you're at."

"I couldn't stop," I told her. "I didn't even realize what I was doing."

My days took on a rhythm based around the 12 Step fellowship. I still saw my old friends and Matthew, but meetings became the center of my life. They gave me something to hold on to, some hope for a path that would lead me out of this unbearable way of being in the world. I went to a meeting, often two, on most days. My home group met five days a week at noon in the church across town. So, except for days when work interfered, I drove through midday traffic to the meeting. I had taken up smoking cigarettes—American Spirits, organic, in the maroon pack. Without additives, they burned slowly; half-a-cigarette lasted me through the drive to the meeting; the other half got me back to work and calmed a tiny edge of my endless anxiety.

Even with meetings to go to, my days ground on me. Another physically-debilitating depression had settled in. The warming spring air sandpapered my skin. The bright spring sun glared against my eyes. I remember my housemate placing a branch from a flowering magnolia tree in a vase on the kitchen table. I saw its elegant grace and burst into tears.

Spring had been a difficult season for me for most of my life. In late April 1983, a few weeks shy of my ninth birthday, my appendix had ruptured and nearly killed me. That traumatic encounter with my mortality had haunted me ever since, particularly in the springtime, as April warmed into May. I often became sick during that season; even before my diagnosis with manic depression, I frequently sank into a springtime sorrow.

The depression in April 2002 was exhausting. When I wasn't at meetings or at work, I usually hid at home, curled up in bed. After the last hospitalization, my Dad had given me a television set—the first one I'd had in years. At first, I hadn't wanted it, but it was proving to be a huge blessing. The reception was terrible; it got only PBS, so I watched news shows and documentaries, anything to help distract me. TV brought a blessed relief from having to spend time with my own thoughts. I could relax and forget myself.

I watched every minute of Ken Burns' documentary on the Civil War and tried not to think about the soldier ghosts who had shared my home a few short weeks ago, whose wounds I tried to ease with homemade morphine. Memories like that were dangerous, humiliating, terrifying. And they touched off a deep and painful longing. I did not know what to do with that yearning. I wanted to be stable and well, yet still I craved those strange places between life and death, sanity and insanity. I had to shove those feelings out of my mind and just keep putting one foot in front of the other.

For the first several months clean, I simply dragged myself through the motions of living. In the midst of wild unhappiness, I had three basic truths around which I structured my life:

1) Killing myself was not the right thing to do.

2) No matter how much I wanted to escape, using drugs would screw up my life worse than it already was.

3) My brain was inescapable, uncontrollable, and fucked up.

The third fact frightened me most. Once again, I found myself staring into a completely alien future. Was it possible to live happy and healthy and free with a manic-depressive mind? I had no idea. Since my diagnosis in 2000, I'd existed at the extremes: the wild rapids of mania and hypomania or the chronic gray suffocation of depression. The anti-depressants prescribed to me never touched the despair; only cannabis had helped to lift that clinging sadness. Now, without pot, would I simply have to learn to live within a constant depression?

I went to ninety 12 Step meetings in ninety days, stringing the key tags on my key chain to mark weeks and months of clean time—white, orange, green, red. Before long, I was taking on helping roles in my home group meeting: setting out and cleaning up materials, handing out key tags, and eventually leading meetings. With my sponsor's guidance, I began to write my way through the Steps—sometimes on my own, sometimes with a group of women who gathered on weekends. Sarah gave me assignments. She pushed me to peel away the layers of meaning in the Steps, to explore how they related to my experiences.

Step one was pretty easy for me. I knew my powerlessness over drugs and had vivid recent proof that my drug use made my life unmanageable. I did not particularly like calling myself an addict, but I fit the 12 Step definition. I had used compulsively, unable to stop once I got started. I kept returning to my drug of choice, getting high obsessively, despite the destruction, despair, and degradation it facilitated in my life. Self-centered fear motivated all of my actions. I didn't have to read far into the 12 Step literature before concluding, "Ok, yeah, fuck, I'm an addict."

The second step was harder. Much harder: *We came to believe that a Power greater than ourselves could restore us to sanity.* What the hell did that mean? Sarah had me write about each key term in the step—Power, restore, sanity— and each one of them stumped me. A Power greater than myself: I'd been a believer most of my life, though I had stepped away from organized religion years ago. On Pine Mountain, in 2000, I had come face-to-face with a gigantic Power, felt myself lifted up to some great Spirit's reckless, astonishing beauty. An extraordinary, vast, ecstatic experience.

The years since had brought exile. A huge gulf separated me from any divine higher power. Indeed, I could not touch my connection to anything Sacred without listing into terror, like a ship lost on a deadly ocean, floundering in high seas. I could not meditate—the experience of relaxing my mind and communing with quiet felt too much like sliding back into mania. I did not believe that a godly power could restore me to sanity; my experience suggested instead that my higher power had picked me up on Pine Mountain and cast me down into madness below.

As for "restoring" me to "sanity," I had no idea what that meant. What did sanity look like? I was manic depressive—had I ever been "sane?" I could look back over my life now and see oscillations of intense moods and strange thinking going back into childhood and intensifying in college as I experimented more liberally with drugs and irregular sleep. What would it mean to be *restored* if I didn't know what *sanity* meant?

"Go back to the words of the step," Sarah told me. "It doesn't say God. It says 'Power greater than ourselves.'"

"Yeah, but power has a capital 'P'," I said. "That means God."

Sarah laughed. "Look, this program has worked for *lots* of non-believers and confused believers over the years.

Try this. Does coming to meetings help you to not get high?"

"Yes."

"And does that help you stay stable?"

"Yes."

"Were you able to do those things on your own?"

"No."

"So meetings and the Fellowship itself are literally a power greater than yourself, don't you think? And for now, try substituting the word 'stability' for 'sanity.' If you stay stable, maybe you'll come to understand sanity."

Sarah was an amazing sponsor. Amazing. Her sense of humor was unshakeable. She did not lecture; instead, she asked questions, sometimes leaning on me to shift my perspective but never bullying. One of her most consistent pieces of advice when I got muddled and frustrated and caught up in my own sorrow or anger or self-pity was, "You're ok. You're right where you need to be." Sarah instilled confidence somehow, and those words calmed me down: *You're right where you need to be.* Even when it seemed patently absurd that I "needed" to feel the way I felt, I let myself at least consider the possibility. It helped.

Meetings forced me out of my den of self-pity. It was effortlessly easy to get lost in the gloom of my depression; I felt so heavy in heart and spirit. And yet, every time I went to a meeting and listened to other peoples' stories of addiction and loss, I was reminded of my incredible good fortune and privilege. I still had strong relationships with friends and family. I still had a job. I had miraculously dodged arrest. I had access to health care and treatment. Like any good treehugger activist, I was broke, and yet I had avoided incurring debt.

Going to 12 Step meetings kept me from giving in completely to depression and self-pity. Working the Steps started a process that continues today—the on-going work of taking responsibility for my actions while also forgiving myself for my brain chemistry and my mistakes.

The Third Step remains my favorite: *We made a decision to turn our will and our lives over to the care of God as we understood Him.* I don't remember exactly when or why this step started to make sense to me. I do remember experiencing brief glints of relief from pain when I tried to put this step into action. When I first read Step Three, it seemed breathtakingly pretentious—turning over my will and my life. Seriously? And yet the 12 Step program emphasized ideas like this: Surrender to win; Let go and let God.

In 2002, I was barely holding myself together. The idea of giving up my will seemed both dangerous and inviting. On the one hand, I could scarcely handle my life. Depression and the traumatic repercussions of my recent manic/psychotic episodes hounded me. Going to work and to 12 Step meetings took huge amounts of effort and self-control. Truly giving up my will might render me unable to function.

On the other hand, my decision-making had not proven to be worth a shit over the last few years. Although blessed by great good fortune in many important ways, my interior life was a shambles. I was bereft, heartbroken, confused, empty. Self-loathing shadowed all of my thoughts. I had no idea who I was.

So, although I still couldn't get my head around the "God" in the step—Sarah and I agreed that I should ignore the "Him" part altogether—I could still pray. I could still run the words through my head and mean them even if I didn't have a destination in mind for the prayer: "Please take my will and my life. Please guide me, help me do the next right thing, because right now I don't know what the fuck I'm doing." It helped.

I took my medications—lithium and Effexor—every day. I told Sarah that I felt like a hypocrite in meetings, saying that I was clean while popping pills.

"I mean really, what's the difference? I'm messing with my head either way."

Sarah said, "Come on, Christina, you don't believe that. If you quit taking medication, what happens? Would you stay clean?"

"No. I know, I know."

"Then what's the problem? Do your bipolar meds get you high? Do you want to take more of them than you need?"

"Lord, no."

"Then you're not abusing them. You're taking them because you need them to stay healthy, and if you don't stay healthy, you won't stay clean."

Sometime in late 2002, a few months out from my one-year clean anniversary, Sarah invited me to come to the meetings that she and others in the fellowship organized at the regional jail. We checked in at the front desk, leaving our coats and purses, then passed through a metal detector and a series of locked doors. The meetings occurred in a narrow hallway that ran alongside the cells for the non-violent female drug offenders. We sat on the other side of the bars from the women who sat in a tiny common area facing us. Most of the women were so young—younger than me. Most had had hard lives.

I remember one woman saying, "Everyone in my family smokes crack. Every one of them. And all my friends. When I get out of here, where am I supposed to go? I want to stay clean, but where do I go?" They spoke of their terrors and regrets. Many of them awaited trial or sentencing, and some faced decades of prison time for prescription fraud or drug distribution. While I had met many people in the 12 Step rooms who had done time, it was much different to actually be inside the jail with people experiencing direct and dire consequences of drugs and the nation's messed up drug laws.

During these meetings, I often felt that I had little to offer; my life had been so comparatively sheltered. And yet, the stories of addicts seeking recovery share some common themes. My addiction had taken me to psychiatric wards instead of jails, but the doors in both places were locked tight.

At the end of the meeting, we'd join hands through the bars and say the Serenity Prayer. Our group walked out, picked up our coats, and hugged each other goodbye in the parking lot. I would often sit in my car for a few minutes before driving home, feeling a quiet awareness of gratitude. Before the heavy cloak of depression closed back in around me, I pushed myself to breathe deeply and say Thank You to whatever higher power may or may not be listening. I was moving slowly, but I was starting to get better.

ELEVEN

In early February of 2003, something very unexpected happened. At work one afternoon, the phone rang, and it was Adam. I had seen him occasionally at forest-activist gatherings in the years since Pine Mountain and sent poems and notes to him and Loki regularly, but our contact was always tentative. Each time I saw him in person, I felt embarrassed and confused. Although he treated me with kind friendship, a great distance separated me from him. I was in so much pain in those days and so exhausted from trying to understand what had happened to me—why my mind had gone so terribly wrong—that I simply withdrew. Keeping my defenses up and strong, with Adam and with everyone, seemed the wisest course of action.

But Adam called in 2003 with an invitation. The annual Bloodroot Gathering would be at Blanton Forest again over Memorial Day weekend. Would I help him plan it? The event always had a team of organizers. Adam

was no longer the director of the organization, but he acted as lead coordinator of this event. "Help me bring this to
birth," he said. "Let's do this together."

I hung up, startled and rattled. My life had become
very quiet, focused on stability and recovery; the unexpected invitation brought memories of manic mountaintop glory and tragedy rearing up in my mind. But perhaps
I could go back, without getting high, and understand a
fraction more of what had happened on Pine Mountain in
the year 2000. And to have the chance to work with Adam—perhaps there too I could come to peace with that
strangely dear and painful friendship.

So, I said yes. Of course I said yes. And we set to
work. Adam and I made a good team. We had a similar
sense of poetry and symbolism to shape a theme for the
event and a similarly obsessive work ethic. He was a wiz-
ard with logistics and pacing for the program. But it was
more than that. Working with Adam gave me renewed
strength. I felt a confidence and competence that had been
absent from my activism since my diagnosis. He was endlessly encouraging, asking my thoughts and advice, com-
plimenting and reinforcing my efforts and ideas. Blanton
Forest had meant so much to both of us. In the work of
organizing the Bloodroot Gathering, the connection between us found an easy, constructive outlet.

A subset of the planning team met up at Camp Blanton in March; we needed to scope out the facilities, gain

inspiration, and spend some time together. On my first venture back into Blanton Forest, a small group hiked up to the Sand Cave to spend the night. Gabe was there— Activists in Aprons would be coordinating food for the event—along with three other friends who worked with environmental groups in Kentucky and North Carolina. Despite the camaraderie, the mood of the group was heavy. It was March 19th. We had chosen the spring equinox to visit the site. President George W. Bush had chosen the 19th as a deadline for Saddam Hussein to leave Iraq. The U.S. teetered on the brink of a war based on trumped up charges that Iraq had weapons of mass destruction.

To my relief, I felt surprisingly relaxed being back in Blanton Forest. I had feared becoming overwhelmed by grief or mental chaos. But Gabe and Adam were kind, almost solicitous, aware of my troubled relationship with this place. And the forest itself seemed peaceful and familiar in its early spring starkness. I had only seen Blanton Forest drenched in May sun, full of flowers and leafy-green. With winter barely past, only the deep breathing hemlock, pine, and spruce trees shadowed the mountain; the gray branches of deciduous trees spiraled empty arms into the sky.

We built a campfire and ate together in the Sand Cave, just below where "Jonetta" still glowed crimson on the cave wall. After dinner, Adam and I sat a little apart from the others. He had carried his guitar up the mountain and asked if he could play me some songs.

"I wrote a bunch of songs when I came back to Blanton in 2000," he said. "I'm not quite ready to play for a larger audience." He looked momentarily shy, which surprised me; I thought of him as unshakably confident.

The temperature was falling quickly, so I pulled my sleeping bag up around my shoulders and sat propped against a tree, listening to Adam's voice wind through the dusky forest. I remember one song in particular, a haunting piece about the sudden death of his dear friend years ago. He sang with his heart on his face, his voice raw as bone. Again, the vulnerability surprised me; he was trusting me with these songs.

Later, we talked about the summer of 2000 when Adam had returned to Blanton. It was thick in the heat of July, around the time that I had emerged from my second hospitalization and started the plummet into depression. He had camped for several weeks here in the Sand Cave and nearby, moving around the mountain and occasionally meeting local people—one of whom, Bill, now worked as the caretaker at Camp Blanton. I felt again a stab of deep envy that Adam had been able to spend so much time in this beautiful, sacred place without losing his mind.

Adam played the guitar softly as he told me these stories and then paused.

"This place feels like home," he said quietly, turning to look at me. "Like you and I have been here hundreds of times before."

I sat very still, like an animal that tries to hide in plain sight. Hundreds of times before... Was that innocent hyperbole or something else? Something related to the strange connection I felt with him? Or to my bizarre visions of a yogic fertility ritual, the strange delusions from 2000 that caused me to cringe with shame and embarrassment whenever they came to mind? Hundreds of times before... What did that mean? Did it mean anything?

I had always felt overwhelmed by Adam—this very public figure, so well-loved by so many people—and his unexpected comment hit a nerve that made me intensely aware of my brokenness. With two years of dire manic depression and one year of timid stability under my belt, I did not trust my brain or my body, my instincts or intuitions. I did not trust my place in the universe or my ability to have friendships and be loved. I was quite convinced that everyone, save perhaps my immediate family, only loved who I had been in the past—the quicksilver being hopping nimbly up this mountain at the turn of the millennium. Surely, no one, particularly not someone like Adam, could care deeply about the *me* of today, with my self-hate, my heavy body, my knotted, sorrowful mind.

And so Adam's words confused me. Why would he say that? Or maybe I was going crazy and hearing voices—his voice had sounded strange. Did this mountaintop have the power to turn my mind inside out again? I sat silent, feeling embarrassed and lonely, wanting to cry, to put my head on his shoulder and hold onto his hand, to ask what he'd meant and what the heck was going on, but I couldn't. I couldn't do it.

Adam had looked away, quietly playing the blue guitar. Owls called from the far side of the ridge, and stars appeared above Sand Cave. As the night settled in, Adam rolled out his sleeping bag nearby. In my mind's eye, I see us on that mountaintop: two seekers camped out in Nature's great temple, miniscule in the face of the mountain, befuddled by the beauty and star shine and each other, trying to do something of worth to help the Earth, while the world whirls around us, and war comes with the dawn.

In the very early morning, before a friend climbed the mountain with news of the U.S. military's overnight invasion of Iraq, I walked barefoot with Adam to Watt's Creek where it rumbled beneath the boulders of the Maze and down the mountain. We slipped into a cave below the stones. Cold water slid over slick, black rock into a small pool, and our skin steamed as we took turns dunking underwater. I felt surprisingly calm; my heartsick confusion of last night washed away in the stillness. I don't think that we spoke at all—although I seem to remember laughter—as we enacted a silent ritual of cleansing and clearing away, an unspoken baptism. Equinox: a turning point, a new beginning. I wondered briefly if this was the same pool where I'd dropped the broken millipede and turtle shells years before—rebirthing Turtle Island.

This time on Pine Mountain, though, was wholly different than in 2000. I occupied a humble, heartsick, and self-conscious place rather than that reckless, golden chaos in my mind, the cresting manic sense of grandiose power. I still carried a combination of vivid shame and longing that coupled together whenever I thought of that mountaintop experience, but the hunger spoke more softly now, a muted call instead of a scream. One year, one month, and ten days had passed since I'd last gotten high. I had a black key tag strung on my key chain now, marking one year of clean time in the 12 Step program.

This was a different life, one I did not care to trade for madness, even the gorgeous madness I'd experienced in this forest. And on that March morning in 2003, the world around me respected my wishes; nothing reached out to whirl me into frantic dancing, not the great jagged mountain, not the thick-trunked trees, not Adam. He was quiet that morning, intent, perhaps a little sad.

Adam left me alone up there in the Sand Cave on the morning of the equinox and headed down the mountain with the others. Left me alone in the chill damp quiet to breathe with the blue- and green-streaked sandstone, to commune and let go. I had so much emotion tied up in this space. How many hours had I spent here in my mind over the past three years? How many hours hurting and yearning toward that golden mountain light? But now, instead of casting flames of wild power, I felt small, held in perspective by the massive rock walls of the cave. Small and a little empty, as though I had been forgotten and the magic had moved on, as though God had possessed me and then left me behind. But alongside that sadness was gratitude. Finally: gratitude. I was grateful to be here, to be stable within the physical embrace of forests and rock and water, to be stable inside my painful friendship with Adam.

I emerged from the Maze on my way down the mountain to find Adam and Gabriel and the others sitting in the path, waiting for me. They were quiet as I approached. Gabe had Adam's guitar. He had written a song years ago that had become one of the anthems of our circle of treehuggers—"Waltzing with the Mountains"—a favorite around campfires and a favorite of mine: "There is a mountain stream so pure/ it's purer than any heart/ Where rains from clouds come pouring down/ it's where the ocean starts." I always imagined Gabe playing the song as a lullaby for his daughters. He played it for me that day, his voice sweet and sad among the grey trees. I sat down quietly with the group, tears in my eyes, feeling honored and cared for, grateful, as though something had come full-circle and started anew in my life.

We returned to Blanton one more time before the Bloodroot Gathering, arriving two days before my birthday. Adam and I had meetings with some amazing local Harlan residents who were helping us organize the event. Later, we walked around the camp, compiling long to-do lists while continuing to hammer away on a final program. The event was shaping up to be the largest Gathering to date, bringing together people from campaigns across the country along with passionate local Appalachian activists and even a few celebrities. At the same time, we were trying to coordinate sound systems, parking, food, facilities, and sleeping spaces for several hundred people in a ramshackle Boy Scout camp held together mostly by dust and good will. It would be an adventure.

The rest of the group left on the morning of May 7th; I spent my twenty-ninth birthday hiking alone and barefoot in a black dress up Pine Mountain. I lay down on the altar rock in the Sand Cave and gazed up at the single rhododendron bush in bloom at the cave's edge high above. No fear. No madness. Deep muddy soil, drifts of pale rain and patches of vivid blue sky. Early spring wildflowers. My beating heart. No fear.

Between the 12 Steps and planning the Bloodroot Gathering, that spring was the happiest and most grounded I'd been since my diagnosis with manic depression in

2000. I felt the strength to make other changes in my life. Despite on-going challenges, Matthew and I had continued our stumbling relationship. The 12 Step program recommended not making any major life changes in the first year of clean time, and I had clung to that as a reason to stay with him. During the fall of 2002, we grew more distant, spending less time together as my depression eased and I became more involved in 12 Step recovery.

In some ways, our relationship unraveled very gracefully; as we grew less intimate, we became better friends. There was more laughter, more healthy argument, more space. Unfortunately, the weird possessive and controlling tensions that had permeated our relationship from the start continued to rear their heads. We could not find a balance. Finally in the spring, as I was driving to Harlan for one of the planning meetings, he called my cell phone and started yelling. I don't remember why he was angry, but I do remember yelling back, finally, telling him to cut it out and leave me alone: "Just forget it. Don't call me. Don't ever yell at me again." We spent time together occasionally in the months to come, but that phone call marked an end point, a fundamental change.

I arrived at Camp Blanton several days before the Bloodroot Gathering to do the last-minute ground work and to enjoy the beautiful quiet before the crowds arrived. Bill, the camp manager, adopted me, sharing breakfast and coffee with me every morning. He urged me to stay in his guest room, but I declined politely and pitched my tent on the far edge of the camp next to Watt's Creek. The days dawned perfect and clear and cool; the dazzling sky painted the surface of the lake bright blue. I ran errands, wandered in the woods, and did the inevitable troubleshooting of a big event in a rural community. Everything was cobbled together—the availability of our folding chairs and party tents depended on whether the local funeral home needed them during the weekend.

But it was beautiful: the planning, the event itself, the people, the forest, all of it. In my memory, that Bloodroot Gathering—spread over all four days of the Memorial Day weekend—appears as a sparkling, shining, laughing whirlwind. Extraordinarily well-choreographed and completely chaotic. Over 300 people from across the country and from all walks of life attended. I was the gal with the clipboard, keeper of the lists, tag-teaming with Adam to make announcements at every mealtime about new logistical details. In hindsight, I realize how extraordinary it was for me to have stood in a position of leadership and authority in this place: Camp Blanton, where, in 2000, my sanity had publicly started to unravel. Now, I very publicly helped to orchestrate a remarkable event.

On Sunday afternoon, Adam and I put aside clipboards and shoes to lead a hike up the mountain together. We met at the trailhead with a hug and sparkling eyes, excited and reverent at the prospect of showing off this mountain. I encouraged the group to try hiking barefoot: "You see more things without shoes. It's amazing. I even remember the names of plants better when my feet are in the dirt." The group started up the trail, crossing through the cold water of Watts Creek. Everyone seemed a little giddy, discovering new things about the forest via the nerve endings in their soles and toes: squishy moss like a damp-wringing sponge, dry hemlock needles that prick against the skin, curved rocks, warm earth. I watched, amused, while Adam explained the American chestnut reintroduction program like a snake-oil sales pitch: "We can promise you a future filled with American chestnut trees!"

The group hiked slowly with frequent pauses to identify plants or discuss geological features of Pine Mountain. As we neared the top, Adam steered me a little way apart from the group. He wanted to tell me something. In a sincere voice, almost as if in confession, he apologized for leaving me here back in 2000, for traveling on without me.

I murmured something about it being in the past, saying, "You didn't know how messed up I was. You don't need to apologize."

"No, you don't understand," he continued, his voice turning plaintive, almost pleading. "I could have helped you, but I just left you here. It was a betrayal."

Something in that word—betrayal—made me suddenly want to rage at him.

"Why are you telling me this *now, Adam?*" After three long years. Words tumbled through my head that I didn't say aloud: I don't want an apology *now.*

Here in this place, as I was finally reconciling with some of the painful experiences of 2000, I didn't want to think of Adam and Loki pulling away in the blue Vanagon, kicking up dust, leaving me behind. I didn't want to think of that as a betrayal. What if he could have helped me, if he somehow could have used the strange intimacy between us to keep me from the hospitals and restraints and humiliation?

I didn't say anything more to Adam, just sped up, eventually breaking away from the group walking up the mountain. Just get me away from him. Past the Sand Cave toward a part of the forest where I'd never been. Don't tell me that you could have helped me and didn't. I don't want to know. I pushed through rhododendron tangles savagely as branches sketched red lines on my skin. All the heat and chaos and confusion at Gabe and Erin's farm... the hellish despair of that long winter... Would it have made any difference if Adam had not left me behind at the camp in 2000? In all honesty, I doubted it, but the thought still brought a searing pain. For years I had so desperately wanted to change the past, now I just wanted to get over it, to move on. Shut the fuck up, Adam.

Just then, unexpectedly, the ground disappeared in front of me. I stood on the edge of a small cliff, stopped to gauge the height, and then jumped, yelling as I fell—a raw sound of emotion that I'd never heard before from my throat.

The cliff was not high. Maybe six feet, but what I'd taken for the forest floor was a thick blanket of dry leaves, piled two or three feet deep along the base of the cliff. My feet struggled to find the ground and slipped sideways, knees twisting, until I came to rest, covered in leaves and dirt. My anger evaporated as I sat up laughing. Around me, the world had changed. I gazed out upon a magnificent sight—American chestnut saplings filled the forest understory, the long green banners of their leaves streaming in the breeze. And beyond, more rhododendron in bloom, leading down a gentle slope. Further still, a green grove of oak and poplar and walnut trees that were tall and thick and old beckoned to me.

I stood, brushing leaves from my dress, and walked to the closest chestnut sapling. I knelt down, running my fingers against its smooth, silver bark and saying prayers that somehow these trees might be spared, protected from the insidious orange blight that had destroyed American chestnuts as a canopy species. The fungus traveled on the breeze from tree to tree, waiting as the tree matured and the bark grew furrowed. Then the blight burrowed in through the cracks, webbing beneath the bark, killing the cambium tissues, and choking the tree. Precious few American chestnuts showed natural resistance to the blight. Infection meant an all but certain death.

I wondered sadly, stroking the bark with my fingers, if it hurt a tree to die this way. Did they feel pain? I wanted to be a healer—that was really all that I'd ever wanted, in all the manic chaos, what I most truly wanted was to heal the aching wounds of the Earth. I wanted to be the bone woman, the witch doctor, bringing lost species back to life and setting them loose again on the ridgelines. I slipped my fingers between my legs to where old womb blood had dripped softly for the past few days and caught red drops on my fingertips. I caressed the bark of the chestnut tree softly with the blood, leaving orange-red tracks on the young tree's silver skin, still intact. My blood for yours.

Tears touched my eyes, but the sight of so many saplings, so beautiful in the green spring, gladdened my heart. I brushed my hands through the long green leaves as I walked, smiling softly, into the rhododendron thicket. I moved more slowly now, ducking and darting through the angular tangle. From time to time, I caught rustling sounds, like the scurrying noises squirrels make in dry leaves. But as I reached the far side of the rhododendron, the rustlings congealed into footfalls, and I turned just in time to see a form of dark fur tumble out of the dense vegetation.

My first thought was "dog," and I almost began to extend my hand, to reassure it, and then I saw the claws. The endless long claws. The brown snout. Thick black coat and black eyes. Black bear. It was a small bear, probably a yearling. In the moment, foolishly, I failed to look for a mother bear. Black bear rarely harm humans, but a mother will take forceful action to protect a cub.

The bear looked dazed after its tumble from the bushes, and it stared at me, sniffing, from about ten feet away. I felt dizzy and enraptured, not at all afraid. Instead, I wished that I could reach out and touch it, feel the fur, smell what a wild bear smells like. But I stayed standing, my hands raised in a gesture of reassurance and distance, saying, "Stay away—you don't want to trust a human."

At the same time, inside my mind, I was whispering: *Thank you, thank you for letting me see you—your beautiful face—for letting me see you here in this place.* After a few moments, the bear turned and trotted away, then paused and came back again, curious, closer to me now, still sniffing. And then the bear leaped and turned and ran, fast, into the rhododendron thicket. I was left behind, breathing hard, heart thudding as though I'd just run up the ridge.

But the mountain was not done with me. I walked slowly on into the grove of old trees that filtered soft green sunlight through their canopy. I followed the gently rolling knoll—a saddle on the mountain ridge—dipping down then back up. I stopped in the low point and stood still, arms lifted to spread and share the blessing of this place, and felt light glowing off my shoulders, light expanding... and then I jumped nearly out of my skin at a sudden loud racket of wings. I must have frightened the wild turkey that rose now, clumsy in flight and flailing against the air, as it fumbled off the forest floor into the arms of an old oak.

And then—it happened so fast—out of the same tree, a golden white ghost came flying straight at me. Day blind and startled awake by the awkward turkey, it stretched broad tawny wings and gazed black-eyed upon me from a pale face. The song of its wings—an invisible velvet rustle—revealed its identity. Fifty feet away, the owl swerved, arcing its wings to make a sharp turn, back downslope, disappearing into thicker forest, leaving behind the lush whisper of its flight.

I stood still for a long time, my mind tracing over each event of the past hour—chestnut trees and bear, the turkey and the owl. I felt the curve of rock and soil against my bare feet, warm sun and shadow on my face, spirals of breeze against my skin. A rain shower fluttered by, dusting prisms in my hair and on the tips of leaves. The soft water brought out salamanders—gleaming red efts— brilliant orange, resting on emerald tufts of moss. They were everywhere. I began to walk further into the trees but stopped for fear of crushing the tiny creatures as they emerged into the new rain.

A few people were still milling around Sand Cave when I finally climbed back out of the heavenly grove. One of them, a friend from Charlottesville, said, "Oh good! We were wondering when you'd reappear." Adam had asked them to wait for me while he led the hikers back to camp. It felt good to be looked after, good to be among friends, but I chose to walk down the mountain alone, breathing slow and savoring the day. The gold-green glow of that wild forest on Pine Mountain had embraced me again, but this was altogether different from the mind-bending experience of 2000. My feet were bare, my skin laced again with blood, my face flushed, but my mind remained clear and calm. Nothing to hide, no fear, no sense of self as unmasked divinity, just me, awash in gratitude for the grace of this day.

I stopped at Knobby Rock and stood for a long while, gazing out at the valley in the early evening light. I was replaying a vision that had come into my mind often during the past year. The vision took place here, on these rocks: a re-telling of my 2000 pilgrimage, a reinterpretation. The vision had such a taste of reality that I sometimes forgot it was fiction.

In my vision, I see myself walking down Pine Mountain in the slight rain that fell those fateful May days of the new millennium. I wear the dress made from purple hemp. My feet are bruised, bloody and bare. I am a pilgrim, carrying nothing but my breath. At Knobby Rock, I stop and lift my face to the grey skies. I know that this place, here, marks the crossing-over point between Spirit and Society, between the mountaintop world that melded my brain into God and the sad-faced human valley below.

In reality, in the year 2000, up there on the mountain ridges, I had dreamed and prayed and sought to give up my self, to be a sacrifice, to do whatever I could to save both nature and humanity—those two inseparable entities. I had walked down the mountain to Knobby Rock with my mind on fire, thinking that I had been successful, that my work was done.

But in my visionary version of events, as I gaze up at the grey sky, I am offered guidance. Something tells me to cross over from Spirit into Society and return. Return. *Go down from this mountain and return. Not as a sky god with an aura of arrows, not as conqueror or hero, but as a subject. Return into bondage, dependent on the machine you sought to transform. Lose yourself, lose your mind.*

But why? Why?

A voice from the sky, a voice in my mind, replies: *Trust me. Return to the valley. This is your heroic practice. Trust me. I know.*

In my vision, my eyes are clear and I understand. I am not called only to be a wandering, ethereal mystic, speaking in tongues on the mountaintop. Instead, this wild ecstasy will bind me to the human world, to mental illness, stigma, and brokenness, to medicines and treatments. I am to learn to heal myself on that path, and maybe, somehow, in the process, be of service to a broken humanity. In my vision, I understand the blessings of the mountaintop and this transition into the human world. I understand the purpose in the harrowing to come.

My vision felt so close to real life. But in reality, in 2000, I'd had no clarity at all, just a brain fraying and scalded by THC and intensifying mania. I had walked down the mountain and the weak joint in my brain had cracked—leading me into insanity with no notion of what was to come.

Below in the valley, I saw mist rising, curling itself into a dragon that loped slowly off among the trees. I blinked and looked around, reorienting myself back into 2003. I'm ok. I took deep breaths to clear my head, to ground myself. I'm ok—Bloodroot, the Gathering— I should get back.

I looked for Adam as soon as I returned to the camp. I had no reason to hold onto my anger. He had meant the apology as a kindness. And if that apology burned my already-broken heart, that was not his fault. No one could have predicted the chaos that had unfolded in my life after the 2000 Bloodroot Gathering at Blanton.

Adam was in the dining hall, in the milling mass of people waiting for supper. He caught sight of me, and his face lit up. People seemed to part between us as he raced over. I don't remember what I said—something incoherent and excited: "Bear! Turkey! Owl! Chestnuts!!!" And Adam laughing as he said—or I think he said—"We *can* promise you a future filled with American chestnuts!" I had no idea what he meant, or if I was hearing him right; I didn't care. I was laughing too as Adam pulled me into a hug that was somehow like a dance.

Quietly, he said, "Write about it. Will you write about what you saw? And send me what you write?" I nodded, surprised. I had sent him such vast quantities of my strange writings over the last three years; I was pleased that he still wanted to read my thoughts.

That last night of the Gathering, I fell asleep in the back of Adam's Vanagon after a quiet, late-night talk about the event, our work together, the magic of this place and time. Nothing sketchy, just talk and then sleep. There was a gentleness to it, a building of trust and friendship, and a kind of closure. Sleeping beside Adam back in 2000 after the thunderstorm drenched my sleeping bag stood at the beginning of a turbulent, destructive time. This night in 2003 at the end of the Gathering was a validation that my connection with Adam was a good thing—often confusing to me—but not responsible for the pain of mania and depression.

The Monday of Memorial Day dawned cool and grey. In the afternoon, as the camp emptied out, I wandered around the dining hall and along the lake shore while manic memories from 2000 jostled in my head. I still could not fathom the strangeness of that time. Thinking of it made me feel disconnected from myself. Something in those memories remained achingly precious to me, and yet so much pain and sadness and shame had followed May of 2000.

Gabe and Erin's daughter Laurel came to sit beside me on the rock wall beside the lake. I felt another jolt of memory from three years ago: the little girl placing a green net on my head here on this spot, saying, "I'm so glad we caught you!" She must be seven now. I wondered if she remembered at all, if she remembered me losing my mind at their home. Today, she pointed at a huge dragonfly, perched perfectly still on a stone nearby.

"Why isn't it moving?" she asked.

"I don't know, Laurel. Let's take a look."

We knelt down to peer closer. It was the biggest dragonfly that I'd ever seen, with long, black-veined, shimmering wings. We got so close that we could see it breathing, but the dragonfly remained in place.

"Maybe it's cold?" Laurel suggested.

"I bet you're right."

Erin walked over just then to give me a hug. They were packing up the truck to head home to the farm.

"It's so good to see you doing so well," she said. "Come visit, ok? Come soon." I hugged her goodbye, then looked up as Laurel tugged my arm; the dragonfly had taken flight, darting low over the lake's surface.

Adam and I left at the same time this time, heading off in opposite directions to our homes. Bill, the camp manager, came out to wave us off. He leaned in my car window and said: "Don't forget now! The same road that takes you away from here can always bring you back!"

INTERLUDE

A part of me would like to end the story here. There is a poetic satisfaction to the circularity of my story between the 2000 and 2003 Bloodroot Gatherings. But stopping here would present a very partial portrait of life with this disease. The 2003 Bloodroot Gathering occurred at the tail end of the initial, acute phase of my manic-depression, but I was far from recovered.

Recovery from mental illness, for me, has been a long process of discovering how to weave stability into day-to-day living. Part II of this book charts key moments and experiences of my learning, changing, and healing. In between were long periods of daily life: sometimes plodding, sometimes wrestling with symptoms and treatment, always seeking the right balance to stay clean, stable, and perhaps to seek again toward joy.

My recovery has taken a bipolar track—one external, focused on relationships and confidence and learning to live again in the human world—and one more internal and difficult to articulate. At some point in my recovery, I realized that parts of me that I'd always deeply treasured had become toxic in the chaos of mania and its aftermath. My inner life, my imagination and creativity, my experiences of Nature, God, and Love had all become dangerously entwined with the shame that followed mania's powerful delusions. It took years to recognize and accept that my manic depressive experiences could have both transcendent and pathological components—it didn't have to be either/or.

Thus, strangely, in order to reclaim love for myself, I've had to forgive manic depression for ravaging my life. Acceptance is too neutral a word; I've had to fall in love with this chronic illness and with my strange, fragile, chaotic brain. I've had to learn to respect them both and their power: the ability to give insight and grace and healing, but also to devolve into destruction and despair.

Alongside the internal journey, recovery has also been a dance between myself and others. My family members loved me with an unflinching ferocity that refused to allow me to self-destruct. A creative, respectful doctor with good listening skills managed to win my trust and help me sort out medical treatment. The 12 Step program members offered me a life raft and an instruction manual. I had a handful of friends who I trusted with my diagnosis, especially including Catherine who showed me that manic depressives can be happy, healthy, and deeply alive. Matthew reflected back to me the pain and confusion that manic depressive behaviors can cause friends and family; he helped me generously and as best he could through an extraordinarily difficult time. Loki, Adam, EQ, and other Bloodroot friends resurfaced regularly to remind me that Nature and Love and God still existed, and that I might be able to find and feel them again.

But of all the people who have helped me recover, no one has invested more time, energy, pain, perseverance, and kindness than a man named Danny, who arrived in my life in September 2003. He pushed and struggled and challenged and argued and loved me with a tenacity that I could barely fathom—"Why would anyone want to put such commitment into a crazed, broken creature like me?" This force of nature took the form of a roving treehugger musician with hair curlier than even Gabe and Erin's kids and an extraordinary instinct for joy.

Part II

"Bipolar disorder takes no prisoners
but humbles the grandest and the littlest
and asks us to rise again from our ashes."
– K.S.

TWELVE

The afterglow of the 2003 Bloodroot Gathering lasted into the summer and fall. I had more energy for my activism. With the help of some friends in the movement, I organized a roadshow of presentations in western Virginia in cities whose drinking water came from the George Washington and Jefferson National Forests. For the presentations, Loki and our friend Christopher dressed up as George Washington and Thomas Jefferson, pontificating elegantly about their namesake national forests. I hired a musician to travel with us and leaven the presentations with emotion and entertainment. I had one singer lined up already when my funder suggested that I hire Danny as well.

Danny and I had met five years earlier at a Bloodroot Gathering in eastern Tennessee. I caught the tail end of his Friday night set, walking into the room just in time to hear him sing, "I've been healing and growing wild/ playing Twister with my inner child" sung at high volume with great energy and humor. I laughed and thought, "Oh my, I like this guy!"

Our friendship really began on a late-night road trip to Asheville, NC later that year. He made his way as an itinerant eco-troubadour—in his words—playing the campfires and coffeehouses of this great land, making hundreds of dollars a year. He performed at environmental action camps and gatherings, direct action trainings, Earth First! Rendezvous, and acts of civil disobedience. He, along with a handful of other performers, helped create a common culture among the disparate eco-groups across the country. Home was Austin, Texas or Eugene, Oregon, though in the late 1990s, he mostly lived on the road. Danny only occasionally owned a car, usually traveling by bus or friend or hitchhiking. I picked him up on the way to a conference in Asheville, and we talked and talked, swapping stories about God and love and politics. I found him incredibly funny; we had an easy resonance.

On that same trip to Asheville in 1998, Danny inadvertently helped convince me to take a leap of faith and quit my quiet, stable job in a university library to become a full-time volunteer activist. He told me a saying that he'd learned to live by, something he'd picked up in his travels: "Trust the road, and the road will provide." A few months later, with that phrase in mind, I decided to make the jump.

Danny and I stayed friends through the years, running into each other at activist gatherings. He could be tricky sometimes. He tended to drink a lot, and one night got a little friendlier than I liked. Another time, at an event during the summer of 2002, as I was barely hanging on to my mind and trying desperately to stay clean, he offered to be my sobriety buddy for the weekend, and then changed his mind when the whiskey came out at the campfire.

That hurt, and so, in 2003, I hesitated to hire him to help with the roadshows. But overall I knew him to be a good person, a light-hearted light-bringer, and so I called him in Texas to see if he would come out to Virginia. He turned me down the first time, saying that we didn't need two folk singers—one was more than enough. But when the first musician that I'd hired broke his wrist two weeks before the roadshow, I called Danny back and begged. He said, "Ok. I'll do it. Send me a bus ticket."

The roadshow team was unwieldy; six guys and me, traveling in a huge rental van. We gathered in Harrison-burg, Virginia the night before our first presentation. I arrived with my own car full of costumes, petitions, and pamphlets. Danny came out to greet me with a hug.

"Come inside," he said. "I want you to hear something."

He positioned me beside the couch, called the rest of the group together, and sat down cross-legged on the floor with his guitar to sing.

Oh Virginia/ You were my first love/ for twenty years you held me while my path was being found/ my eyes upon your mountains and my feet upon your ground/ You showed to me the way, set my feet in motion/ taught me a profound love for the forest and the ocean/ And I'm blessed again to walk upon your shores/ Oh Virginia/ I could not have asked for more.

It went on, a celebration of the state's beauty and a call for its protection. Danny had written *Oh, Virginia* that day on the bus to Harrisonburg. This was his first time playing it. When he finished singing, I was on my knees. The song spoke to my heart, to all the work I'd put into trying to protect some fragment of Virginia's wildness, and I couldn't stay on my feet. It felt like he'd written the song for me.

The week of shows was chaotic and under-attended, but we did pick up some good press. On Thursday afternoon, the crew had some time free in the city of Lynchburg. We wanted to be outside in the open air, so I found a green strip on the map, which turned out to be a long greenway park by the James River. I flopped down on the grass with a book while the guys played frisbee. A short time later, Danny hollered at me from up the hill. He was holding a bicycle built for two.

"I traded some guitar repair for an hour's rental. Come on. Sit up front. You can steer."

I had been feeling tired and blue, the familiar low-level depression resting its gloom on my shoulders. But Danny's grin made me laugh, and so I climbed on and we rode, wobbling, down the road, picking up speed along the dirt trails through the park. The roadshow guys whooped and cheered when we rode past, "Alright Danny!"

The week wrapped up at a conference in Ohio. The crew arrived at the camp late on Friday night and rolled out our sleeping bags on picnic tables beneath a shelter. In the morning, we climbed back into the van to find a breakfast joint. I sat in the back, facing Danny. We were arguing about something in a friendly way. The van passed in and out of early sunlight shining through the trees as he gesticulated. One ray of light fell in Danny's eyes and lit them up, deep brown like chestnut wood with concentric circles like tree rings. I stared, entranced, and heard an audible click in my head. In that instant, Danny went from being my sweet, goofy pal to being suddenly very attractive.

We spent that evening curled up on the front porch of one of the cabins. On Sunday, after the conference ended, we took a walk into the beautiful green forest near the Hocking Hills. A muddy, mossy trail led us into a field of boulders with great trees growing in between. The stones reminded me of the Maze on Pine Mountain. Danny and I climbed up on one of the massive rocks to have the talk.

"You know I think you're awesome," Danny said, grinning.

"Yeah," I smiled back.

"Well, I have to tell you—I've been single for the past year, and that's also been really awesome."

I laughed. "I hear you. I'm only a few months out from an intense relationship. I'm not looking to be seriously involved with anyone, even someone of your awesomeness."

We agreed not to try to create a partnership but to enjoy each other's company when we had it. And then we stood up and hugged each other, and the whole world swayed around us. We both felt it. I saw the forest light waver like heat mirage above a desert, like a boundary between worlds shifting. We pulled back from each other with startled faces.

"Maybe," Danny said, "We should reconsider."

We spent the next few weeks meeting up in different places around the region. I put hundreds of miles on my car, driving out to Midwestern towns where he was playing gigs to meet him, taking time off work or bringing work along with me. Ohio, Illinois, Indiana. It was an exciting, heart-leaping kind of time. We went together to the annual Reunion at Adam and Danielle's farm, where people grinned to see us paired up. Danny started coming back to Virginia more often, staying with me or visiting his parents in the southwest part of the state.

Danny already knew about my manic depression. He had not, thankfully, been around me in the most acute extremes of the illness, so he'd never witnessed full-blown manic madness. We had crossed paths in the last three years only while I was slogging my way through depressions. We'd talked about my diagnosis long before the romance began, so I never had to struggle with the question of when or how to tell him.

Much of our first year together was mellow. We had a great deal of openness and honesty in our relationship and a ton of laughter. But I was not a great partner. I remained mired in self-pity and self-absorption, assuming that because of my illness, my needs trumped his. Danny took care of me a lot, but he would also push back.

"But I feel bad!" I would cry piteously.

"Well, I'm sorry about that, but being bipolar is no excuse for you being an asshole," he'd reply. I heard that line many times for many years before I grasped the obvious: treating Danny badly because I felt bad about myself was not acceptable to him and not a good way to live.

So our life together was rife with both joy and challenge. In the summer of 2004, we took a road trip together to a wedding in Montana. Danny would be playing in the ceremony and helping lead the dance band. He'd been wary of having me come along on such a long trip, knowing that I could be emotionally difficult. We camped along the way and made plans to visit Yellowstone and the Tetons on our way home.

I brought along three grant proposals that were due during the time we'd be away. Once we arrived in Missoula, there were beautiful places and people to see. I helped out with food preparation and decoration—everything but my grant proposals.

When the wedding was over, I finally started writing. I was slow, discombobulated; it took me so much longer than I thought it would. I was embarrassed, ashamed, pretending:

"Are you almost done?" Danny would ask every day.

"Yes! Yes, I'm nearly finished." But I wasn't, and Danny waited, not going to visit friends, not going out in the wilderness, instead waiting for me to get done so we could leave and have the adventures that we'd planned.

I didn't understand why he was so angry when we finally drove away from Missoula. I have a distinct memory of looking out the car window at the remains of the Fort Missoula Internment Camp, where Japanese and Italian Americans were held during World War II, and feeling trapped by Danny's words, unable to comprehend why he was so furious. It took hours for me to grasp that I had held him hostage, that he had believed me when I said, "I'm almost done!" and so he'd waited, and waited.

In hindsight, my behavior seems bizarre to me. I was scrambled up in my head, not even thinking about Danny, just embarrassed at my own fumbling disorganization, impatient with myself, not thinking—or at least not thinking right. At the time, I thought he was being unreasonable. I kept arguing, "I didn't mean to... I didn't realize..." We had to skip the National Park visits to get back in time for a family commitment. We fought the whole way across the country.

The reality was that in the course of my illness I'd forgotten how to look out for other people. My whole mind was focused inward to try and protect myself from further hurt; I had nearly lost my ability for interpersonal empathy. Instead of trying to understand how Danny felt, I snapped my shell shut and waved my claws blindly, trying to defend myself against unknown, unidentified threats.

Danny and I split up after the Montana trip. He did not want to be in a relationship with someone who couldn't see beyond her own skin. He moved back to Oregon and I went home to Charlottesville, feeling sorrowful and reflective. We talked occasionally on the phone, but when I took a trip to Oregon for a conference that fall, he made no attempt to meet. A mutual friend of ours saw me at the event. She touched the side of my face, smiling, "He loves you, you know that? He loves you."

He did, too, because he came back to Virginia late in October to help with a fundraising concert that we'd previously planned together. After the show, we stayed at Sean and Roxanne's place, on that idyllic mountainside. I talked him into getting back in the relationship.

"I understand why you were so angry. I wasn't appreciating you or looking out for you, and I'm so sorry. I can do better than that."

I don't know whether Danny believed me, but he agreed to give it another try. I really did mean what I said, but my relationship skills hadn't been particularly fantastic even before 2000. In the years since, as I struggled to digest the trauma of manic depression, I was extraordinarily self-obsessed. Not in the sense of vanity—not at all—I still actively hated myself in many ways. I hated having manic depression and having to take medications and being fat and having to avoid drugs and alcohol and most of all I hated feeling bad, always, always feeling bad and sick in my soul. I was extremely self-conscious, while also being unaware of what I was doing much of the time. My focus remained on trying to hold myself together.

On some level, I wanted to stay out of sight—to keep safe by hiding out. And yet part of me clearly longed for the brightness and energy that Danny brought with him. He had such a light, a joy-bringer, surrounded by music and laughter and friends. I craved that even as I feared it. In those early years, I looked to Danny to be both a shield and a safety net. Somehow he managed to give me that without giving in to my self-pity.

In hindsight, I scratch my head when I consider why Danny stuck with me. I was a toxic, childish creature for many of those early years, too traumatized to be self-reflective or to figure out how to go about healing. Danny has told me that he's not sure why he stuck around either. "Most of the time," he'd say with a half-smile, "when I wanted to leave, God would tell me not to."

Thank you, God.

◆

In addition to the challenge that Danny set for me to be a more decent and gracious human being, other events both large and small stretched me to reach beyond self-pity and fear. In the fall of 2004, while Danny and I were split up, the natural world called me dramatically out of my comfort zone. Most of my contact with nature was in the local parks those days, walking the greenway or the reservoir trails; I did not venture out much into wild places. My confidence in myself to navigate the mountains stayed at a low ebb, despite the wonderful experiences in Blanton Forest.

In the fall of 2004, I drove out to Shenandoah National Park to visit my parents. Along with their neighbors, they had gone cabin camping at the Lewis Mountain campground since I was a child. The September day was clear in Charlottesville but unsettled; Hurricane Ivan had come ashore on the Gulf coast and was traveling north along the Blue Ridge. I drove out from Charlottesville into the rolling hills of Greene County with music turned up loud, never noticing the intensifying colors in the sky—purple, black, then a nauseating green.

I drove around a long curve in the road, and sudden rain crashed against the windshield. Ahead of me, a white fold of cloud, beautiful as an angel descending, draped down from above, lowering, taking shape over the road. I finally recognized it as another wind blast rocked the vehicle: Tornado! Adrenalin leaped into my bloodstream, and I slammed the car to a halt, reversed into a turn lane, and jumped out, leaving the door open in my flight. I threw myself down a steep roadside ditch and hugged the ground as the trees bent sideways and the wind made a sound like I'd never heard nor dreamed.

After a short, intense time, the violent wind quieted. The tornado moved off to the north, taking off roofs and knocking down trees. The rain fell gently again. As I climbed out of the ditch to the roadway, I saw jags of white cloud hanging over the Blue Ridge and thought sudden and sharp, like a jolt of electricity, about Adam and the view from Pine Mountain, the rise and fall of the water cycle. Adam had been kind and friendly the past year—clearly happy for Danny and me. Sometimes the difficult intensity of my manic times with him seemed like nothing but a dream.

I pulled up to the campground at Lewis Mountain still covered in mud and eager to tell my story. "Yes," my parents said, "There've been tornadoes all along the mountains—We tried to call to let you know—Why didn't you check the weather!?"

What could I tell them? I was glad for that moment, for the fear and danger and opportunity. Tornadoes had terrified me since childhood. Our family visits to Iowa in the summertime often coincided with tornado outbreaks. Yet here, I had acted on instinct, nerves, and adrenalin and taken powerful, self-directed action for my own safety and survival. For the first time in a long time, saying that I felt grateful to be alive was not a mealy-mouthed platitude but had a sharp flavor and loud sound, like the bite of metal or clang of bells. I felt a keenness in my bloodstream and body that I had not felt in a very long time. It was good to be alive.

♦

The human world remained more difficult for me than the world of storms and wind, and my inability to see far beyond the trauma of manic depression continued to cause troubles for my relationships. Soon after Danny returned to Virginia in 2004, he was offered an organizer's job based in North Carolina with a campaign trying to outlaw mountaintop removal coal mining. He would be traveling to target Congressional districts giving presentations to build support for a bill in Congress. After years as a musical performer in the movement, this was a serious job for Danny, and he was very excited. His family came from the Appalachian Mountains, just beyond the region where coal mining occurred; his connection to this project ran deep.

A series of odd events, including the offer of a year's worth of funding from a friend, gave me the opportunity to work alongside Danny on the project. I had been ready to leave my job with Virginia Wildlands for the past several months. We had a new board president with whom I had constant friction, and after five years, I was ready for a change. The opportunity to work on stopping mountaintop removal—the practice that had so horrified me back in 2001—also held tremendous appeal. Danny was wary. Working together with a partner was always dicey and working with a partner in my state might be downright destructive. But he took another tremendous leap of faith with me and agreed to give it a try.

As part of our training, we drove to Knoxville for a conference in January of 2005. The group put us up in a hotel where I had a restless night, then we spent the next day meeting new people at the meeting. After that, we drove on to the small mountain town where our project was based. Something happened on this trip—I don't remember exactly what combination of factors—I might have forgotten to take my meds that morning, or perhaps I just had too much sugar, not enough sleep, the heightened energy of new places and people, but I ended up freaked out. Sitting in a Mexican restaurant in North Carolina, quietly fighting the urge to scream, I put a name to it:

"Danny, the room's too hot."

"The room's too hot? What do you mean?"

It took me a while to explain, but he got it, instinctively, resonating with my discomfort. He got it. The music was too loud, the people too close. The world was filled with sharp edges and my nerves raked up my spine like barbed wire. I wanted to pull my hair or devolve into panic: the room was too hot. It became our code phrase for times like this, when I couldn't easily slow down my mind or talk myself into calmness, feeling again like an animal caught in a leg hold trap, wanting to chew off my paw. We got a room at a local motel, and I took some extra lithium. It was an eye-opener for Danny, I think, to see me on the edge like that. For me, I got to see another facet of the gift that Danny was to me; his presence and understanding helped ease me into sleep and a quieter frame of mind. Still, the rawness of that day—our first day in this new community together—was not a good omen.

On my first day of work in late January, I met with my new boss. We sat down in her office while she laid out terms for my employment. I'd thought that the situation was already settled. We'd talked on the phone back in December and made a plan, but the details she laid out in January bore almost no resemblance.

"But that's not what we agreed on," I said.

"Well," she replied, "that was never put in writing."

"What?" My jaw really did drop. I had known her for years and thought of her as a friend. Why would we need to put something in writing?

"These are the terms," her voice firm with finality.

"You've got to be kidding!"

I wish I could say that I stood up at that point, stated that I found her behavior unethical and would not work under those conditions. But I did not. I agreed, numbly and with a growing feeling of nausea. I didn't see any way out. I had already quit my other job. I was stuck. I was also afraid—unwilling or unable to stand up for myself. So I didn't say anything, just sat there, feeling violated and ill.

This too was not a good omen for the start of a new job. I felt like a limp rag, disempowered and kicking myself for failing to advocate on my own behalf. The first several months of the job were a nightmare, full of my bad choices and self-pity. First and worst, I absolutely collapsed as an activist. My job was to locate and recruit groups and individuals to host Danny's presentations.

Without my work, he would have nothing to do. But I couldn't do it. I wilted. I had been foundering in that endless low-grade depression even before taking the job, and now I crashed. Danny finally had to step in and help me make the phone calls and find the host groups. The situation reminded me of how my mother, back in 2000, pulled me up by the arms as depression weighted me to the floor, trying to help me write the big grant proposal.

Danny was hurt, disappointed, angry. His trust in me was broken—again—but he continued to help me. We slowly filled up weeks of outreach presentations for him to do, and he set off, talking to church groups, Rotary Clubs, reaching outside the choir. He was tireless, often putting in hundred-hour weeks while on the road.

Meanwhile, I talked with Dr. McLean, who was still my psychiatrist, about the depression. He suggested that I try another mood-stabilizing medication to complement lithium's effects. Studies were coming in that showed mood stabilizers to be more effective than antidepressants when dealing with bipolar depression. The lamotrigine he prescribed had a remarkable and rapid effect. I felt as though the lenses of my glasses had been wiped suddenly clean after years of looking through dirt and smear. I felt so much better. Lithium held me stable— kept me from the radical upswings—and now this drug, finally, seemed to be putting a foundation under my feet to end those terrible, dragging plummets into despair.

And then I did something astonishingly stupid. I stopped taking Effexor, cold turkey. I was so eager to get off of it once and for all; I just stopped. Even after the dreadful experiences I'd had doing the same thing a few years back, still, even so, I did it again. McLean told me not to; he said to titrate down, but I was fixated: I wanted Effexor out of my body.

Within a few days, it was indeed out of my body, and my brain had once again slammed into rebound shock. All of the wretched symptoms returned: the electric jolts and swiss-cheese holes in my brain, the vertigo and nausea, the weird tingles in my hands and feet, dizziness, brain fog—I couldn't drive; I could barely walk or speak. I spent beautiful spring days at a friend's place in the mountains, staggering around the house, trying to focus my eyes. McLean worked with me to ease some of the symptoms— enough so that I could still do my job—but the extraordinary discomfort continued for months.

Over the course of the spring, I decided that I ought to move to North Carolina. I'd been splitting my time between Charlottesville and the place where Danny was living in the NC mountains. The commute was six hours long, and I felt ready to leave Charlottesville. The move uprooted me from my 12 Step community. In some ways, I wanted this. I had remained active with the Fellowship since 2002, although travels with Danny had lessened my meeting attendance. I continued with Step work—

slogging through the "searching and fearless moral inventory" of the Fourth Step and sharing it with Sarah with great relief in the Fifth, attempting with my Ninth Step to make amends to people I had hurt during my active addiction.

For some time, however, I had felt uncomfortable going to meetings while dating Danny. Having a relationship with someone actively using drugs or drinking was not exactly encouraged in the Fellowship because of the potential for relapse. Danny drank. He drank more than he wanted to sometimes. He'd spent two years sober back in the '90s, going to 12 Step meetings regularly, so he'd self-identified as an alcoholic in the past. This had given him a lot of empathy for my situation over the years, but it also caused me irrational worries that if I talked to my sponsor, Sarah, about Danny's drinking that she would tell me to stop seeing him.

In reality, she never would have said such a thing—she would have asked questions and helped me think things through and probably told me "you're right where you're supposed to be"—but I was not in a good head space. I kept it a secret, and the secret drove a wedge between me and the 12 Step program. When I moved to North Carolina, I went to a few meetings, but the Fellowship I attended had only a handful in the area, spread out in distant towns. The local group was tiny. I felt uncomfortable there. In truth, I would have felt uncomfortable any-where, so I just stopped going.

My family helped me drive the moving truck from Charlottesville to North Carolina. Years later, Danny told me about sitting in the truck with my Dad, watching me carrying a lamp up the stairs to my new apartment. He got along extremely well with my parents and often compared notes with them about my mental health.

"That kid needs a break," my Dad said.

"No," Danny replied. My father looked surprised.

"No," Danny said again, "That kid needs to make her own breaks."

During 2005, my health never really recovered from the shock of Effexor withdrawal. In July, another physical crisis hit, which may or may not have been related. What-ever the exact cause, it had the feel of a shamanic illness—some diseased part of my spirit coming to the surface. In July of 2005, after years of swallowing stress and anger—from this job, from my manic depressive diagnosis and all its implications—my digestive system gave out completely.

On Danny's birthday, we went to a B&B in Hot Springs, NC for a weekend vacation. My old colleagues in Virginia Wildlands had given me a gift certificate as a go-ing-away present, and Danny and I were looking forward to a chance to relax together. We had plans to hike, soak in the hot springs, and enjoy the creaky, historic B&B. But almost as soon as we arrived, my digestive system began to malfunction; by nightfall, I was as sick as I had been since my appendix ruptured in third grade. A high fever shook my body, pinching my head into a blinding headache, while my stomach violently rejected any substance put in it.

I stayed sick for the next ten months. The fever and vomiting subsided in a few days, but I could no longer digest food properly. By the grace of the federal government's COBRA program, I still had health insurance and, for a time, used it almost every week. Even with batteries of tests—needles and scans, invasive cameras and biopsies—the only thing the doctors ever determined for certain was that my body was not absorbing fat.

The summer turned surreal. I could not eat solid food, so my head swam in a kind of vague daze all the time. I lived in my bed or at the doctor's office. I knew almost no one in the little mountain town, and Danny was frequently away, so I was often alone. One night, after watching a documentary on PBS—the one station my tiny television could tune in—I realized how reminiscent this time was of the months spent crawling out of depressions: the bedridden aloneness and exhaustion. Yet now, despite the constant sickness in my stomach, I was not depressed. Instead, I felt a sense of urgency. The fall season of Danny's outreach presentations was coming up fast.

Sick or not, I had to get my act together. I had to make my own breaks. I could not abide fucking up again like I had in the spring. I needed to regain my self-respect, and Lord knows, I owed it to Danny. He believed so deeply in this project and worked incredibly hard. For each series of presentations he did in the target Congressional districts, he took along residents of the Appalachian coal mining region who lived in the destructive shadow of mountaintop removal. They were doing critical work; they deserved my best.

So I pushed myself. I couldn't eat or digest food, but I could set up internet service at home and work from my bed. I started researching groups in our target districts, started on the outreach phone calls and emails. The project director planned to send Danny to districts in southern Louisiana at the beginning of September and then other southern districts along the Gulf of Mexico, maybe Texas and Florida.

Unfortunately, even with my better efforts kicking in, our project seemed star-crossed. Our plans were decimated one-by-one by hurricanes. Katrina smashed the Louisiana outreach effort, then Rita and Wilma washed out Texas and Florida. I began to find a certain grim humor in the endless obstacles: "Just don't send Danny to the Outer Banks, ok? My cousins are there on vacation."

Finally, the director sent Danny north for the remainder of the hurricane season. As for me, I simply put my head down and butted my way through. It was far from graceful, but I did my job.

My contract ended at the end of 2005. December found me ragged and bitter. Danny and I had met and exceeded the target number of presentations for our contract. We did it, but at a huge cost to our relationship. The management at the organization had been wretched, and the unethical behavior of my initial hiring had continued throughout the year. I had no desire to continue with this group, nor did they have any desire to keep me.

But more than that, I did not want to look for further activist work. I wanted to stop. I was angry. I wanted a life without the constant heartbreak of watching Earth and people destroyed. I wanted a job without backstabbing and betrayal, without petty tyrants who run nonprofit groups as their miniature fiefdoms and care more for funding and recognition than effectiveness.

More than anything I wanted my health back; I badly needed to get better. Despite the multitude of tests, the gastroenterologist turned up no explanation or treatment for my illness. At the end of December, he turned me loose.

"I can't find anything wrong with you. I don't know what else to try."

"But what am I supposed to do?"

He sent me on my way with a shrug and a prescription for a pancreatic supplement that I'd tried once before; it had helped briefly.

"Maybe it'll help you again." He shrugged a second time.

I had started losing weight at an accelerating pace. Earlier in the autumn, I noticed a new slimness to my face, which pleased me at first. I'd never lost the weight that I'd gained so rapidly while taking Zyprexa back in 2000. Lithium also had weight gain as a common side effect, and my metabolism had clearly changed in the past five years. When I got sick in the summer of 2005, I was the heaviest I'd ever been. I was initially grateful to lose some of the weight, but things were getting out of hand; my body was turning frail and transparent.

Danny and I went to Illinois to visit friends for New Years. He stayed to record an album during the month of January and to get away from North Carolina. His experience with the managers of our project was even worse than mine. Danny was heartsick; for years, he had wanted to be an environmental organizer and had done incredible work for this organization. But the management took advantage of him. It was an abusive situation, and he badly needed to step away and do something different.

January of 2006 found me alone in the North Carolina mountains with rapidly-deteriorating health. Now that I no longer needed to fight my way through the job, now that I could relax, my exhausted body fell apart. In the bitter winter, I could not stay warm. I wrapped myself in blankets, sat in front of a space heater, or simply stayed curled up in bed. I rarely went outside. The winter's teeth bit into me; the mountain wind seemed to slice through my clothes. My mirror showed a pale face, growing dark-eyed and sunken, with colorless lips. Without fat absorption, I could not absorb fat-soluble nutrients.

I remember sitting in a rocking chair in the kitchen, facing the sun that fell into the apartment in long blocks of light. The heat was on; the sunlight felt warm on my face, yet my feet and hands were numb. The blanket around me was not thick enough to stop the shivering.

And yet, a real change began in my life that January. My thinking began to shift. I was starting to care about myself again. The self-loathing remained present, but less powerful. Like the need for rapid action to avoid the tornado in Virginia, I finally began to recognize that I had to take a more active role in healing myself in other ways. Up to this point, my life had been centered on surviving, hanging on. The 12 Steps, medication—these were all about keeping myself from oblivion, keeping myself from going headlong back over the edge into psychosis or suicidal depression. I always felt like those extremes were just a breath away, and all my energy had to go into protecting myself from them.

Now, having completed my work contract, I found myself with a small triumph: I'd finished the job successfully. That horrible, excruciating job. I had survived it and finished it by fighting my way through what seemed like an impossible situation. I'd given something of myself for Danny and for a larger cause—it wasn't anything huge or heroic, but it had required me to put aside my self-pity and push myself. While coping with two debilitating illnesses. Huh. Maybe I had more strength than I realized. Maybe I could put some of that same dogged energy into getting well.

And so, in January of 2006, I began to do two things to invest in caring for both my body and my soul. First, I began to reconnect with spiritual things. I needed to offer up prayers for healing but wasn't sure how to do it. I did not follow a particular tradition or worship some specific deity; instead, I prayed to a presence I thought of as God/Goddess—that entwined male-female entity I first met in a moccasin flower on Clinch Mountain years ago. I also read some books about structured prayer and ritual and learned to light candles and cast circles, to raise my energy and lift my prayers to the sky. It felt wonderful, a gentle reconnection with something precious and long lost to me.

The ritual component, in particular, helped me focus. Straight-up meditation had left me floundering in my own mind, and prayer had been extremely difficult since the divine whirlwinds of mania hit. I'd lost the experience of communing with God and Nature, of feeling those vast energies within me and around me. Whenever I began to experience that kind of connection, my brain felt like it was sliding into manic patterns, and I panicked and shut down.

But structured prayers came with a kind of recipe book—I could build a ritual and set it in motion within a circle of safety, without losing control. These were simple rituals, not like the chaotic maelstroms I built in my mind on Pine Mountain. I simply called circles and lit candles and asked God/Goddess for help healing my body.

My second new tool was research. Since the onset of digestive illness in July, I had spent hours searching the internet for some clue. Could there be a connection with my sudden discontinuation of Effexor? Or with the new medication, lamotrigine? What about water-borne illness, or chronic allergies, or—? I had researched and ingested homeopathic and herbal treatments, trying to find something, anything, to help me recover. In January, I went back and retraced my steps. I got a copy of my file from the gastroenterologist and read every page. I went over the events of the past year. What new things had happened in 2005? The two biggest shifts were the medication changes and my level of stress. 2005 had been a fast-paced, intense, painful, difficult year, following on the heels of five more excruciatingly painful, difficult years. I wondered if such a thing as cumulative stress existed.

Finally on a random alternative health website, I found the missing link. Hypochlorhydria, or low stomach acid, can knock the entire digestive system out of whack.

The syndrome didn't directly explain all my symptoms, but it could cause a cascade effect. Chronic stress could cause hypochlorhydria, and I had a massive freight of chronic stress. A simple test for the syndrome was to mix apple cider vinegar with water, sip on it, see if you feel better. I hurried to the kitchen. The effect was instantaneous. I lay back on my bed with tears slipping into my hair as the incessant low burn in my belly eased. I finally had a place to start.

It took three more months to find a balance that allowed my body to function properly again. When I got an annual physical exam with a family doctor in July, I was still anemic, my liver enzyme levels were a mess, and I had lost a quarter of my body weight. It was a crazy illness, coupled with painful struggles with work and relationship. And yet, 2005 marked the most dramatic turning point in my recovery. For the first time since my manic depressive diagnosis, I'd had to stand up and dig in and fight, unsupported. I found ways to reconnect with a Higher Power, and I learned a hell of a lot about manic depression.

In hindsight, I am amazed at how little I knew about my disease in 2005—five years after my diagnosis. Doing the research to heal my digestive system meant digging into all kinds of information about my mental illness. I poured over the prescribing information for all the medications I had taken for manic depression. I learned about the weight gain from Zyprexa and lithium. I learned about the horrible SNRI discontinuation syndrome that occurred when I quit Effexor. I learned that Dr. Sesti really was experimenting on me: in 2000, Zyprexa was not approved for long-term treatment of manic depression. I learned about the potential for suicidal thoughts and behaviors when starting some new medications, including the one that had propelled me—groping to stay alive—into the hospital in May 2001. I read and read and learned so many things that would have helped me if I'd taken the time to look them up before.

I stayed in North Carolina until early May of 2006. While slowly rebuilding my health, I looked for work. I made a little money consulting on fundraising for some non-profits and helping to plan the 2006 Bloodroot Gathering. This event would be held in West Virginia, near the region where mountaintop removal coal mining takes place. On Memorial Day, at the end of the camp, we planned a pilgrimage out to a family cemetery in the middle of an MTR mine. The mining company had "protected" the cemetery; it sat perched on a hillock in the midst of the mine's desolation. Generally, the company did not permit visitors, but in the face of public scrutiny they allowed a group of us, including descendants of the families buried in the cemetery, to make the trek.

Visiting that cemetery was among the more moving events of my life. A security guard, sweating in the heat with a gun on his hip, led us out across the sunbaked mine site, scraped clear of living things. The cemetery lay within a tiny grove of trees on a tiny tuft of land with the mine's vast moonscape all around. We went in among the trees, joined hands, and said words of grief, prayer, and hope.

Adam was there, and we walked together for a time. We'd stayed in touch in the years since the remarkable 2003 Bloodroot Gathering at Blanton Forest and continued to collaborate on projects. Later in the summer, I sent him a note about a thought that came to me on that walk to the cemetery. At Blanton Forest, in the manic heights of 2000, some words had come into my mind like guidance from beyond: "Be patient. Things will get worse before they get better, but the tide will turn and run swifter than you can dream."

For some reason, I had always interpreted this as referring to the political realm. It had never occurred to me until that day, walking up the hill to the cemetery, that it could be a message for me as well.

"Falling off the knife edge," I wrote to Adam, "was the start of things getting much worse, and the work of getting better is slow, fierce, pounding—and inside it, still only glimpsed from time to time, a clear-burning flame of something better in me than I yet can dream."

THIRTEEN

In April 2006, I got a job at a university library in Manassas, Virginia, not far from my parents' place in the D.C. suburbs. Danny was back from Illinois and dealing with a depression of his own. 2005 had been incredibly hard on him. I had played a big part with my terrible performance at the beginning and my on-going tendency toward self-centered arrogance. Between that and the organization's abuses, the job was eating him alive. In the fall, I had jokingly offered to buy him a mandolin that he'd been coveting if he'd quit in December. He laughed, sort of, and said, "Alright."

That tremendous strain between Danny and me continued into 2006. In May, he helped me move my stuff from North Carolina into my parents' basement. He stuck around at loose ends for part of the summer while I started work at the library. But the D.C. suburbs had no appeal to either of us as a place to settle. In some ways, I'm not sure why I took the job. The position paid well, and I needed a place to rest, to continue to recover my health, and to figure out what would come next, but Northern Virginia was not a good fit for Danny or for us as a couple. We pieced together a solution: I would stay at my parents' place, work, and save money while he went back out to play music. We had cell phones for the first time in our lives and could talk anytime. We would take things as they came and try to stick it out together.

From May of 2006 until August of 2008, I lived in the cool quiet of my parents' basement. After I left home for college, I had never really come back. Following my diagnosis with manic depression, I had resisted moving home for fear of becoming completely dependent. But by 2006, I was grateful for the opportunity to move back in. The basement became a place of rest and refuge, and my parents were delightful. Now that I was no longer savagely ill, we began to develop a lovely friendship between equals, between adults. Spending time with them was the greatest gift of the two years I spent in Fairfax.

During the summer of 2006, I completed my withdrawal from environmental activism. At the time, I was still serving on boards of directors for both Bloodroot and Virginia Wildlands. Something happened that summer—I can hardly remember what—some small conflict within Bloodroot that made me outrageously angry, so angry that I frightened myself. My response was way out of proportion, and I realized that I wasn't going to do anyone any good being an angry, reactive presence within these organizations.

I had so much anger, overwhelming anger—toward myself, my former employers in North Carolina, my manic depression, the politicians who were ignoring climate change and expediting coal mining in my beloved mountains, and on and on. I had to step away. I had to get better. I resigned from both organizations. Ten years after I first gave my heart to forest activism, I was done. Working in a library again. Anonymous, quiet, with no idea what to do next.

In the two years that followed, I did my best to just let go. I worked as the Evening Supervisor at the library and lived a hidden life. My work hours—from 1pm to 10pm—were pleasantly out of step with the rest of the D.C. suburbs. I dodged the endless traffic, went jogging midmorning, and grocery shopping at midnight. The job was lovely. Being responsible for a library felt like a breeze after my job in 2005—a pleasant mix of challenges and boredom. I made a handful of good friends but mostly kept to myself.

For two years, I was able to catch my breath and practice the art of feeling good again. What a remarkable thing—feeling good. My medications seemed to be working well. I was getting plenty of exercise, sleep, good food, low stress. I suddenly found myself with energy and creativity again.

In hindsight, I probably had a touch of hypomania, although perhaps it was just the joy of getting well, but there were nights at the library, especially in 2007 and 2008, when a powerful energy thrilled in my body and reached out toward the stars. When the library was quiet, I sometimes spent my nights pumping up the volume on my iPod while I shelved books, dancing in my office. I felt joyfully restless, wondering what would come next for me. I began to spend more time pondering my manic experiences—all the mythical and historical components, the quest for healing between Earth and man. What did it all mean? Did it mean anything?

The library was around the corner from the Manassas battlefield, a vast swath of golden waving grasses surrounded by D.C.'s outer suburbs. Two major Civil War battles had been fought on that ground. I would go there sometimes in the summer and wander the battlefield, picking ticks off my ankles. I tended toward the bloodiest patches—Young's Branch, where the 5th New York Zouaves lost one hundred twenty-four men in five minutes of fighting; the Confederate cemetery at Groveton with its eerie lack of gravestones, just one tall plinth to mark the unknown bones of two hundred sixty-six men buried there. In the summer, when the library closed early in the evening, I often climbed the hill to the New York monument to watch the sun set behind the distant Blue Ridge Mountains.

And yes, I did speak to ghosts there, even channeled a beautiful plea from them ("give us back the land so loved, not to own, but to befriend, to be friends"), but I was grown-up and grounded this time. Instead of trying to locate codes or cosmic solutions, I turned to fiction. Sitting at my parents' kitchen table while they were out of town during the summer of 2007, I wrote a wild, science-fiction faery tale. Multiple themes from my manic episodes swirled into the story, but best of all, it was funny—healing, joyful, silly.

I titled the story *Southeast of Twilight*, named after a town in West Virginia nearly destroyed by mountaintop removal coal mining. The heroine has manic depression and can pass back and forth between the world of the living and the world of the dead. She is aided by Bob Dylan and an army of Civil War ghosts who want to invade the living world to reverse climate change. I knew that it was loony—I wanted it that way. The writing allowed me to separate out the bright and positive themes of my active disease and spin them into a love story. And it was a love story, full of my love. In the end, the heroine—using combined forces of personal will, divine Spirit, and magic—calls a whirlwind that obliterates a mountaintop removal coal mine. She rebuilds a mountain on the site and opens the door for lost species, like the American chestnut, to return. The heroine's name is Lucy, "bringer of light."

My job gave me other unusual opportunities to explore my slow-growing confidence. One evening in the library, a powerful line of storms spawned alarms and tornados across the region. As the supervisor, I took charge of rounding up the patrons and moving them from study spaces next to the floor-to-ceiling windows into an interior safe room. As I moved around the library, I could see the sky going eerily dark; my knees turned watery, but I kept going. With the last patron safely out of the way, I paused by a window to look up and saw the clouds beginning to rotate, something descending through the trees.

I'm not sure how I got from that window to the safe room, but I arrived just in time to see a fist of wind slam the ground outside, taking down tree limbs and three light poles. A full-fledged tornado dropped from that same storm a short distance away, tore off a few roofs, and leaped the interstate. We were safe, no damage beyond the light poles, but I walked a little straighter nonetheless. I'd faced down an age old fear a second time by taking responsibility for other peoples' safety. That felt brave. That felt good.

While I tested out my strength in Virginia, Danny settled temporarily in Texas. He worked for a friend's cabinet-making business and built guitars after-hours. With much of the rest of his spare time, he went to AA meetings. His rough year in 2005 had included a lot of seriously problematic drinking. To say he hit "rock bottom" would be a misnomer, but he landed in a place of deep hurt, knowing that alcohol would continue to cause havoc in his life and undermine the good. So, he stopped. Just stopped, and began going to meetings every night.

On his walks home after meetings, he'd call me—I'd just be leaving my job at the library—and that was our time together: the best time of the day. I used my vacation leave to travel to Texas. Danny lived in the Hill Country south of Austin—a beautiful little town called Wimberley, in a house on the banks of a spring-fed river with a rope swing out front. Being apart was both lonely and good. We were healing up. At the end of 2007, we decided to get engaged.

◆

That same year, I began to encounter some of the stigmas and misunderstanding surrounding manic depression. Over the summer, after picking multiple ticks off my legs, I started feeling fevery. Worried about Lyme disease, I went to see a doctor, who discovered something new— my thyroid was enlarged, the goiter likely caused by lithium. My doctor sent me to an endocrinologist who looked at my chart, then looked me over briskly.

"Bipolar? You know, it's not really a big deal. It's just like having diabetes. I don't understand why people make it such a big deal—it's very treatable."

I stared at her, caught between embarrassment and unexpectedly intense anger. Oh really? Just like diabetes. Are diabetics usually admitted to the hospital in restraints with a needle full of anti-psychotics? Are they treated in a locked ward? Do their minds become alien and uncontrollable? I didn't say "bullshit" out loud, but it layered my tongue and choked me.

For seven years, I had kept my diagnosis a tightly-held secret from all but my closest family and friends. When it came up in the 12 Step Fellowship, no one seemed to judge; even if they weren't familiar with the disease, most addicts understood the experience of helplessness, despair, loss of self, shame.

But hearing a medical professional say something so clueless and cavalier stunned me. I'm sure that her motive was to be reassuring and kind, but it felt like a kick in the gut. This mental illness—mental *otherness*—that had ravaged my life was a HUGE deal. Very treatable? Sure, I suppose, if you're lucky enough to get a good doctor and find medications that actually work—it had "only" taken me five years to get truly effective treatment.

But her statement reflected a more profound misunderstanding. Any chronic illness is a hard and heavy thing to carry, often changing peoples' lives radically. But manic depression had obliterated me—my identity, my confidence, my spirit and sense of self. My *mind* had betrayed me. For years, I had no idea how I should feel, how I could feel, what it meant to be human, to have emotions. For years, I had no idea who I was—all sense of prior identity was stripped away by my extreme behaviors, the diagnosis and hospitalizations and medications and shame.

Although it did not kill me, I lost my life to manic depression. In this brief conversation with the endocrinologist, I began to understand how few people would understand this, how few would fathom the devastating grief and terror of losing control of one's mind and of one's freedom.

For many years, I had dealt with this reality by hiding my diagnosis. Only my family, my closest friends, and the people who had been part of my life during the uncontrolled period of my illness knew. I never told an employer or a new friend. In a very real sense, I stigmatized myself rather than letting someone else do it to me. This put an immediate distance into all my relationships. I had a secret, and I used it as a shield.

I had good reason for hiding my identity. People can be ignorant and unkind. When I left my job at the library in 2008, the staff and patrons had a going-away party for me. I sat with a piece of cake in front of me untouched while I listened to a conversation unfold around me. A medical student who frequently studied at the library was describing her training rotation in a psychiatric ward. Those crazy people. She was always afraid that they would hurt her. Especially those manic patients. Oh my god. The things they would say... She went on.

Colleagues and library patrons were laughing at the story. I felt like I was going to pass out; my hands shook, and that old familiar sweat ran down my spine, leaving trails of shame on my skin. The words sat on the back of my tongue—"I have manic depression. I am manic depressive." I could not say them out loud.

Among my library friends that day, I observed something very common, encountered time and again—a desire among many people to distance themselves from mental illness. I can understand why. It is frightening to consider losing control of one's mind, and no one can know with absolute certainty that it will not happen to them. So we turn the mentally ill into the Other, laugh at them, or diminish their experiences into something comic or tragic, leaving no middle ground.

◆

My first steps toward going public with my illness were very slow. My parents and Loki had nudged me over the years to talk to people who shared my diagnosis. With Catherine in my life and the 12 Step program, I felt like I had enough support, so I resisted my parents' efforts.

Loki had a bit more success. He had remained a brother to me over the years, finding small ways to help me heal, including bringing two people into my life who gave me some comfort. In 2001, the heart of my first depression, he introduced me to his long-distance girlfriend, Natasha. I remember sitting with them in a restaurant, struggling with words to explain my condition while anxious chills flashed hot then cold across my skin. Natasha had taken lithium for a time; I was never quite clear on her diagnosis, but she was such a lovely, grounded, brighthearted spirit that she gave me a glimmer of hope.

Loki also reminded me about a well-known forest activist and mutual acquaintance who'd been quite public about his manic depressive condition. He regularly attended a wilderness gathering that I helped to organize in Virginia. The man hugged me when I confessed my story and winked, "We should start a new group—call it Bipolar Bears for Wilderness."

These were not small steps, simply saying the words out loud to relative strangers took enormous effort. Perhaps, in hindsight, I was fortunate that the first instance of a truly public revealing happened unexpectedly and from an unexpected quarter. Although I had resigned from my official role in Bloodroot, I continued to go, when I could, to Reunions and Gatherings to see friends and stay in touch.

For the 2009 Bloodroot Gathering in Kentucky, Adam asked me to give a short talk to the whole group, a kind of mini-keynote. I was thrilled and spent hours putting together my ideas. I would speak about the concepts I'd described in *A Patchwork Theology of Soil Liberation* long ago, about the challenges of working to save the land because the land has been imbued with the traumas of the past.

Adam introduced me. We'd had our usual sporadic interactions over the past many years—always friendly and loving but more infrequent in the last year or two since I'd resigned from the Bloodroot board. He seemed off-kilter at this event—frustrated, tired, and unhappy. But I was astonished when Adam stated in his introduction that I'd survived an intense psychotic episode, that I'd gone through a wormhole and come back intact.

Later, while apologizing repeatedly, he tried to explain why he'd introduced me that way: he'd meant to express admiration for my strength and resilience, not to shame me in front of my peers. But his intentions didn't matter. I had walked to the podium with my jaw hanging open, mouthing the words, "What are you doing?!" to Adam. I had stood in front of the audience, my shirt already damp from the usual embarrassed sweat that accompanied acknowledgment of my manic depression.

But I gave the speech anyway, as I intended, ignoring Adam and his words. I was proud of myself for pulling it off and furious with Adam. How could he, of all people, after all we'd been through, think that it would be ok to "out" me in front of my peers? Although the Bloodroot community was probably one of the safest places to be outed, my intense fear of stigma descended like a gray cloak. People must be looking at me strangely, I thought. I wondered if they'd listened to my talk differently since they had Adam's description of me in their minds.

I thought that might be the end of my friendship with Adam. I stayed angry at him for at least a year. Since 2000, the ambiguity and intensity of our friendship had often been exhausting; in my mind, he was always freighted with the astonishing strangeness of our times together on Pine Mountain. I couldn't think of that place and time without thinking of him, and I couldn't look at Adam without at least an echo of embarrassment about my bizarre brain. And now this. It broke my heart.

He wrote me a beautiful letter that summer, full of apology and appreciation for me and for our friendship. I read it once and thought seriously about burning it. Instead, I put the letter away in a filing cabinet and forgot about it. When I discovered Adam's letter again, years later, my life was very different. I was able to hear the love in his words and realized—to my great surprise—that being outed in 2009 had been a gift. I had not dissolved into tears or run away; I had stood on that stage and said the words that I wanted to say. Adam's introduction had created an opportunity to find another interior reservoir of strength.

♦

My next "outing" was self-selected and deliberate. After Danny and I got engaged in December 2007, we began to look at options that would allow us to live in the same place. I hemmed and hawed—life was so easy in my parents' basement—but finally made a decision to go to grad school. I didn't have much sense of direction or a particular career goal; I just wanted to see if I could do it. Academics had always been a strong suit for me—I loved school. Could I, as a fairly-functional manic depressive, complete a Master's degree?

I picked History because of my fascination with Virginia's traumatic past but ended up studying more recent times—20th century environmental history in the Shenandoah Valley—at a university in Harrisonburg, Virginia. I loved being back at school and out of the suburbs, but it was a high-stress, often painful time. I found that I could do the academics—I had the intellectual capacity and skills—but I could not keep up the pace. As an undergraduate, pulling all-nighters was no big deal, but now, with this disease, any kind of sleep disruption had destabilizing consequences. The stress of juggling multiple simultaneous assignments was impossible. At the end of the semester, I gathered my courage and registered with the university's Disability Resource Center.

Until that fall, it had never occurred to me that my illness counted as a disability, yet it fit the legal definition by substantially limiting one or more of my major life activities. As usual, I felt embarrassed and uncomfortable taking this step; it seemed like an admission of weakness. I still had an internalized concept that I should always be self-sufficient: "I can handle it!" But at the same time, registering with the DRC felt courageous. I had taken responsibility for myself and my needs, figured out a strategy to cope with the realities of manic depression. I wasn't ducking out of work, just asking for extra flexibility, extra time. My professors responded beautifully and gave me exactly what I needed. I ended up loving the experience of grad school, my research, and my thesis advisor. The History department selected my thesis as the best in my graduating class.

Meanwhile, the folks in the Disability Resources Center made a lasting impression on me with their kindness and gentleness. Even at age thirty-four, I went in quaking in my boots. The director who reviewed my file gave off a palpable sense of empathy. Afterward, she introduced me to her colleague, who looked to be about my age, saying, "Anthony knows a lot about stress reduction." He grinned and shook my hand like an old friend, "Hey! How're you doing? What do you know about Buddhist meditation?" We talked for a while in his office, decorated with brightly-colored Father's Day paintings by his young daughters, and I left feeling lighter.

When I graduated in 2010, I decided to continue in the education world and try getting a Master of Fine Arts in Creative Non-fiction. I didn't want to go into a PhD program in History, but I liked the idea of teaching in academia. West Virginia University admitted me to its MFA program with a full-ride and a teaching assistantship. I would get classroom teaching experience. It would be another opportunity to push myself.

Danny was supportive as usual. He had moved with me to Harrisonburg in 2008 and found it to be a challenging place to get his footing. He kept being offered jobs that didn't pan out. Meanwhile, I was stressing my way through the first semester of grad school. That first winter, the conflict in our relationship grew almost to the breaking point. We had a standard fight that occurred over and over: he'd calmly express a concern or frustration with something I said or did; I'd get immediately angry and defensive; he'd become upset that I couldn't just hear him out; and then the conflict would escalate. I had not yet learned how to live beyond myself, how to empathize with Danny in our day-to-day life. So much of my energy still remained protectively focused inward. And he was tired, lonely in a new city where neither of us knew a soul.

By 2009, positive things began to unfold for Danny—he started his own guitar repair company and spent a few weeks on the road playing music with an old friend. By the time I graduated in 2010, Danny had a job building guitars in Staunton, Virginia, just south of Harrisonburg. He agreed to rent an apartment there for us to share while I rented a dorm room in Morgantown, WV. I commuted home most weekends. Right from the start, I felt pretty sure that I wouldn't complete the degree at WVU. It was a three year program, and the distance from Danny seemed unsustainable; the time-consuming work of teaching two classes per semester pushed my own writing projects to the side. In spite of wonderful colleagues and professors, I didn't think I could keep up with the program and wasn't sure that I wanted to.

In October of 2010, I took a weekend trip to Maine to attend a memorial service for my maternal grandmother. She had died in June, but we delayed the memorial until all the family could be there. It was a lovely time together, preceded by a very busy week with many late nights doing homework and prepping to teach. While in Maine, I felt my mood begin to topple, a rapid sinking in my body and mind that would have once terrified me, thinking that I was descending into full-blown depression. My brother asked if my feelings were caused by sorrow over my grandmother's passing.

"No," I said. "This is something different. It's manic depressive depression, not grief. It's my brain acting up."

It was a surreal experience. Thoughts of suicide meandered through my head, along with gut-clenching sensations of despair, and yet I could separate myself from them. The thoughts and feelings were induced by my illness, not my soul. I could treat them as symptoms. And so, I took care of myself. I canceled class for the day after I returned from Maine. I talked to Dr. McLean and made a temporary adjustment to my medication. I slept for 15 hours after returning from the airport, then took a walk in the sunlight. I spent the week being gentle with myself. Within a short time, I felt well again. Manic depression was slowly becoming familiar to me, still unpredictable and mysterious, but perhaps, at least sometimes, an illness that I could navigate.

FOURTEEN

2011 was my watershed year. A cascade of events pushed me to get well on a new level. As in 2005, the final catalyst that forced me to take responsibility for my healing was Danny, and specifically my desire not to lose him. I was home from Morgantown on winter break, and we'd had a series of spectacular fights. As I brought him coffee one morning, trying to be sweet and make up, he said, "You know, I have my own demons, but when you're not here, I never go to sleep angry. I never wake up angry."

That hurt like a slap in the face. He was happier without me. And I was lonely and sad. The fall semester had been good in many ways, but I was exhausted. I felt independent, yes, but it was a dragging independence. So I had the strength to pull heavy weights around behind me on my own, so what? Danny's comment woke a desperation in me. I didn't know what else to do. I had tried to change my attitude, my way of dealing with the world and with him, but I still had this terrible habit of taking my hurts and angers and fears out on him. What could I do to get better? One more self-help book, one more plan for behavioral change, one more round of counseling, talking and talking but getting nowhere? I had done so much of that over the years and nothing seemed to stick.

Later that day, memories of another fight we'd had earlier in the fall came to my mind. We were driving out to a party in Danny's truck. I said something mean, and he told me that he didn't like it. For some reason, that time, I noticed my response: the nerves in my body yanked taught, my fists knotted, my shoulders ducked into a defensive crouch. I was physically primed for a fight—not just a war of words but a vehement body-based need to defend myself that was far, far out of proportion from the momentary disagreement between Danny and me.

The memory stuck, and in the days after Christmas, as I struggled to figure out what the heck to do next, my manic depressive tendency to link together divergent ideas kicked into gear, and pieces began to fall into place. First: The medical emergency I'd had as a child—the ruptured appendix at age eight—had haunted me all of my life. My memories of that near-death experience and the traumatic hospitalization remained excruciatingly clear nearly thirty years later, along with the memory of sorrow that surrounded the event. Since then, I'd felt a tremendous protectiveness toward my body, especially the deep double-scar that marred my lower abdomen. I'd carried a life-long intense defensiveness: an instinctive, hair-trigger reactivity that saw everything as a threat, including and sometimes especially my kind-hearted sweetheart, Danny.

Second: Years ago, in the drug rehab program that followed my last hospitalization in 2002, a counselor mentioned a form of therapy called EMDR—eye movement desensitization and reprocessing. We'd reviewed my medical history during the rehab intake process, and I'd told her about the appendicitis and my disturbing, recurring memories.

She said, "It sounds like you have post-traumatic stress disorder."

I laughed uncomfortably—I didn't like this counselor at all. She was hostile and mocking to other participants in our group therapy sessions.

"Really," she said, "it's true. You have flashbacks, nightmares, body memories, right?"

"Sometimes, yeah," I said.

She proceeded to tell me about EMDR and described a bit of the process.

"You'd either follow my fingers back and forth with your eyes, or listen to tones in one ear and then the other." It sounded like hypnosis to me. No way.

"I can take your insurance!" She looked overly-eager, as though I was a particularly intriguing lab rat, and it creeped me out.

"No. No thank you." I left quickly, out into a gray rain that coated the streets.

Eight years later, as a grad student at the university in Harrisonburg in 2010, I was seeing another counselor—a very different kind of lady—who worked in the on-campus counseling center. Danny had read a book about bipolar disorder that recommended both medication and therapy as treatment. I went to the counseling center at his urging and met a wonderful woman named Cheryl.

"Just keep coming by," she said once we reached the university's eight-session limit. "We'll hang out for an hour unofficially. I like talking with you." A year into our time together, my appendicitis experience came up, and Cheryl too said, "Your symptoms sound like PTSD." I protested that PTSD was a much bigger deal—something that happened to combat veterans and victims of natural disasters, not a sick eight-year-old.

"No, that's not true," she said. "PTSD is what happens to people who experience any kind of trauma and then have after-effects that disrupt their lives."

In my 2011 midwinter desperation, as I sought to heal my relationship with Danny, the pieces began to line up: perhaps my reactivity, my defensiveness, my wound-up-tight, fight-or-flight fears had a connection to PTSD from a long-ago yet terrifying medical emergency. I remembered the rehab counselor's recommendation of EMDR therapy and poked around on the web. Searching "post-traumatic stress and eye movement" brought up pages of information about EMDR. The practice still seemed peculiar to me, but the American Psychiatric Association, the Department of Defense, and the Veterans Administration all recommended it for treatment of PTSD. My graduate assistantship provided good health insurance; I had nothing to lose.

By some remarkable grace, an EMDR practitioner lived just an hour away from Morgantown in rural Pennsylvania. Paula was a retired psychiatric nurse and a trauma specialist. In addition to her counseling work, she went to disaster sites with the Red Cross to offer trauma assistance. She was the real deal.

On my first visit, I told Paula that I'd done years of talk therapy counseling and had never been able to touch some of the most troubling aspects of my personality, like being constantly alert to possible dangers all around me...

"Oh, that's called hypervigilance," she told me blithely.

...Or my habit of frightening myself, staying always on edge by looking for worst-case scenarios, trying to figure out just how bad or dangerous any given situation could be.

"That's right," she said. "Very common. It's called catastrophization."

"You're kidding," I said. "Catastrophization? There's a name for it?"

"Oh yes. Yes, you have PTSD alright. Come back next week." She grinned.

I cried the entire drive home. Something told me that I had just tapped a deep and important vein in my life's story. I felt grateful and broken all at the same time. The scar tissue in my abdomen burned and twisted.

For five months, through the long winter and slow spring, I carved out time between classes at WVU to drive to Pennsylvania twice a week for sessions with Paula. I have never worked as emotionally hard as I did with EMDR therapy. The process was strange and grueling. Paula speculated that this was because my trauma was so old and deeply-ingrained in the habits of my life. For someone dealing with a more recent experience, the process would be difficult in other ways, she said, but the trauma itself would be easy to locate.

In my case, I was chasing down childhood memories and encountering the depth of fear I had experienced at age eight. Events that would be minor to an adult had been terrifying to me as a child. One particularly visceral memory involved the smell of the rubber oxygen mask being lowered over my face as I struggled on the operating table. In another memory, I remembered frequently imagining what it would be like if I had died. I could see my gravestone, twined with ivy. I could feel the crushing sorrow of my family as they came to visit. I remembered receiving a transfusion: how strange it felt to lie still watching someone else's blood flow into my arm. And when an IV needle came loose in my vein one night, I woke covered in blood. And my incredible envy when school friends came to visit: They could leave! They weren't tied up to beeping machines and dripping bags! And they could eat! I longed for food to chew and swallow instead of fluid nutrients pumped into my arm for 21 days.

I remembered the near-death experience itself with a howling clarity. Sitting on the invisible window sill hovering above the bed, looking down at my small, overheated body. I could feel my unbearable skin—fever raging, the brutal cold of the hypothermic pad making me scream. I remembered the grief and longing: I did not understand what the window represented, just wanted to cross through and be among the golden sunlit fields on the other side. At the same time, feeling the complicated confusion of not wanting to leave or hurt my family. My parents' faces were so full of fear, hardly believing what was happening as they watched me begin to die. My child's mind interpreted it all as my fault. So much pain for a little kid.

I remembered tastes and smells—the blessed alcohol rub that preceded the cool hush of morphine, that drench of narcotics taking the raw teeth out of my pain, and then the anger inside me when the doctor told the nurses to stop the pain shots because I liked them too much. Such a

short period of time—not quite a month in the hospital—
yet so deeply inscribed in my life. A weary sadness lay
over me during those days and beyond. Sadness that I
could not run or play in the beautiful springtime, wondering in the back of my brain if I would ever recover, and
my family's intense emotions of fear, grief, and worry that
my childhood radar picked up and carried without understanding.

Most days, Paula and I interspersed discussion of
memories and current physical and emotional reactions
with the eye movements. We would gauge the level of
distress a memory caused to me, and then the eye movements, back and forth, whittling down the memory until
it lost its power. Paula explained the theories about why
EMDR worked:

"Because of the way trauma occurs, the memories become embedded in our brains without being processed.
Sometimes, we might not even understand what happened—like you as a kid. You didn't really understand."

"No. They explained it to me, but I didn't understand.
And I didn't know that I'd almost died."

Paula nodded. "Exactly. EMDR is helping you pull out
the memories of the experience and file them in healthier
places. It's not that you'll forget. No, no, no. The memories aren't dulled or minimized in their importance, just
that they lose the incredible power to... Well, for example—" she pointed at my abdomen, "—make a thirty-year-

old appendectomy scar feel like it's going to bust wide open."

For months of my therapy, my scar became almost torturous. I would lie awake at night in the half-light of my apartment, curling first into a fetal ball, then stretching out my side, trying to stop the agony in that scar. It burned, and the pain was full of terror. Sometimes I could feel the scalpel in my flesh and had to bite down hard on my pillow to keep from screaming. Only months into the EMDR treatment did I realize how bizarre it was: my scar was healed and had been for decades; the organs beneath the scar functioned just fine. All of the burning, aching, bursting feelings were a fiction, played out by some terror in my brain.

That realization was a breakthrough for me, emerging from the maze of traumatized memory into an understanding of my body's physical reality. I remember when it hit me; I was driving back to Staunton after a session with Paula in Pennsylvania. The pressure of the seatbelt against my scar became almost unbearable. I squirmed and twisted, finally pulling over to unbuckle the seatbelt and get out of the car. "How in the hell did I live through thirty years like this?" And then it hit me. I had in fact lived. I had lived nearly thirty years beyond that terrible illness. My body had healed a long, long time ago. I felt astonishment and a slow-dawning sense of freedom. The fear inside my scar had been so powerful that it could erase reality. All these years. All these many years.

Before EMDR, I had no idea how deeply I distrusted life. The world was full of threats. Everywhere, all the time. It had long felt safer to veil myself from life and distance myself from my body. But, much like lithium, years ago, had opened up a space inside me for healing to begin, EMDR opened space for me to learn a few things about trust.

The EMDR process helped me to be calmer, more relaxed, with more space in my brain. I didn't have to worry so much, to spend so much time building barriers in my mind to keep myself safe. I began to ponder the concept of trust. Learning to trust myself, to trust my body's strength and ability, to trust the world and the universe. Tragedy is real and most everyone meets with it from time to time, but focusing my life around it meant that I was losing my life. Safety is both an illusion and a reality. If I believe that we live in the hands of god (and I do), then there is a greater safety beyond the unpredictable dangers of our daily lives—an overarching, encompassing safety.

I called Adam early in 2011. By the beginning of the spring semester, I knew that I would drop out of the MFA program in May. I was pondering other possibilities, including applying to online MFAs that I could do from Staunton. Because of the many projects we'd worked on together, I'd asked Adam to write a recommendation letter for me to get into grad school, and I needed him to send another copy. When I called, he seemed grateful to hear from me.

"I've been wanting to call you, to talk," he said. "I've had your number out on my desk for the last week." Adam had been through a harrowing time over the winter holidays—a health emergency and a time of darkness that followed, a confusing transition.

"I'm sorry that it's been hard for you," I said and then paused. "But, you know, Adam, I think it's going to be really good for you to go through some dark times." It was an odd thing to say—I knew it as the words left my mouth—and Adam seemed a bit put off. But I was certain in my bones that it was true and felt excited for him to see what would come next. He was retiring from activism—really, finally, stepping back and away after twenty-plus years of leading Bloodroot.

I sat on the couch for a long time after we hung up, looking at my hands and wondering. Always when Adam was around, doors seemed to open in my mind. My intense anger with him in 2009 had eased away over the years. I couldn't bring myself to ditch the friendship, although he remained a sore spot, a representation of the emergence of my mental illness. And yet that on-going inexplicable familiarity and dearness held me. I wanted to understand it, to hear Adam's perspective, to find an explanation, but I didn't have energy—not now. Still, he came to mind from time to time over the following months. As my EMDR sessions dug shards of traumatic memory out of my body, I wondered if Adam too was digging—trying to excavate his darknesses and find the next phase of living.

During the spring semester at WVU, I took a non-fiction workshop and started writing this book. I felt nauseous and terrified when I brought the first two chapters in to be workshopped. Showing this material to my class of twelve would substantially increase the number of people who knew my diagnosis. I had told so few people over the years. Even as we discussed my writing in the neutral voices of academia, I felt ashamed, embarrassed, wondering if my fellow students would now question my abilities and assume things about me based on my mental illness.

Yet that first day of publicly sharing my story brought a remarkable gift. One of my peers told me that, after reading the draft, she'd called a friend and apologized. The friend had manic depression. My classmate had never understood why he acted the way he did. She thanked me for giving her insight into a person she cared about deeply. It gave me a reason to keep on writing: telling my story could expand understanding of manic depression and perhaps help with healing.

Meanwhile, home life with Danny began to improve. Our standard pattern of conflict—The Fight—occurred with less frequency and virulence. We had more room for our other great love—talking and pondering the mysteries of the world. Dialing down a lifetime of defensive reactivity on my part proved to be slow going, but Danny was interested in the process of EMDR and sympathetic. I think we both held out hope that this would help us transition to a kinder, calmer relationship. When I told him that I planned to leave the MFA program, Danny encouraged me.

"Don't get a job right away unless you have to," he said. "I can bottom line rent. Take a break, step back for a little while and figure out what you're doing."

In early May, after classes had finished but before the semester was done, I drove home from Morgantown through a lovely spring evening. My route took me past Berkeley Springs, WV, a pretty resort town near the Virginia border. The springs bubbled up in the middle of a park, so I left my shoes in the car and wandered through the grass to the pools and waterways that crisscrossed the grounds. Sunset was beginning to soften the air, turning it pink and cool. I felt a remarkable peace and gentleness, just breathing and walking, greeting others in the park without fear. Being so calm inside felt incredibly odd to me; usually, I carried anxiety around like a heavy handbag. This quieter state reminded me of another time. When did I last feel this way? So glad to be alive, so at peace in the universe, in the hands of god?

When it struck me, I was caught between laughter and anger. Hypomania had felt just like this, back in the spring of 2000, when fear left me and joy took its place. Before I jumped the barriers between sane and insane, for a couple of months, I had simply felt really, really good: free in my body, free in my interactions. Now in 2011, I was grounded and stable but still felt good—really good. Wow... I thought, I wonder if it's possible to live this way?

In early June, Danny and I decided to get married—in July. The sudden decision occurred because my health insurance policy from WVU was set to expire. If we married, I could be on his insurance at work. We'd been engaged nearly four years, so why not? We had a tiny, sweet wedding in Staunton with immediate family. Our big day turned out to also be the hottest day of the year, so instead of standing under the trees on the courthouse lawn as planned, our friends locked the door on their music store for half an hour so we could say our vows in the air conditioning. Appropriately, given Danny's love of guitars, our wedding pictures have rows of musical instruments for a backdrop.

With Danny's generosity, I was able to lean back that summer, relax, and write. It was scary, exciting, and hard to write with as much honesty as I could summon about my experience with manic depression. With the rest of my time, I looked for jobs and mostly just meandered through my days. My mind drifted. Little tasks like putting away laundry could take up an entire morning. Not because of depression or boredom this time, it was just that I could allow myself to be slow and easily distracted. I would sit on the back porch for hours watching things: sunlight turning emerald as it passed through summer leaves, crimson cardinals hopping on the power line, spinnakers of rain that dropped from a sudden thunderstorm, the spiraled petals of red roses growing in a broken brown bucket.

I felt strange. On the one hand, I saw myself as an unkept promise; all the potential of my younger life—the academic excellence and passionate activism—seemed played out and gone. My college friends were accomplishing great things, while I had no profession, no real achievements, no particular goals. On the other hand, I felt happier than I'd ever been, enjoying the process of withdrawing from my stress addiction, resting, letting my mind become still. Trying to trust the process, to feel my way along to the next right thing.

FIFTEEN

In October, I drove with EQ to the annual Reunion out at Adam and Danielle's farm in Ohio. It was good to be there, good to see them and Loki and other old friends. Adam's retirement from Bloodroot put us in similar places—standing in a transition zone, uncertain of which way to go next. But while I was learning to be more relaxed and happy, Adam seemed terribly sad. It felt like we had both now come down from the mountaintop and become our simple, scared, fragile human selves.

When EQ and I left, early on Monday morning, Adam and another friend met us at the car. As I hugged Adam goodbye, the history of heartache and hurt between us ran through my mind, stretching back to Pine Mountain and that golden light, that door between worlds. Tears came fast into my eyes, and I wanted to step away from him and hold on to him at the same time.

Then something odd happened, something new. I could see a light begin to dawn behind my closed eyes—a clear light rising, easing out and surrounding us both, so lovely, blending with the morning sun that tangled in the trees, and growing, radiating, so bright I knew that our friends standing nearby must see it. I wasn't crazy or high, I swear—nine and a half years clean, nowhere close to manic. Instead, it felt like a wordless, shared prayer to sweep out the sorrow. *I remember everything.*

I stared out the car window as EQ and I drove away. My heart felt shaky, sore, and strange. Watching the forest around their place give way to farm fields, I wondered at that goodbye, at that light, and my bond with Adam all these years. I shook my head. He had been such a tumultuous force. Did I really want this connection, and this man, in my life? A thought came into my mind then, immediate and quite clear: "You don't get to choose. This is something that *is* and will remain."

Yes, I thought. Yes, I knew that.

I'd never fully trusted Adam before or been sure if I could believe him when he spoke of treasuring our friendship and connection. But what if Adam had actually meant what he'd said, and I had been too stubborn or scared or self-conscious to believe it? The glowing light around us that morning felt like confirmation.

The possibility of coming to peace with Adam started a cascade of thoughts: maybe I don't need to understand everything or always be in control, maybe I don't need to constantly protect myself from what other people might think or do. Maybe I really can relax and trust—not just Adam, but everything: my manic depressive brain, my ability to live with honesty and honor and courage in this world. Trust.

Adam seemed like a lynch pin once again. This friendship that had confused me for so long and been so deeply tied to my first manic trauma, now felt suddenly, extraordinarily simple. Really, it didn't matter what exactly had happened on Pine Mountain or why we shared this bond. It was enough just that the friendship existed. My goodness, what a concept—to trust, relax, let go, appreciate the joy of existence, appreciate the existence of love.

I gazed out the window for a long moment, resting my thoughts on these novel ideas. Could I be sane and stable and also experience seemingly impossible things, like a great glowing light that surrounds a friendship? Could I be healthy and crazy at the same time?

Hmmm… I would like that.

EQ's car zipped down the two lane through farmland and forest, the golds and ambers of autumn framing a perfect blue sky. In my mind, I began composing a note to send to Adam. Perhaps I would title it, "I saw the light." I grinned. I might have laughed out loud.

EQ glanced over at me, smiling.

"Are you alright?"

"What?" I turned from my thoughts to look at him, feeling brilliantly happy. I had turned a corner. "Oh yes, EQ. I am so good."

I would close the letter to Adam with these words: "Whatever our connection is, wherever it comes from, wherever it goes, fighting against it seems to generate pain. Embracing it brings more love into the world. I get that now. A love and a light and grace and gratitude." I smiled at the orange stripes of sun slanting through the autumn trees. Thought of Danny back at home, the quiet joys of our life together, the great love and strength and grace and gratitude he brought into my life.

"I am a lucky gal, EQ."

"Yeah?" He grinned.

"Incredibly lucky. Amazingly lucky! Fortunate in my family, and friends like you."

♦

June 2012: The crowd sat in front of us, a sea of grinning faces of friends and neighbors that I'd known all my life. EQ and Loki had seats in the front. Gabe and Erin sat together a few rows back; they'd been friends of Danny's for years before I'd met any of them. Ruby and James laughed and hugged my parents. My brother leaned against the wall where he'd been chatting with Catherine. Danny and I stood in front, dressed up and giddy, grinning back at this gathering of beloved people here to celebrate us and our marriage. The tiny wedding that had occurred last summer gave us legal status, but this was the real celebration.

Danny had organized the music; I had written the ceremony. We sat down together to review the plan just an hour before the event began, so everything was slap dash and improvisational. The ceremony had rapidly turned into a comedy act, with us playfully riffing off each other to the audience's laughter. Now came the serious part.

"This is the time when we talk about each other and say nice things," Danny said.

I stepped up to the mic and smiled at him. "I'll start." I had written out what I wanted to say but set it aside. I would remember.

"I've noticed in the past year or so, that when people ask me how I'm doing, my answer tends to be, 'I'm great! Things are really, really good.' It wasn't always this way. Danny and I first got together in a pretty dark and difficult time of my life. I'd usually say something like, 'I'm doing ok, hanging in there.' I can attribute that shift in attitude almost entirely to Danny." In the audience, I saw Gabe and Erin look at each other and smile.

I choked up for a moment—a flush of memories—and pulled out my notes.

"Maybe I should read this after all," I muttered in the microphone. The audience laughed. I turned to Danny and addressed myself to him: "You have a stubborn refusal to live a life that's focused on 'NO,' on being negative, or harping on the dark and difficult parts of life. 'Those times will come'—you like to say—'so why make the good times bad?'" I heard the audience shift, saw people nodding.

I continued: "'Sorrow and loss are always with us,' you tell me, 'but dwelling there is a waste of this precious gift we have, this time together on this planet, as part of this community, as friends and sweethearts.' You show that to me every day as you breeze around town saying, 'Thanks for making today the best day of my life!'"

Danny looked a little teary-eyed, a lopsided smile on his face. I continued, "When we first met, I thought that was just the way you were—that you had a light-hearted personality, and you do. But I know now that it is not just boyish goofiness that keeps you going, it is the work of a man seeking to let his light shine in the world." Now he was definitely teary-eyed. "You make a conscious effort, every day, to be a joy bringer, and your generosity has transformed me and my life."

I folded the paper and smiled at Danny. He had taught me through his combination of love and boundaries that I could take responsibility for my health and my actions; that I could make full use of my strength, capabilities, and creativity; that I didn't have to be afraid. He had taught me so much about joy.

♦

Late on an October afternoon in 2012, I climbed over the blue boulders in the Tye River beside Matthew's land, tucking my bare feet against damp moss and lichen. I had recently started spending time with Matthew again after many years. Loki had invited us both over for dinner, and we'd sat on the couch telling jokes and cracking each other up. A few weeks later, we both went on a group hike up Massanutten Mountain and spent the whole time catching up, watching for wildflowers, and exclaiming over the American chestnut stump sprouts along the trail. It was a pleasure to remember why I'd enjoyed Matthew's company so much years ago and another great joy to find that Matthew and Danny hit it off tremendously well. Danny and I lived in Staunton now, in the Shenandoah Valley, two miles from Loki's house and thirty miles, give or take, from Matthew's land by the Tye, this gorgeous place in the Blue Ridge.

The October day was fantastic—one of those blue sky autumn afternoons that make the Virginia mountains heavenly. I'd come out here alone a handful of times over the years, slithering down the steep slope from the road and wading through the rapid water. Wandering the quiet forest here usually brought a mix of emotions—gratitude to be again in this gorgeous place mixed with hints of that old longing for the manic whirlwind.

Today, I needed some time in the forests, time to think big thoughts and renew my mind. I paused on a broad rock part way across the river to take deep breaths of cooling air and listen to the gurgling rush. I thought about coming here with Adam and Matthew back in 2000, the last cleansing before my manic pilgrimage into that golden mountain light. I leaned back, looking at the sky and lacing my fingers across my belly. *I don't miss it anymore.* The words came into my heart, so quiet and true that they startled me. I don't miss it. I don't miss the chaos and fever, or the mirage of unbridled, infinite freedom in mania. I don't miss it. I know where it leads.

Above me, the twisting hands of sycamore leaves reminded me of my poetic dreaming at the turn of the millennium. The season of friendship, the healing of kinship. My grand quests, seeking to heal Virginia's squalid history. I still believed in those things. My heart still rang with the truth of that need. And the ghosts still whispered, the Earth wept and sang to me, but I no longer carried an unrealistic burden. No longer lived in panic that I wasn't doing it right, that I hadn't figured out the puzzle, and that the healing was entirely my responsibility—mine alone. No. I was human again, not supernatural. I smiled to myself, thinking that even a super hero would need stronger super powers than lithium to fix human brokenness.

Somewhere along the line, I had stopped looking backwards. The life I'd left behind no longer filled me with yearning. It seemed now like one particularly dramatic piece of my story, not the sole defining moment. Besides, my latest incarnation was really good. A quiet life, a ton of love, a great job.

In March of 2012, I'd started working at the same Disability Resources Center where I'd registered as a grad student three years before. Anthony, the smiling staff person who'd talked with me about Buddhist meditation, hired me to help students needing assistive technologies and alternative formats. He and my other colleagues were inspiring as proponents of disability rights and self-advocacy; they encouraged students to speak openly about their disabilities when they felt ready. In my application cover letter, I had mentioned my disability and this book, but I had not—so far—shared my diagnosis with many people. Why would I want to volunteer for stigma?

But there was a growing sense in me that I needed to stop stigmatizing myself and find my voice again. When Danny and I threw our wedding party last summer, our dear friend Erin had said to Danny, "She's doing so well. She really needs to be helping other people with manic depression." And just a few weeks ago, the university's new president had given a speech on diversity. He quoted a basketball player from Rutgers; she and her teammates had just been racially stereotyped and insulted by a radio DJ. The team responded with public grace, inviting the DJ to meet with them in person. When asked why, the player said, "We want people to see who we are. We want to be recognized and valued for who we are."

The words rattled around in my head. People with diagnoses of mental illness are stereotyped and discriminated against; we should be recognized and valued for who we are. And yet, why on earth would I want to go public about such a deeply feared and misunderstood illness? People will label me with this diagnosis, and that will undermine the respect I have gained—why would I risk that? Why?

I stretched again, tipping my head back along the rock so my chest lifted toward the sky. I could feel my heartbeat in my brain. Why. Because I am not a monster, nor a caricature. I exhaled and spread my arms wide across the boulder. I had learned and benefited from and, in a sense—no, really, for real—had come to love this illness. It remained intensely difficult, with times of rawness and anger and fear, but what deep relationship does not include such things? And besides, this condition had shaped my thoughts and creativity and wisdom; it created and re-created my mind, and I loved my mind.

I sighed and sat up. A few tears had slipped from the corners of my eyes, and my heart echoed with old hurts. I will not let my diagnosis be all that defines me—but I do not want to be someone who hides.

The sun had shifted in the sky and fell now at an angle over the Tye. It captured the reds and golds in the leaves, amplifying the colors so that the whole space—from the river to the mountains to the sky—seemed to vibrate. I wanted to get up to my favorite spot on Matthew's land—the wide flat stone, my kneeling place—and spend some time in meditation before the day began to darken, but not yet.

This rock in the river held me. Power and mystery in the stones and the curling, constant water that sculpted these mountains. Nature and Love and God. Unknowable things: huge, yet close at hand, in my heartbeat and blood stream, in my mind. *I believe in this. I trust this.* I could hear it in the ringing water and bird calls, feel it all along my skin, moving through me, pushing these thoughts into my consciousness, pushing me.

POSTLUDE

A few months after that day at the Tye River, I went to a party and met a psychiatrist's daughter who reminded me about the grim history of treating mental illness. A few days after that, I saw the cemetery behind old Western State Hospital, row upon row of blank grave posts spread out stark against new snow. I began to realize that the purpose, for me, of writing honestly about my manic depressive diagnosis was much more than a therapeutic exercise. I have learned things about myself—yes— but also about ghosts and history, psychiatry and stigma, and about survival, healing, resistance, joy. About Nature and Love and God.

The pall that looms over my home state of Virginia comes from the still-smoldering histories of Jamestown, slavery, indigenous genocide, Civil War, segregation, eugenics, fear, hate. In my manias, was I wrong to identify those themes, to seek their healing? No.

Do ghosts from this still-bleeding history haunt my home state? I am certain that they do.

Do the implications continue to haunt our national and cultural consciousness? Of course.

And what about the radiantly beautiful Central Appalachian Mountains and forests that so overpowered my mind in 2000. Are they threatened by short-sighted greed? By logging and coal mining and fracking for natural gas, by pollution and poisons and encroaching development? Yes, and again and again, yes.

In the prelude to this book, I suggested compassionate resistance as a tool for responding to these realities and to the stigmatization of Otherness—a way to unmask the energies of domination and exploitation that are forever trying to command humans and the Earth that gives us life. The goals that I described, of naming, truth-telling and staying alive, may sound like small steps, but for me, since my diagnosis, they have been important accomplishments, particularly the effort of staying alive long enough to recover and embrace joy.

Joy is not an easy proposition in an oppressive society. Joy needs space. It requires hollowing out room enough to breathe. Looking back at my story, I see that constant theme throughout my recovery: discovering the liberating, internal space provided by lithium and EMDR and seeking to find or create or hold onto external space to be myself—the awkward, odd, moody, quirky, uncomfortable creature who believes passionately in strange things and struggles with a powerful, intangible illness of the mind. I see myself trying—not to erase the extreme experiences—but to manage them. I see myself seeking to reincorporate the beauty that mania showed me in healthy ways, to enact methods of healthy madness.

There is not room for this in the western medical model—although western medicine and its medications have been central to my healing. And at times, in the worlds of alternative healing and spiritualism, I have faced rejection for accepting this diagnosis and taking medications. But a space for healthy madness exists, clearly, because I live here happily, talking to ghosts, continuing my quest to heal history, experiencing love in impossible ways, while simultaneously working a good job, swallowing my prescriptions twice daily, holding on to dear family and friends, planting a garden, writing a book.

As a person with a mental illness, I am not a monster or a stigma or an outsider to the human community. But I do not belong to dominator society. My mind and my heart live outside, in a space I clawed out for myself, where there is room for my strangeness, and for Nature and Love and God, for impossibilities, for joy.

Joy is the heart of resistance, but change is its goal. To unmask, disarm, and dismantle a society based on domination takes many types of actions, large and small. Here is something that is both tiny and enormous. Let the cat out of the bag: you are not straight, narrow, or "normal;" you do not conform to set standards; it may be that you are not quite "right." But there is space for you.

Try this: Destigmatize yourself and carve out space in your mind to breathe and to live from your own sweet heart's core. Dominator society rejoices in self-hatred and conformity; it encourages hatred of others.

Try this: Make your space a place that celebrates the odd and extraordinary, dare yourself to welcome the discomfort and confusion that often accompanies encounters with the strange and new and Other. Relax. Enjoy it.

The Earth and the Universe will continue to exist in splendidly wild and unpredictable ways. Take off your shoes. Step outside and see what unfolds.

ACKNOWLEDGEMENTS

As I hope this book makes clear, I survived long enough to begin to build a recovery by the grace of my family, specifically my parents, Norman & Nancy, and my brother, Eric. I learned how to be generous and alive again by the grace of my patient partner, Danny Dolinger. I do not use the word "grace" flippantly. These four are creatures of light and goodness and the heroes of this story.

Hear All The Bells began in Kevin Oderman's creative non-fiction class at West Virginia University. I feel special gratitude toward this group. It was frightening to begin to share my story publicly, yet they responded to my writing with care and gentleness. Kevin continued to mentor me even after I left the MFA program, and my classmates showed me that my story could help people—and that, to my mind, is the best thing that stories can do.

A heap of other beautiful people read the manuscript in its many revisions and helped me to clarify and refine it: Nancy & Norman Wulf, Danny Dolinger, Liz Beavers, Emily Mitchell, Lucy Weston, Steven Krichbaum, MA Jones, Rodney & Heather Webb, Andy Mahler, Josh

Tyree, Joe Meador, Bill Gardner, Doug & Inga Taylor, Ernie Reed, Jared Featherstone, and Kate Winslow.

Thank you to Charlotte Drummond for connecting me with Anne M. Carley of Chenille Books. In one brief consultation, Anne shifted my perspective on self-publishing, helping me to understand it as a valuable tool for advocacy and outreach. She began by asking me a deceptively simple, exceptionally useful question: "What do you want to do with this book?"

To the numerous other wonderful people whose love and support helped me so much during these years, well... so many of you are in this book, and I gave you pseudonyms, so it wouldn't make much sense to list you here, would it?

Truly though, I have been surrounded by the most extraordinarily loving and supportive communities of people during this journey. No words can truly do justice to your good and wild hearts.

My gratitude, love, and joy to all y'all, always.

LETTER TO A FRIEND

My dear friend –

I am both sorry and grateful to hear of your recent diagnosis. It is a painful experience, I know, but this might also be a turning point, the way out of much mental chaos and pain.

I have some ideas that may be helpful as you set out on the path of living life with a diagnosis of manic depression, but I should start with two disclaimers. First, of course, I'm not a doctor—none of this is medical advice. Second, every person with bipolar disorder (I usually call mine manic depression) has a different experience. Our symptoms vary; our experiences with diagnosis, hospitalizations, and recovery vary. Please understand that what happened to me may be nothing like what has happened to you and that what has helped me get well might not work for you. We each find our own way.

Having manic depression is hard, but you can recover and connect with your joy. You can feel good and live life fully. Hold on to that hope, because it is real. Alongside the suffering, you have and will continue to gather wisdom and insight that few others on this planet have. So hang in there and work and study how to become well.

I have a few tips that might help along the way. They break into two basic categories: the practical, day-to-day care of body and mind, and the spiritual, philosophical, existential quests and questions of identity, self-acceptance, joy and despair. Because I'm manic depressive and get annoyed by easy categories, I'm going to mix them up and just try to tell you what I know.

Have you had to walk out the doors of a hospital or a doctor's office with this new diagnosis—"manic depressive" or "bipolar" or "mentally ill"—emblazoned on your chest? Have you come back to earth from a manic episode wondering how to return to daily life once you've been up that high and out that far? How do you fit yourself back into the straight and narrow after your mind has taken you to such strange places—the ragged outer reaches of depression and mania? Even if it was all delusion, how do you set that aside, become "normal?"

My simple answer: You don't. You can't. You find another path between those two extremes. You find a third way out.

The difficult reality is that no one can do this for you. No medication, no counselor or partner or guru or parent or friend can find that third way, because it is your way, your quest, the answer to your riddle; it is deeply personal, deeply yours.

I am a strong proponent of medication being part of that third way, in large part because manic depression is a progressive disease; it gets worse; it is unpredictable; it has an extremely high rate of suicide. Please do not risk your life by rejecting medication.

Doctors may tell you that you will need to take medication for the rest of your life. And then in the next breath, they'll explain that medical science still doesn't really understand what causes manic depression or by what mechanisms medication helps to stabilize a manic-depressive brain. So be aware that the future is wide open—who knows what new treatments and understandings will emerge in our lifetimes?—but for now, medications are among your most powerful tools for recovery.

You will have to work to find your way through the pitfalls of treatment. Medications can dull and numb the wild, careening, creative senses of hypomania and mania and may take a long time to chew through the bleak, dead weight of depression. However, I know from experience that **it can be done**, that medication can provide stability without turning your life into a dull gray blur. I *feel* and experience as deeply as I did before my diagnosis; my moods are as wild, weird, and sometimes difficult as ever, but they do not take over my entire body and being. They do not drag me beneath the waves until I cannot breathe.

I wish I could tell you that I found that balance quickly. In reality, it took years of experimentation and stubbornness to figure out the medications and lifestyle that allow me to feel in touch with myself and in love with my mind again. But that's life, isn't it, really? Everyone has to struggle and search to find what works for them, for their health, for being happy and alive. You and I are not so different.

I also won't pretend that my life is all stability and ease now. Bipolar disorder is difficult—sometimes it is extremely difficult—and every day is a balancing act. My point is simply this: don't reject medication out of hand like I did early on. If your symptoms are milder, medication can give you a stable base to work from. If your symptoms are severe, medication can save your life.

Lithium saved my life; no doubt about it. I am a huge believer in lithium. My psychiatrist refers to it as "the gold standard" for treating manic depression. Lithium has the longest and best track record of anything else that's available. It's also an element on the periodic table, so it truly is natural medicine.

Unfortunately, many doctors hesitate to prescribe it. I am speculating here, but I see two major reasons for that. First, to be effective, lithium blood levels have to stay within a fairly narrow range. A person taking lithium has to get periodic blood tests to check lithium levels; in the first months of treatment, the tests must be fairly frequent. I think doctors worry that patients, especially during those fragile early months, won't follow through.

The other big reason that doctors don't prescribe lithium, I believe, is that no pharmaceutical reps are promoting it. Lithium carbonate is a salt; you can dig it out of the ground or evaporate it from lithium-rich waters. Since lithium can't be patented, no one makes big money when doctors prescribe it. Meanwhile, pharmaceutical companies put a lot of time and money into promoting their newer, not-as-well-tested drugs, and I think some doctors get swept up into trying out "the next big thing."

I had a terrible experience with this before getting hooked up with my current psychiatrist. My previous doc put me on a brand new drug and had me take it in a way that had not been tested or approved at the time. It did *not* work for me, and I spent a miserable, sometimes-suicidal year before finding an ethical doctor.

Speaking of which, if you have the flexibility, find a good doctor! Few things were as important to my early recovery as finding a doctor who treated me as a competent, capable, insightful, intelligent human being with a challenging, often bizarre, but also treatable medical condition. I have the same doctor now and feel incredibly fortunate: he listens to me, returns my calls, and respects my assessments of my health. When I go to a new doctor now for some other health issue, I ask a lot of questions; if a doctor is too rushed or arrogant to answer them, I don't go back.

This brings to mind another huge challenge facing people with mental health conditions of all kinds: equitable access to health care and treatment. This is one of multiple justice issues surrounding mental illness, and there is a vast amount of advocacy work needed. For one example, when you feel better, take the time to learn about people with mental illness in the criminal justice system—how many thousands of people who belong in treatment are instead incarcerated.

Having limited access to health care can create immense challenges. For instance, you may have less flexibility with regard to accessing good doctors and locating one who will work well with you. Hopefully the doctor who diagnosed you will have provided guidance to resources, but if not, look for community health groups, wellness centers, free clinics, etc. Virginia has community services boards. Some hospitals run support groups. Check the internet, get on the phone. This is a time to ask for help, even if you're like me and you despise asking for help.

If, for whatever reason, you have a crappy doctor and you don't have the option of switching to another one, your best bet is still to learn as much as you can about your illness and your meds and your body. If you have a doctor who is abusive in their behavior, bring a family member or friend with you. It can be tough to stand up to a bad doctor. We're taught to think of them as infallible, and bad doctors will exploit that concept. We've got to talk ourselves into thinking differently. You or your insurance or taxpayer dollars are paying your doctor to help you get better. The goal for both you and your doctor is full remission of your condition. Psych yourself up and don't settle for less.

Psychiatrists have a tough job—they're supposed to treat symptoms of a mental illness, but they can't tell how you feel inside your head and inside your body. Be honest with them. If you feel horrible, especially if you feel suicidal, tell someone!! If you feel like you're skating onto jittery, manic ice, then call for help! I didn't want to do it either, but I am so grateful that I finally spoke up, asked for assistance, took the lithium, etc. And if your doctor proves unwilling to listen or does not treat you with respect, *please* try to find another doctor. Their role is to help you get well, to put your illness into remission. Do not settle for less.

Still, even the best doctor will only see you for short periods of time every few weeks or months, so you will have to self-advocate. I cannot overstate this. You need to understand your condition in order to effectively address your problems. School yourself in manic depression. Please! Do your research. You are your best advocate. The more you understand your brain, your diagnosis, the medications, the needs of your body, the better off you will be. There is so much information out there—on-line and at the library. Keep an eye out for legitimate sources: there's a ton of free, scientific literature and lots of personal stories of recovery. Some of those stories may seem scary or discouraging. The bottom line is that, while you may not be in total control of your destiny (no one is), your choices have a heck of a lot of influence on your destiny. You can recover.

Sadly, many people with mental conditions settle for half-measures. After my diagnosis, when people asked me how I felt, I remember thinking, "I don't know. Apparently I'm mentally ill, how am I supposed to feel?" And in reality, I felt awful. Depressed and self-conscious and ashamed and awful! It was a terrible time in my life.

In hindsight, I'm disappointed in myself for not taking a more active role in trying to get well. In those early days, I didn't read about the medications I was prescribed; I just took them without question. Huge mistake! Please read the information that came with your meds from the pharmacy. Look them up on the web and get familiar with what they are supposed to be doing. What kind of drugs are they? Mood stabilizers? Atypical anti-psychotics? Anti-depressants? Learn about what those are and what they do and why your doctor prescribed them.

Be aware, however, that the internet has many discussion sites where people share stories of terrible side effects and misery caused by one medication or another. Don't get freaked out—everyone's experience varies. I have a friend who cannot take lithium because of the side effects it caused for her. Instead, she takes a medication that I tried and could not tolerate. Every experience is different.

Medication regimes for treating bipolar disorders are changing all the time. For example, more recent research shows that most standard anti-depressants are not appropriate for treating bipolar depression—they may trigger mania or simply be ineffective. I took an SNRI anti-depressant for nearly five years that never really did anything for me, but at that time, studies were unclear. Once I got off the anti-depressant and onto a second mood stabilizer, everything turned around for me.

That's a good example of a painful reality of treating manic depression: to a real extent, medication is prescribed by trial and error. There is no one-size-fits-all treatment, and it can take a long time to find the right combination. In the process, you will invariably encounter difficult side effects—some will subside as your body adjusts; some may be intolerable and require you to change medications. I wish it wasn't like this; I wish treatment was easy and straightforward, but at this point in history, it's not. You have to be very patient, especially right at the beginning, while you wait to see if the meds you've been prescribed will work on your symptoms. And then—this is the really hard part—you may have to try again to find what works best for you.

There are some day-to-day physical tools that may help you during these difficult times and throughout your recovery. In essence, they are the same health practices that benefit everyone: good sleep, exercise, diet, social interaction, meditation, meaningful work or other activities, etc. It's just that for us they have an extra layer of importance: they are tools for stability, methods that allow us to pursue lives of joy and meaning. Indeed, exercise and sleep *are* medicine, crucially important for the health of a manic depressive mind.

As a central part of my on-going health and stability, I *try* to exercise every day (I don't, but I try!). Even in the worst hurt of depression, I would drag myself outside to walk most days, and it helped. In hindsight, I wish I'd pushed myself further into full-on, sweaty, out-of-breath, elevated-heart-rate, aerobic exercise. For me at least, that type of exercise is most beneficial for helping regulate my moods.

Any kind of exercise, however, is good for us and our brains. It lifts my mood when I'm depressed and helps me work off excess energy when I'm a little hypo or anxious. Not to mention that exercise can help keep off the weight gain that seems to accompany just about every psycho-tropic drug on the market. My best days—physically, mentally, and emotionally—are always days when I've gotten some kind of exercise.

I do my best to eat healthy and whole foods. I take some supplements too that might be helpful: fish oil supports mental stability; n-acetyl cysteine (NAC) helps diffuse lingering, low-grade bipolar depression; B vitamins and vitamin D may lift moods and energy levels. Look them up, read the studies, talk to your doctor. Fish oil and NAC require specific dosages to be effective. Make sure to check with your doctor and/or pharmacist to make sure they don't interfere with your medications. These supplements have worked very well for me in complementing my medication regime, but like all these things, may not work for everyone and could be harmful for some.

What else? I *try* to sleep at least seven hours a night (I don't, but I try). Regular sleep is critical; it is crucial; without it, you will get sick again. Read up on circadian rhythms and their role in manic depression. Read about cortisol and stress and try to find time to chill—meditation, quiet wandering outside or gardening, or just being in silence. These times help me stabilize my addiction to stress and ground myself and remember who I am. One of the most helpful things for me in terms of mental self-care is to remember that my life is bigger and wider than whatever mood I'm experiencing in the moment.

Speaking of addictions, for many years I self-medicated my manic depression with marijuana. It accelerated manias and eventually tore up my brain chemistry. You may have been told that pot is harmless, but the reality is that any chemical that interacts with your brain chemistry can be dangerous for bipolar people. This includes alcohol, hallucinogens, narcotics, stimulants, depressants, etc. All of it. Even sugar and caffeine, crazy as that may sound, if you ingest enough, can rattle your stability.

I was well and truly bummed to give up cannabis. I loved the stuff. But over time, using it damaged me. Since giving it up, my life has only improved. Spending time in 12 Step rooms helped me so much in my early recovery. Meetings got me out of the house and into the company of others who faced serious struggles, helping me to keep my challenges in perspective. I also had the chance to be of service, and that went a long way in helping me slowly rebuild a sense of self-worth.

I have been fortunate to have friends and family who would not accept my extreme self-pity or my sense of weakness. They refused to allow me to use my illness as an excuse not to grow and flourish as a human being. My husband is particularly strict about this, which sometimes pisses me off. I whine, "But you don't understand!" And then I realize that he is right. He may not understand the vagaries of living inside a manic depressive brain, but he certainly knows the challenges of living in this difficult world. Mental illness is a hell of a big challenge— disorienting, disturbing, self-eroding—bit it did not erase me, and thus my responsibility to live bravely and ethically remains, and perhaps increases.

You should know that even with treatment and without illegal drug use, I still often have very intense and volatile moods. Meditating can help to calm that down. A counselor once gave me a very helpful meditation—to view one of my wild moods like a train passing by—it comes in loud and dramatic, but then it keeps moving, passing me by; I can let it go.

That said, I am grateful for the strong and powerful moods, even if they can be jarring. I welcome the ability to feel intensely. For a time, as I adjusted to medications, my mind and thoughts often felt flattened, a feeling that I hated. I'd rather have the occasional jaggedness of being too up or too down than feel flat. I am grateful to have a doctor who supports that. He works with me to keep my medications at a level where I can feel deeply and thrive.

I try to have a good social life, though to be honest, that remains my biggest challenge. During my first two years of unfettered manic depression, I developed serious social anxiety. I was terribly afraid of what people would think of me, and I just hurt all the time, especially when trying to interact with people who I'd just met. I didn't know how to relax and be myself because I had no idea who I was.

In over a decade since then, that anxiety hasn't entirely gone away. Sometimes I have to fight with myself to go out to a party; once I'm there, it's fine, I have fun, but there is a deep-seated anxiety that I must overcome first. I love my family. I love the friends I already have, but I struggle to make new ones. That concerns me, and I'm not sure how to remedy it. The upside is that I love my own company; solitude suits me; I really do love my own mind.

Still, there is a fine line between being solitary and isolating. Most of all, I would challenge you to not be afraid. Try not to hide out. Most people will not judge you nearly as harshly as you judge yourself. Indeed, what I felt as a crimson "M.D." scrawled on my chest, most people—friends and strangers alike—never noticed. It is so easy to self-stigmatize; I still do it. And it is so unnecessary. People who stigmatize mental illness have probably had little contact with people who have our diagnosis. Being open about who you are and about your strength and goodness can be a transformative thing. It can change peoples' hearts, minds, and lives. It can also be hard as hell.

Your family and friends will probably be key parts of your recovery. Try to be honest with as many of them as you can. I know that too can be difficult. Help them understand what symptoms of manic depression look like.

They can help you recognize if your moods are starting to go haywire. That is one of the weird phenomena of manic depression—we don't always notice the symptoms. Especially hypomania, because it can feel so good! And, frankly, *you* have to figure out where the line is—when are you in a really good and productive mood and when are you hypo? My line is when the symptoms become disruptive: for example, when I cannot sleep or when I cannot fully control the words coming out of my mouth.

Work with your family and friends to set up a contingency plan describing what they should do if you get really manic or really depressed. How do you want them to help you? If they have to take you to a hospital, which one do you prefer? Make sure they have phone numbers for your doctor. I felt embarrassed as hell to have to do this, but in reality, you're creating safety and a degree of control for yourself in case your ability to reason and make decisions becomes compromised. It's worth it.

Expect to hit rough patches. For example, I have found that consistently, when we set our clocks forward and back for Daylight Savings, it rocks my world for a few weeks. I don't know why—some combination of disrupted sleep and circadian rhythms, I suppose. My mood goes dark, anxious, raw. My life is all sandpaper on my bones, and my husband is a jerk, and my friends secretly hate me, and I am tired of being alive. Or, I am jittery as a boiling kettle, rattled, off-kilter, fighting to sleep.

On those occasions, and in other times when moods dip and swirl in ways that cross the line, I do several things. Talk to my doctor, and if he concurs, take a bit more or less lithium. Become more disciplined in taking care of the basics: sleeping enough and well, eating enough and well, and exercising, always—my advice for every occasion—get hot, out of breath, tired. It brings immediate relief. Getting outside in the daylight is crucial too, I've found, to help my body adjust as seasons change.

Mostly though, getting through the rough patches is a matter of being patient. Trusting that the painful moods will pass, that I will re-stabilize back into my own strange mind. There is always fear though—I can't help it—a fear deep in my gut of again losing myself and my mind, fear that the medications will stop working, and I will be unable to find my way back to self and sanity and joy.

But in the midst of that terror, what is there but to continue, to try and go on unafraid? Everyone on the planet is born into a particular set of circumstances, specific challenges, dangers, and fears. As people with a mental illness in 21st century America, we have a great many more options to help create a good life. Our predecessors with manic depression had no real treatment options and most lived terribly difficult lives.

Throughout much of western history, people with mental illness have been treated horribly—confined, experimented on, lobotomized, sterilized, killed by neglect or by targeting. But the same types of things have happened to so many other groups! The list of human cruelty is horrifically long. Mental illness really is just one more way of being human in the world. We help others by being open, by not denying our existence, and by trying to live good lives.

Here are two final thoughts for you before I wish you luck and good fortune as you seek your third way out. First, I encourage you to cultivate a deep and healthy respect for the power of manic depression to harm your health, turn your life inside out, potentially kill you. But I also encourage you not to live in fear and not to reject this condition; it is so deeply a part of you.

Second, once you are stable and if it feels safe for you, consider exploring the delusions and insights and weirdness of your extreme experiences. I believe that manic depression is indeed bipolar—it has two realities. One is that the disease is devastating and dangerous. Another reality is that this madness brings new perspectives, new insight into the world. There are often pockets of wisdom within the dangers of insanity. Just be careful.

My personal goal is to find methods of healthy madness—to keep my balance and be a generous, good person within this day-to-day world while also exploring the mysteries of my mind and the broader human experience. For me, these are components of a worthy and meaningful life, a way to be of service to human understanding of the world.

We have a unique perspective, you and I. Most people on the planet don't have minds like ours that periodically go out of control and lead us into strange places. They don't have the endless distraction of keeping a mental balance either, but every human being has their own difficulties and their own path. If that path is an escape route out of the destruction, cruelty, and domination that haunts human existence, then we are headed in a good direction.

You and I have no choice but to find our third way out, and so, you and I can help lead the way.

Peace to you, dear friend. I wish you the best.

With love,
Christina